ON THE COLORS OF VOWELS

VERBAL ARTS :: STUDIES IN POETICS

Lazar Fleishman and Haun Saussy, series editors

On the Colors of Vowels

Thinking through Synesthesia

LIESL YAMAGUCHI

Fordham University Press
NEW YORK   2024

This book was a recipient of the American Comparative Literature Association's Helen Tartar First Book Subvention Award. Fordham University Press is grateful for the funding from this prize that helped facilitate publication.

Fordham University Press gratefully acknowledges financial assistance and support provided for the publication of this book by the University of California, Berkeley.

Cover Credit: Plate 14, S. Ishihara, *Tests for Colour-Blindness*, 24-plate edition, Tokyo: Kanehara Shuppan Co., Ltd., 1971.

Copyright © 2024 Fordham University Press

All rights reserved. No part of this publication may be reproduced, stored in a retrieval system, or transmitted in any form or by any means—electronic, mechanical, photocopy, recording, or any other—except for brief quotations in printed reviews, without the prior permission of the publisher.

Fordham University Press has no responsibility for the persistence or accuracy of URLs for external or third-party Internet websites referred to in this publication and does not guarantee that any content on such websites is, or will remain, accurate or appropriate.

Fordham University Press also publishes its books in a variety of electronic formats. Some content that appears in print may not be available in electronic books.

Visit us online at www.fordhampress.com.

Library of Congress Cataloging-in-Publication Data available online at https://catalog.loc.gov.

Printed in the United States of America

26 25 24   5 4 3 2 1

First edition

Contents

	Introduction: After "Voyelles"	1
1	*Klangfarbe*: Vowels in Helmholtz's *Sensations of Tone*	21
2	The Interaction of Color	49
3	Mallarmé and the Tension of Timbre	65
4	The Colors of the Universal Alphabet	84
5	*L'être imaginaire*: Saussure's Colored Vowels	103
	Conclusion: Remarks on "Synesthesia"	121
	Acknowledgments	141
	Notes	143
	Works Cited	185
	Index	203

III §31 Wir reden von "Farbenblindheit" und nennen sie einen Defekt. Aber es könnte leicht mehrere verschiedene Anlagen geben, von denen keine gegen die andere offenbar minderwertig ist.—Und denk auch daran, daß ein Mensch durch's Leben gehen kann, ohne daß seine Farbenblindheit bemerkt wird, bis eine besondere Gelegenheit sie zum Vorschein bringt.
—LUDWIG WITTGENSTEIN, *BEMERKUNGEN ÜBER DIE FARBEN*

III §31 We speak of "colour-blindness" and call it a defect. But there could easily be several differing abilities, none of which is clearly inferior to the others.— And remember, too, that a person may go through life without their colour-blindness being noticed, until some special occasion brings it to light.
—LUDWIG WITTGENSTEIN, *REMARKS ON COLOUR*

Introduction: After "Voyelles"

Voyelles

A noir, E blanc, I rouge, U vert, O bleu: voyelles,
Je dirai quelque jour vos naissances latentes:
A, noir corset velu des mouches éclatantes
Qui bombinent autour des puanteurs cruelles,

Golfes d'ombre; E, candeurs des vapeurs et des tentes,
Lances des glaciers fiers, rois blancs, frissons d'ombelles;
I, pourpres, sang craché, rire des lèvres belles
Dans la colère ou les ivresses pénitentes;

U, cycles, vibrements divins des mers virides,
Paix des pâtis semés d'animaux, paix des rides
Que l'alchimie imprime aux grands fronts studieux;

O, suprême Clairon plein de strideurs étranges,
Silences traversés des Mondes et des Anges:
— Ô l'Oméga, rayon violet de Ses Yeux!

Vowels

A black, E white, I red, U green, O blue: vowels,
Someday I will tell of your latent births:
A, black corset hairy with the shiny flies
That bumble about vicious smells,

Gulfs of shadows; E, candor of vapors and tents,
Lances of proud glaciers, white kings, rippling umbels;
I, purples, spat blood, lovely lips laughing
In anger or penitent inebriation;

U, cycles, divine vibrating of viridescent seas,
Peace of pastures strewn with animals, peace of furrows
That alchemy impresses upon broad, learned brows;

O, supreme Clarion call full of strange, strident strains,
Silences traversed by Worlds and by Angels:
Oh Omega, violet ray of Their Eyes!

—A. Rimbaud[1]

"I invented the colors of vowels!" Arthur Rimbaud declared in the summer of 1873, dashing off his statement with an emphatic exclamation point. The poet, not yet nineteen, had sequestered himself in the attic of his family's farm in Charleville, his extravagant escapades in Paris and Brussels already behind him. As he slips into the series of correspondences that inaugurated his sonnet "Voyelles," his enthusiastic exclamation modulates quickly into contempt:

> Black *A*, white *E*, red *I*, blue *O*, green *U*. — I fine-tuned the shape and movement of each consonant, and, with instinctive rhythms, I flattered myself with inventing a poetic idiom that would be accessible, one day or another, to all the senses. I reserved the translation rights.
>
> A *noir*, E *blanc*, I *rouge*, O *bleu*, U *vert*. —Je réglai la forme et le mouvement de chaque consonne, et, avec des rythmes instinctifs, je me flattai d'inventer un verbe poétique accessible, un jour ou l'autre, à tous les sens. Je réservais la traduction.[2]

No longer extending from Alpha to Omega, as in the poem still unpublished at the time, Rimbaud's vowels here have been deflated of divine ambition, restored to their conventional order (AEIOU). The vision of the poetic feat and the fact of its failure have been made to coincide for one excruciating instant in a text indicatively titled *A Season in Hell*.

Failed as Rimbaud may have felt his vision of vocalic colors to be, however, few—if any—could be said to have established the idea of vowel-color correspondence more prominently than he. A century and a half after its composition, "Voyelles" remains, along with Charles Baudelaire's "Correspondances" (1857) and J. K. Huysmans' *À Rebours* (1884), one of the most emblematic examples of literary synesthesia, and the idea of vowel-color correspondence specifically remains inextricably bound, almost singularly, to the figure of Arthur Rimbaud.[3] At least in literary studies, a book on the colors of vowels could scarcely begin with anyone else. The aim of this book is to broaden literary scholars' gaze beyond this singular reference, suggesting how interdisciplinary perspectives on vowel color might inflect literary treatments of the topic and, inversely, how literary studies might contribute to the multidisciplinary inquiry into synesthesia. But before embarking on the discussion of all that might be said after "Voyelles," let us dwell for a moment on the sonnet itself, as it offers both a microcosm of this book and an initiation to its mode of reading.

One could begin by observing that the "vowels" Rimbaud's sonnet brings into relation with hues expose the many homonyms coincident in the poem's eponymous term. The opening line enumerates the series of vowels that French children learn in school (AEIOU), a series that includes neither all the written vowels of French (which would include Y) nor all the vocalic phonemes of the spoken language (of which there are sixteen). In the sonnet—although, tellingly, not in the disavowal of *A Season in Hell*—the last two vowels of this series are reversed to evoke the Ancient Greek vowels that run from Alpha to Omega, withdrawing the sonnet from the confines of the French classroom and projecting it into the long history of writing vowel sounds (the vowels of Ancient Greek being, famously, the first to be committed individually to writing[4]). Concluding with an invocation of the last Greek vowel ("— Oh Omega, violet ray of Their Eyes!" / — *Ô l'Oméga, rayon violet de Ses Yeux!*), Rimbaud confers a sense of completion and totality upon his composition, now running from Alpha to Omega in an explicitly hubristic attempt to encapsulate all: the beginning and the end.[5]

Of course, Rimbaud's vowels are graphic shapes, as well: although an unwritten /a/ echoes through the color name "noir" [nwaʁ], it is the geometric outlines of the capital A, the resting housefly, and the upside-down corset that seem to motivate the associative series "A, black corset hairy with shiny flies (*A, noir corset velu des mouches éclatantes*)."[6] And one suspects that it is not just the undulating shape of the sea's waves that prompts the juxtaposition of the letter U with "cycles, divine vibrating of viridescent seas (*cycles, vibrements divins des mers virides*)," but also the dual function of the Ancient Latin "V," a letter used to mark both the vowel /u/ and the voiced fricative /v/ so prominently alliterated in the *vibrements divins des mers virides*. The smile of "lovely lips laughing (*rire des lèvres belles*)" associated with the vowel "I" might prompt us to see the letter turned sideways, or to hear a brightness shared between its pitch and peals of laughter.[7] "O," the "supreme Clarion call full of strange, strident strains (*suprême Clairon plein de strideurs étranges*)" invites us to imagine the vowel's timbre in the trumpet's call as the final stanza telescopically propels us through the letter's ring, the mouth poised to pronounce it, the trumpet's horn, and the circles of the ultimate, enigmatic eyes. Ephemerally sounds of music, ancient letters, and anatomical shapes, Rimbaud's *Voyelles* reveal new facets at every turn, emerging unexpectedly in the ripples of the sea and echoing through the memory of laughter.

Readers of the poem have often struggled against this multiplicity. For many, it has seemed that a series of vowel-color correspondences could be convincing only if it were to link colors to one of the many vocalic aspects that the text evokes. Endeavoring to relate Rimbaud's color-vowel assignments to any number of organizational models, from the colored alphabets of children's books to scientific charts of synesthetes' vowel-color connections,[8] commentators have often found the poem lacking: either mechanically reproducing an existing system or, more frequently, failing to do so coherently. They have sought with inexhaustible enthusiasm to locate the associations' origin, excavating the author's personal biography and exhausting his intellectual milieu.[9] But what if the significance of Rimbaud's sonnet were to reside precisely in the complexity of its vowels, which turn out to be musical, graphic, linguistic, symbolic, and even divine? What if the poem's achievement were to lie not in the specific correspondences that it draws, nor in those correspondences' relation to conjunctions observable in the world, but in its exposure of the enigmatic entity we presume to know simply as "a vowel"? Building each association through paratactic juxtaposition, Rimbaud, in his sonnet, invites readers to discern the relationships its syntax withholds. The verbs that would fix vowels and colors in stable syntactic relations are notably absent. Anyone who seeks to discern the logic by which the poem proceeds is thus obliged to confront the multiplicity inherent in the notion of a "vowel." Perhaps it would be right, then, to read Rimbaud's sonnet less as a prescriptive declaration than as an invitation to perceive the variousness of vowels: a prism crafted to diffract their dazzling diversity.

Like the lines of Rimbaud's sonnet, the chapters of this book proceed through a logic of provocative juxtaposition rather than one of narrative progress. Their unifying question, shared with the reading above, asks how the language of color comes into relation with vowels and what it enables in their description. As in Rimbaud's sonnet, the vowels that come under examination here quickly expose the absence of their own definition. They come into focus from the perspectives of various disciplines—physical acoustics, music, poetics, phonetics, phonology—each time only

INTRODUCTION: AFTER "VOYELLES" / 5

to expose the insufficiency of the definition assumed by the discipline. They are identified as vowels by the speaking beings who use them, in a tautological circuit by which the vowels that define the being as one who speaks are, in turn, defined by the speaking being. Rimbaud's sonnet offers an instructive figure for this circular logic. Sounding a homonym with the O inaugurating the final tercet, the Ô of the poem's closing verse is distinguished by its circumflex, the hallmark of apostrophe:

> O, supreme Clarion call full of strange, strident strains
> Silences traversed by Worlds and by Angels:
> — Oh Omega, violet ray of Their Eyes!
>
> *O, suprême Clairon plein de strideurs étranges,*
> *Silences traversés des Mondes et des Anges:*
> *— Ô l'Oméga, rayon violet de Ses Yeux!*

Echoing the vocalic but insisting on the vocative, the *Ô* of line fourteen draws our attention to the emotive expression of the poetic voice just as it addresses the Omega that, in the moment of apostrophizing, is indistinguishable from itself. If, as Jonathan Culler suggests in his classic article, "the vocative of apostrophe is a device which the poetic voice uses to establish with an object a relationship which helps to constitute him [...] He makes himself poet, visionary,"[10] Rimbaud's *Ô* fulfills this function exemplarily, creating a vertiginous *mise en abyme* between the visionary poet (or perhaps, *voyant*[11]) and his *voyelle*. *Voyant* and *voyelle* or, perhaps, *voyant* and *Voyelles*, as Rimbaud's final *Ô* also reminds us that the "you" to whom the entire apostrophic poem is addressed is not the reader but rather "vowels":

> *A* black, *E* white, *I* red, *U* green, *O* blue: vowels,
> Someday I will tell of your latent births [...]
>
> *A noir, E blanc, I rouge, U vert, O bleu: voyelles,*
> *Je dirai quelque jour vos naissances latentes* [...]

The focus of this book is perhaps best figured thus: as a letter decisive in meaning-making (O) and an emotive expression of the voice (Ô!) that is devoid of reference but which in its uttering and recognition constitutes itself as well as that which would pronounce it.

That which would pronounce it in Rimbaud's sonnet is the visionary poet, whose ambition to forge a "poetic idiom (*verbe*) accessible, one day or another, to all the senses" all but explicitly aspires to rival the originary *Verbe* ("In the beginning was the Word," or in French, *Au commencement était le Verbe*).[12] The translation of the *voyant-voyelle* circuit opened up by apostrophe into the Christian Word-made-flesh is not difficult to make out, particularly because, as Culler notes, it is always tempting to see in apostrophe an address to an "ultimate Thou."[13] But Culler diverts our gaze from God to insist instead on the absurd poetic gesture of willing the inanimate into action, contending that in apostrophe, "What is really in question is the power of poetry to make something happen."[14] Invoking W. H. Auden's observation that "poetry makes nothing happen," the twentieth-century critic points out that the poem in question nonetheless continues on, assuring us that poetry "survives, / A way of happening, a mouth."[15] The moment bears stressing here because Culler's shift in focus from the ultimate addressee to the poetic gesture, from the metaphysical to the mouth, is one that recurs, in various guises, throughout the chapters of this book. That which would pronounce the vowel might be God, but it might also be "a mouth"—a mouth that implies a body, if not necessarily a divine spirit.

In his 1991 study of "Voyelles," Jacques Rancière observes a slightly embarrassing resemblance between his reading of the sonnet as "the body of enunciation of the Rimbaldian poem"[16] and the Christian practice of exegesis. "The key to a text is usually a body," he writes:

> Finding a body beneath the letters, in the letters—this was called *exegesis* in the days when the Christian scholars recognized in the stories of the Old Testament as many *figures* for the body to come of the incarnation of the Word (*Verbe*). In our secular age, this is readily referred to as demystification or, quite simply, reading.[17]

The body that emerges from Rancière's reading of "Voyelles" is communal yet profane, and as such it offers yet another orienting figure for this book. In many of the readings assembled here, the language of color describes vowel timbre specifically, "timbre" being the quality of sound that distinguishes one vowel from the next (A from O, E from U), as well as the quality of sound that makes it possible to identify the instrument of a given sound's production (what distinguishes a human voice from, say, a horn). Timbre—or, in German, *Klangfarbe*, literally "sound-color"—may be quantified acoustically, and scientists and linguists of the nineteenth and twentieth centuries sought vigorously to separate it both terminologically and conceptually from the mechanics of sound production. What emerges with almost uncanny consistency in their efforts to separate timbre from sounding bodies is a turn to visual metaphor. Instead of referring vowels back to the human speech apparatus, these metaphors collectively refer them to a master model of color relations that is assumed to be universal. From the metaphorical "brilliance," "saturation," and "chromatism" of vowels there emerges a color spectrum that is also a spectral reflection of the body by which the vowel exists.

So much, then, for vowels; let us turn to their "color." What is the relation of this vocalic "color" to color in the sense of the pigments painters use (*les couleurs*) or colors of light discernible to the eye? And how coherent is the analogy that scattered terms like vowel "brightness" and *Klangfarbe* collectively imply? These are the orienting questions of this book, which investigates "the color of vowels" understood in a particular way. These chapters study utterances drawn from across disciplines that present vowels as if they were visible: bright, dark, clear, chromatic, saturated, blue. Its privileged sites of inquiry are texts in which much hinges on these terms: "sound color"; the brightness or darkness of vowel timbre; the coloration conferred by assonance or rhyme; the "coloring" of neighboring consonants. All of these expressions may be read metaphorically and have long been read so. And it is true that one can grasp some sense, however vague, of the sounds under discussion by translating these ostensibly visual terms into sonorous properties. Such reading is complicated, however, by the existence of adjacent and often identical expressions that demand a different reading. These expressions, equally concerned with the hues and brightnesses of vowels, explicitly intend their visual terms to be understood literally. They do not describe aspects of sound, in other words, but colors that are seen in much though not entirely the same way as the colors and brightnesses of objects observed by all. For some speaking beings, a "bright" vowel is visually bright: in the sense of that flashing silver bike; a green "U" is literally the hue of the emerald lawn, and a burnt-red "A" is precisely the shade of that rust-red brick.

Distinguishing literal from metaphorical observations concerning the colors of vowels emerged as a key concern for scientists of the twentieth century. For experimental psychologists intent on constituting "synesthesia" as a legitimate object of modern science, it was imperative that language use considered indicative of an anomalous biological condition be rigorously distinguished from the metaphorical language used by any and all. The popular voice of neurologist Richard E. Cytowic offers an indicative example:

> Synesthesia (Greek, syn = together + aisthesis = perception) is the involuntary physical experience of a cross-modal association. That is, the stimulation of one sensory modality reliably causes a perception in one or more different senses. Its phenomenology clearly distinguishes it from metaphor, literary tropes, sound symbolism, and deliberate artistic contrivances that sometimes employ the term "synesthesia" to describe their multisensory joinings.[18]

That synesthesia has nothing to do with "metaphor, literary tropes, sound symbolism, and deliberate artistic contrivances that sometimes employ the term 'synesthesia' to describe their multisensory joinings" is by now taken as axiomatic by scholars across disciplines. Yet the vigor of Cytowic's distinction highlights the clear and present danger of the problem. Reports of "synesthesia" in the narrowed, technical sense that scientists of the twentieth century sought to define were notoriously difficult to distinguish from typical language use (i.e., synesthetic metaphor) and especially literary language. There can be little doubt that the twentieth century's codification of synesthesia as a well-defined and widely recognized condition (though, notably, not a medical diagnosis[19]) has been of capital importance to the funding and advancement of its scientific study. What is less readily evident is that the contours of this codification have positioned scholars to achieve the greatest possible insight into the phenomenon. As psychologists Jamie Ward and Julia Simner conclude in their 2020 overview "Synesthesia: The Current State of the Field,"

> ... the current body of work has identified many of the key pieces of the jigsaw puzzle, but has not yet fitted them together. For instance, we know that synesthesia has a genetic component and we know that the brains of synesthetes differ. But we do not know how these two facts are related; i.e., what role these genes play in neurotypical and synesthetic brain development and function. Nor do we understand how this process would differ depending on the type of synesthesia that is manifested (e.g., grapheme-color, mirror-touch, lexical-gustatory). Very little is known about how synesthesia changes over the life span, particularly in the early years in which synesthesia first emerges, and in which normal multisensory perception matures. Similarly, we do not know whether the cognitive profile linked to synesthesia is a necessary outcome of having this condition (two sides of the same coin) or a correlational one. The answer to these questions will be an interdisciplinary endeavor involving (minimally) psychologists, neuroscientists, and geneticists.[20]

Ward and Simner's concluding remarks indicate the remarkable degree to which the contemporary construct of synesthesia remains empirically elusive, as well as the fundamental orientation that scientific studies of synesthesia tend to assume. Research scientists of the late twentieth and early twenty-first centuries aim to identify and describe the biological, genetic, and environmental causes of synesthesia and to elucidate its neural mechanisms and their development. As psychologist Lawrence E.

Marks, another of the field's leading voices, observed at the turn of the twenty-first century,

> To the extent that modern research on synesthesia seeks to elucidate its sensory manifestations and neural underpinnings rather than describe ways that synesthesia helps organize systems of meanings, this research fits comfortably within modern cognitive science, a discipline in many ways heir to behaviorism. Experimental psychologists and cognitive neuroscientists have developed empirical and conceptual tools to evaluate the encoding and representation of perceptual information; but cognitive science still lacks the tools, if indeed any are possible, to deal with the meaningful stories of our lives.[21]

In his clear-eyed consideration of what cognitive science does do ("elucidate sensory manifestations and neural underpinnings") and what it does not do ("describe ways that synesthesia helps organize systems of meanings"), Marks makes it possible to see the serious contribution that scholars in the humanities might make to the interdisciplinary inquiry into synesthesia. One way of understanding this book would be as an answer to Marks. The readings assembled here forge a perspective from which it is possible to see "ways that synesthesia helps organize systems of meanings": systems of meanings ranging from Stéphane Mallarmé's sonnets to Richard Wagner's *Gesamtkunstwerk* and the laryngeal theory of contemporary linguistics (to name just a few). This is what scholars in the humanities are ideally positioned to do. The tools identified as lacking within the cognitive sciences— "the tools [. . .] to deal with the meaningful stories of our lives"—are precisely the ones that scholars and writers of literature have been refining for millennia.

This book's central provocation is to question the methodological utility, in nonscientific disciplines, of assuming a binary division between literal and metaphorical descriptions of vowel color. By suspending the literal-metaphorical divide, the chapters that follow here endeavor to discern the rules by which color language moves as it begins to describe vowels. For if the rules of language are always shared, as Wittgenstein— we think—concluded,[22] then rules constraining color terms might still be discerned, even in the absence of agreement on their sense or reference. This axiom alone would be required: those who speak use color terms in keeping with shared strictures. As players of a chess game move their pawns within constraints, so do speakers evoke green and gold according to established rules that regulate their movements. At no point may any speaker use color terms purely idiosyncratically, for that would constitute a private language, and "it is not possible to obey a rule 'privately':

otherwise thinking one was obeying a rule would be the same thing as obeying it."[23] For color language to mean anything at all, some moves must be inadmissible. "Colorless green ideas sleep furiously."[24] *Do they?* Chomsky asked. They do not.

This book's object of study is thus initially linguistic: "the colors of vowels" are understood as expressions rather than physical-physiological phenomena. Readers who endeavor to locate the book's object of study outside of language may well find it distressingly diverse: inclusive of "vowel color" as well as vowels' colors, *Klangfarbe*, chromatism (*Farbigkeit*), and *coloration*. These terms are not homonymous. They are technical or near-technical designators proper to historical discourses in physical acoustics, experimental psychology, music, poetry, phonetics, and phonology. Although distinctions of sense divide them, they are surprisingly proximal in historical time. Despite Rimbaud's claim, the colors of vowels were not precisely his invention, but they would appear to be an invention of the nineteenth century.

The novelty of talking about the colors of vowels has been most clearly documented in the history of synesthesia.[25] Meticulously amassed in recent years by Jörg Jewanski, Julia Simner, Sean Day, Jamie Rothen, and Jamie Ward, this history attributes the first account of a vowel-color correspondence not to Rimbaud but to the Bavarian medical student Georg Tobias Ludwig Sachs.[26] In his doctoral dissertation of 1812, Sachs observes that "[t]here is much that [. . .] does not belong to the sense of vision," which in himself prompts "a dim representation of different colors" (*colorum quorundam obscura repraesentatio*).[27] These dim representations of different colors accompany many stimuli, including "the intervals of the musical scale" (*intervalla scalae musicae*), "the timbres of musical instruments" (*instrumentorumque musicorum voces*), and "the letters of the alphabet" (*literae alphabeti*).[28] In 1812, associating colors with musical sound was nothing new, to be sure; thinkers from Boethius to Newton and Locke had suggested relations between musical and colored tones.[29] But Sachs introduced a new element for which no precedent has been found: by his account, particular colors correspond not just to musical sounds but also to linguistic elements. Although Sachs's formulation, involving both "letters" and "the alphabet," might seem to suggest graphemes rather than sounds, his specification that "*Ue* (ü)" is gray argues strongly for the (at least partially) sonic nature of the vowels he has in mind. Thus, with Sachs, the question of a correspondence between color and sound appears, for the first time, to involve language.

Even more curious than the historical novelty of Sachs's account is the rapidity with which others begin to report similar sensations. Although the history of synesthesia furnishes no accounts of vowel-color correspondence before 1812, by 1863 the association of colors with letters is regarded as the most frequent type of synesthetic correspondence.[30] Over the next three decades, this observation is repeated and substantiated by larger-scale studies in Germany, Switzerland, and France, with vowels consistently emerging as the element most commonly associated with color.[31] This migration of sound-color correspondences from musical tones and timbres to vowels coincides with the quantification of vowels themselves as musical phenomena. In his landmark publication *Sensations of Tone* (1863), Hermann von Helmholtz demonstrated a correspondence between different vowel sounds and the balance of musical overtones realized in their voicing. Over roughly the same period, French poets from Victor Hugo to Théodore de Banville, Paul Verlaine, Arthur Rimbaud, and Stéphane Mallarmé pondered the brilliance and coloration of vowels as compositional elements in versification, just as Indo-European linguists began modeling universal vocalism in the image of a color triangle. This curious confluence of novel discourses has not been previously observed or critically examined.

Within the History of the Neurosciences, the absence of any reference to vowels' colors before 1812 has been explained with reference to research methods,[32] and it is reasonable to infer that this absence also reflects the scholars' epistemological orientation. Taking the twenty-first-century definition of synesthesia as a largely biological (and partly genetic) clinical condition of pan-chronic validity, Jewanski et al. chronicle past cases of the condition as currently defined, trace its historical nomenclature, and record changing social attitudes toward it. The condition itself, however, is not subject to historicization. Critical examination of the interests driving the creation of the contemporary construct, not to mention the porousness and elusiveness of the construct itself, would seem to be anathema to the team's work.[33] As Jewanski and his colleagues seek to discern which historical accounts might meet the modern criteria, it is not surprising that candidate cases should fall off as the texts available recede into less readily legible, premodern paradigms.[34]

When it comes to vowel colors that have been read metaphorically, the preponderance of nineteenth-century examples is remarkable and uncontested, but its historical novelty is less evident. To offer but one example: in his posthumously published *Essay on the Origin of Languages* (*Essai sur l'origine des langues*, 1781), Jean-Jacques Rousseau contends that it is possible to imagine vowel sounds beyond those used in a given language "by passing from one vowel to another in a sustained and nuanced voice; for one can make out a number of these nuances and distinguish them by means of their particular characteristics (*en passant d'une voyelle à l'autre par une voix continue et nuancée; car on peut fixer plus ou moins de ces nuances et les marquer par des caractères particuliers*)."[35] As the term *nuance* (which shares its root with *nuage*, cloud) designates the subtle variations of hue that result from a cloud's passage over the sun,[36] it is not difficult to see the visual metaphor for vocalic sound in Rousseau's term. Considering expressions that have long been read metaphorically as potentially related to synesthesia opens up a perspective from which it is possible to see that the prehistory of modern synesthesia might well lie in earlier reflections on language, particularly in the annals of poetics.

The case for this longer history is taken up in the conclusion, which reads texts foundational to divided schools of thought on "synesthesia" as fragments of a single story. Placing Charles Baudelaire's "Richard Wagner: *Tannhäuser* à Paris" (1861) in the light of neglected portions of Sachs's 1812 dissertation, this reading draws out unexpected commonalities between their representations of sensory experience. Turning to the literary history by which the synesthetic aesthetics of French Symbolism would derive from Baudelaire's "confusion"[37] of synesthesia with Wagner, the book's closing pages revisit Wagner's writings on the *Drama of the Future*, finding the origin of the *Gesamtkunstwerk* to lie, quite precisely, in the colored vowel. The element in which the arts of music and verse are as yet undivided, the "open sound" of the variegated voice—colored by cleaving consonants—strikes upon sense and the senses simultaneously, providing an affective intensity that is the point of departure for the Total Work of Art.

The point of departure for the Total Work of Art is also the endpoint of this book. As the path toward it winds through forests of symbols, many of which will be unfamiliar to literary scholars, the danger of disorientation is great. Many trees look the same. That the reader be spared the hazards of orienteering as much as possible, I offer a map of the terrain followed by an orienting compass. The first takes the form of five chapter summaries; the second, a brief reflection on Roman Jakobson's "Spectral Sounds."

Chapter Summaries

Chapter 1, "*Klangfarbe*: Vowels in Helmholtz's *Sensations of Tone*," investigates Hermann von Helmholtz's establishment of the term *Klangfarbe* as the technical designator for the quality of sound by which the ear discerns the instrument of a sound's production (harp from horn), as well as the quality of sound by which it distinguishes one vowel from the next

(A from U). With the publication of his *Lehre von den Tonempfindungen* (*Sensations of Tone*, 1863), Helmholtz made it impossible, in German, to discuss distinctions between vowel sounds without speaking simultaneously of their "colors." Why did the Prussian polymath introduce a color metaphor to designate a property of sound whose physical, objective structure he bears the considerable distinction of demonstrating? This chapter elucidates the contours and origins of Helmholtz's terminology, finding that the term *Klangfarbe* extends to vowels only from the moment that vowels themselves are reconceived as musical: as balances of overtones rather than signifying elements of language. Drawing out the contemporaneity of Helmholtz's studies of musical and color perception, the chapter uncovers the traces of a failed quest to establish a physical basis for sound-color correspondence inscribed within Helmholtz's *Sensations of Tone* and *Optics*.

Chapter 2, "The Interaction of Color," turns to the reports of *audition colorée* (colored hearing) collected by experimental psychologists in the 1880s and 1890s. It finds that subjects often describe not just the colors they see in connection with vowels but also how these colors interact with one another in connection with their phonetic and prosodic environments. These descriptions strongly resemble contemporaneous discussions of vowel "nuance," "colors," "coloring," and "coloration" amongst French poets of roughly the same period (L. Becq de Fouquières, Théodore de Banville, Stéphane Mallarmé, Victor Hugo, Paul Verlaine). Observing that the metaphorical colors of the poetic discourse—central to the period's trope of describing poetry as painting—behave in provocatively similar ways to the synesthetic colors, the chapter posits a potential relation between the synesthetic and poetic terms. Turning to the history of poetry from this new perspective, it concludes by observing that in poetics, the language of color indexes aspects of language distinct from both meter and signification, enabling a vision of verse as an art of color composition conceivable even in the absence of the line.

Chapter 3, "Mallarmé and the Tension of Timbre," probes Stéphane Mallarmé's conviction in vowels' universally perceptible qualities, finding these properties imperative to his conception of verse. In his watershed essay "Crisis of Verse" (*Crise de vers*, 1897), Mallarmé describes vowel *timbre* (the French translation of *Klangfarbe*) in terms of brightness, darkness, and coloring, famously lamenting the mismatched timbres of "*jour* [day] and *nuit* [night], dark in the first case, bright in the second." He suggests that these vocalic qualities may "contradict" words' signification and that this potential conflict between sound and sense installs a tension in language that is the condition of possibility for verse.

Although Mallarmé's reflections on the crisis of verse have been generally understood to chronicle the decline of meter and the emergence of non-metrical poetry (*vers libre*), this chapter uncovers another definition of poetry in Mallarmé's writings: one that depends on a tension between vocalic timbre and signification, and which ensures the safe passage of poetry into a meterless world.

Chapter 4, "The Colors of the Universal Alphabet," turns from the imagined, universal alphabet that animates Mallarmé's vision of verse to the universal phonetic alphabets developed across Europe in the mid-nineteenth century. Born of a political will to standardize regional pronunciation and contend with the many non-European languages of overseas Empires, these "universal alphabets" sought to devise a single set of symbols capable of transcribing all possible sounds of human speech. How does one even imagine such sounds? What models emerge to enable their anticipation? This chapter tells the story of the prominent and persistent model that presents vocalic sound in the image of a color triangle. Beginning with the controversy surrounding K. R. Lepsius's vowel-color pyramid (*Standard Alphabet*, 1855), it traces Lepsius's vowel triangle back to C. F. Hellwag's 1781 *Dissertatio de formatione loquelae* and its triangular arrangement of colors to J. H. Lambert's color pyramid of 1772. It then locates a possible synesthetic basis for the vowel-color analogy in the proceedings of the 1892 International Congress of Experimental Psychology, where Sir Francis Galton mentions that Lepsius connected color with sounds and assembles the archival evidence for a synesthetic intuition underpinning Lepsius's vocalic model. Finding Lepsius's vowel-color analogy to rely less on a phenomenal similarity between colors and vowels than on their opposable nature, the chapter concludes by noting the uncanny resemblance between Lepsius's vowel-color pyramid and the vowel-color model that emerges in the twentieth-century science of phonology forged by Roman Jakobson and N. S. Trubetzkoy.

No figure would seem to be more antithetical to the idea of vowel-color correspondence than Ferdinand de Saussure, the founder of structural linguistics and, for better or worse, the name most strongly associated with the principle of linguistic arbitrariness. Yet Saussure also left an account of the colors of vowels in a report published anonymously in Théodore Flournoy's *Phénomènes de synopsie* (1893) and attributed only posthumously by Mireille Cifali in 1983. Chapter 5, "*L'être imaginaire*: Saussure's Colored Vowels," undertakes a close reading of the vowel-color text, asking what prompts Saussure's sensations of color and where those sensations might have left traces in the linguist's corpus. Finding Saussure's colored sensations to be tied to a diachronic perspective on language, the chapter turns to Saussure's oft-neglected publications in Indo-European linguistics to show how his synesthetic perceptions of vowels might have informed his groundbreaking *Thesis on the Primitive Vowel System of the Indo-European Languages* (*Mémoire sur le système primitif des voyelles dans les langues indo-européennes*, 1879). Supplementing the synchronic perspective for which Saussure is principally known, this chapter traces the implicit relationship between orthography, phonetics, and linguistic evolution in Saussure's thought, presenting a surprisingly subjective, sensuous side of "Saussurean linguistics."

Spectral Sounds

In one of his last publications, *The Sound Shape of Language* (1979), Roman Jakobson makes a passing reference to the research of "Saussure's colleague, the Genevan psychologist Édouard Claparède."[38] The reference appears in the context of a discussion of "sound symbolism": linguistic instances in which a particular linguistic sound (typically a phoneme) seems to be intrinsically bound to a particular meaning (typically a quality, such as a color). In his effort to discern the nature of these conjunctions through various attestations in different languages, Jakobson notes a recurring connection between colors and vowels, citing Claparède's observation that "the capacity for comparison between colors and speech sounds seems to exist in each individual in at least an elementary stage."[39] Jakobson's bibliography links the reference back to Claparède's short article "On Colored Hearing (*Sur l'audition colorée*)" (1900)—a piece devoted to defending the integrity of the subjects reporting synesthetic sensations.[40] As Claparède participated in but a single study of such sensations, the research to which Jakobson refers can be none other than Théodore Flournoy's 1893 *Phénomènes de synopsie*, the very work in which Saussure's account of colored vowels appears.

Of course, at the time of writing, Jakobson had no means of knowing that Saussure was among the subjects on whom Claparède's conclusion was based. As it turned out, Jakobson never would know. The towering figure of structural linguistics passed away in the summer of 1982, just months before Cifali republished Saussure's newly attributed "Réponse." What Saussure's most prominent intellectual heir would have made of his reflections on the colors of vowels, therefore, must remain a matter of speculation.

It seems safe to say, however, that Jakobson would have taken great interest in Saussure's observations, for Jakobson maintained throughout his scientific career that there existed "a phenomenal connection between different sensory modes, in particular between the visual and auditory experience."[41] Furthermore, he held that this connection furnished the very condition of possibility for sound symbolism, one of the hallmarks of poetic art. Poetry is not the exclusive domain of sound symbolism in Jakobson's account, to be sure, but it is "a province where the internal nexus between sound and meaning changes from latent to patent and manifests itself most intensely."[42]

The position finds its most lucid articulation in "Linguistics and Poetics," a lecture Jakobson delivered at Indiana University in the spring of 1958. Here, after investigating several instances of sound symbolism in poetry, he offers an explicit definition of the phenomenon:

> Sound symbolism is an undeniably objective relation founded on a phenomenal connection between different sensory modes, in particular between the visual and auditory experience. If the results of research in this area have sometimes been vague or controversial, it is primarily due to an insufficient care for the methods of psychological and/or linguistic inquiry. Particularly from the linguistic point of view the picture has often been distorted by lack of attention to the phonological aspect of speech sounds or by inevitably vain operations with complex phonemic units instead of with their ultimate components. But when, on testing, for example, such phonemic oppositions as grave versus acute we ask whether /i/ or /u/ is darker, some of the subjects may respond that this question makes no sense to them, but hardly one will state that /i/ is the darker of the two.[43]

For Jakobson, the condition of possibility for sound symbolism is a "phenomenal connection between different sensory modes." As these "sensory modes" belong to physical bodies, the connection is entirely "subjective" in nature; it takes place within and by means of the speaking subject. Jakobson's contention that "[s]ound symbolism is an undeniably objective relation," therefore, opposes the term "objective" not to "subjective," as is commonly thought, but to "subject-specific." His claim is that phenomenal connections between different sensory modes, such as one sees in the common perception that /u/ is darker than /i/, possess universal or near-universal subjective validity. Otherwise put, if viewed from the proper vantage point, the connections betray commonalities across all subjects.

In Jakobson's account, this phenomenal connection exists primarily between visual perceptions and minimal units of language, aurally conceived—or, more precisely, their "ultimate components." These components are the phonetic qualities of speech sounds that a given language has opposed: the degree of oral aperture required for the production of a particular vowel, for example (often referred to in terms of an "open/closed" opposition), or the passage of air through the nose required for the production of "nasal" vowels (as in the French *chien*). The example Jakobson offers is Stéphane Mallarmé's: that the "grave" vowel /u/ (*jour*) is "darker" than the "acute" vowel /i/ (*nuit*). This connection between sound qualities and visual perceptions provides the basis for linguistic expectation: for a collective intuition among speaking beings that a particular sound would be more fitting to one particular circumstance than another. Thus, while "[i]n referential language the connection between *signans* and *signatum* is overwhelmingly based on their codified contiguity, which is often confusingly labeled 'arbitrariness of the verbal sign,'" Jakobson explains, the relationship between *signans* and *signatum* in poetry is not strictly one of convention.[44] In poetry, one perceives the possibility of a fittingness between sound and sense, a fittingness that derives from latent synesthetic conjunctions by which the minimal units of language are associated with sensuous qualities.

But whence might such universal synesthetic conjunctions between sound and sense derive? Neither the chapter on "Synesthesia" in *The Sound Shape of Language* nor the discussion of sound symbolism in the 1958 lecture offers any explanation as to why speakers of all languages would intuitively sense /u/ to be darker than /i/. A hurried reader of these texts might well conclude that Jakobson's conviction in this universal intuition is based solely on incomplete empirical data that, by his own account, is plagued by "insufficient care for the methods of psychological and/or linguistic inquiry."[45]

Such a conclusion, however, would be hasty, as Jakobson lays out the basis for this conviction in considerable detail in a much earlier text (albeit one that might not initially appear to have much bearing on questions of poetry). During his wartime exile in the Nordic countries between 1939 and 1941, Jakobson undertook a study of child language and aphasia, which he published in German under the title *Kindersprache, Aphasie und allgemeine Lautgesetze* (1941).[46] The text bears the considerable distinction of being the first to articulate the basic series of oppositions by which infants acquire the sounds of speech, as well as the sequence of losses by which people with aphasia lose them. Rather than consider the imperfect speech of the child and the aphasic as falling outside the realm of linguistic research, as his predecessors had done, Jakobson contended that these inchoate utterances might provide privileged insight into the structures and processes underlying normal human speech.

His argument may be easily summarized. Although each language in the world possesses its own distinctive set of sounds, the basic oppositions underlying them all bear striking resemblances. Jakobson contends that the first opposition to emerge in all infants learning to speak is an opposition between sounds that severely constrict the passage of air and sounds that require it: what we might generally refer to as the opposition between consonants and vowels. One might also understand this distinction "from the motor point of view" in terms of aperture: the degree to which one opens one's mouth. Hence, some variation of [a] is always the first vowel to appear, in opposition to the labial stop [m], as this difference more or less represents the most significant motor opposition available to the human speech apparatus.[47] The first interconsonantal opposition to emerge will oppose a nasal stop (e.g., [m], [n]) to an oral one (e.g., [p], [t]), and the oppositions will progress with increasing refinement until the full soundscape of a particular language has been established. Within the vocalic sounds, the fundamental series of oppositions involves only two steps. First, the child will oppose a wide vowel such as [a] to a narrow one such as [i], enabling babbling strings of *papa-pipi*; the child will then split the narrow vowel into palatal and velar variations, expanding the possibilities of babble beyond *papa* and *pipi* to include *pupu*.[48] These two processes, Jakobson concludes, lead to "a system of three vowels, which is the minimal vocalic system presented by the languages of the world."[49]

A few pages later, this "minimal vocalic system" proves integral to Jakobson's consideration of the "Agreements between the Systems of Sound and Color." Turning to "the penetrating analysis" of the German philosopher and psychologist Carl Stumpf, Jakobson considers Stumpf's proposition that to this basic vowel triangle there correspond "two psychophysical processes — the U - I process, which is connected to the

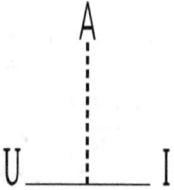

↑ *Farbigkeit* (chromatism)

→ *Helligkeit* (brightness)

FIGURE 1. Jakobson's diagram for the first vocalic oppositions to emerge in all languages (*Kindersprache*, 1941)

brightness (*Helligkeit*) of sound sensations, and the A process, which determines their degree of chromatism (*Farbigkeit*)."[50] *Farbigkeit*, "chromatism," charts the axis on which the first vocalic distinction (*papa-pipi*) is based (what Jakobson refers to as the "wide-narrow distinction"); *Helligkeit*, "brightness," charts the axis established by the second vocalic distinction (*pipi-pupu*) (see Figure 1). Noting the visual metaphors parading as linguistic terms ("brightness," "chromatism"), Jakobson is led to question the strict metaphoricity of the technical jargon. "It is possible to stay within the limits of phonological phenomena concerning the inquiry into sound qualities," he writes,

> and to view the terms light-dark and chromatic-achromatic, as well as variegated or hueless colours, as simple metaphors and to replace them eventually with non-metaphorical terms; but the problem of the phenomenal similarity between sound and colour is becoming more and more evident. Obviously, both series of qualities, lightness-darkness and chromatic-achromatic, are common to sound and visual sensations, and the structure of sound and colour systems shows marked agreements.[51]

By way of illustrating how the apparently "simple metaphors" might indicate a "phenomenal similarity between sound and colour," Jakobson points out that "cases of pronounced coloured hearing, especially in children or retained from childhood, [. . .] show the close connection of the vowels *o* and *u* with the specifically dark colours, and of *e* and *i*, on the other hand, with specifically light colours."[52] Such individuals also demonstrate a "distinct inclination [. . .] to connect the more chromatic vowels with the variegated colours, especially *a* with red."[53] For those who hear colors in vowels, Jakobson thus suggests, the axes of vowel brightness and chromatism simultaneously chart out the relations of both phonic and visual phenomena.

In Jakobson's account, then, the linguistic terms "brightness" and "chromatism" are not "simple metaphors" that might be easily replaced with non-metaphorical terms, as the metaphors signal the phenomenal connection between speech sounds' phonetic qualities and the visual brightness and chromatism experienced by synesthetes. This connection is crucial not only for the study of synesthesia, Jakobson contends, but also for the study of child language and, consequently, language writ large. Suspecting colored hearing to be a vestigial condition, common to all in the last stages of infancy and surviving with varying degrees of strength into adulthood, Jakobson cautiously suggests that its structures might well be integral to the acquisition of speech, our mastery of maximal phonic oppositions aided and abetted by the relationships we perceive between visual shades and hues. As prattling children striving to produce the sounds of language, we might well memorize by means of association, mapping out new motor oppositions within preexisting visual scales. Our intuitive notion of *jour* as "dark" and *nuit* as "light," then, would derive from a synesthetic vowel-color correspondence that was once vital to us but which, ceasing to be necessary as we mastered the sounds of a mother tongue, receded all but irretrievably into oblivion. Such a correspondence would make itself felt only when suddenly realized in an utterance perfectly aligning its elements—or, perhaps, misaligning them so perversely as to make us realize that we had a notion, however dim, of what "perfection" might be.

1 / *Klangfarbe*: Vowels in Helmholtz's *Sensations of Tone*

Every homogeneous substance that resumes its shape after gentle impact may be said to possess a proper tone. Strike a glass, for example, and it will ring with a particular sound consistent and distinct from that of the silver or the porcelain plate. The sound may be altered, to a degree, by a change in striking instrument, point of incidence, or nature of impact, as well as the quantity of liquid rippling in the glass. A rap on a near-empty globe will, as everyone knows, ring out over the dull clink of an over-filled chalice. The proper tone of a given glass thus admits of multiple sounds variable in pitch and volume, subject to the accidents of the moment. But while a glass that has been struck may indeed produce many tones, there is only one pitch that, when sung into its cup, will bring the glass to ring. Varied as the tones born of the stricken glass may be, a consistency nonetheless asserts itself amongst them, too: human beings will link them all, and no others, directly back to the object of their making. Sight unseen, we will know the instrument of the sounds' production, bearing witness to an aspect shared amongst all its tones. The sonic affinities of silent things compose a hidden realm best known to the makers of musical instruments, but their general principle is familiar to all.

This general principle, readily intuited by the untrained ear, has proven less evident in the absence of that organ. A riddle of centuries, the question of just how the tone of one sounding body differs from that of the next bears a considerable history of intellectual inquiry.[1] This inquiry reached a pivotal turning point in the mid-nineteenth century, when the Prussian polymath Hermann von Helmholtz proposed an answer that lay not in the nature of the sounding body—as so many of his predecessors had supposed—but rather in the nature of the sound waves it produced. Helmholtz's argument emerged as part of a larger investigation into the physical and physiological processes involved in the human perception of music. A physician by training and Professor of Physiology and Anatomy at the University of Bonn at the time, Helmholtz was dissatisfied with the gap he perceived between the mathematical study of music on the one hand and the physiological study of hearing on the other.[2] While musical intervals had been figured in mathematical ratios since the Pythagoreans, how the ear perceived these ratios remained entirely obscure. "Musicians, as well as philosophers and physicists," Helmholtz remarked, "have generally contented themselves with saying, in effect, that human minds were in some unknown manner constituted so as to elicit the numerical relations of the vibrations of tones, and have a peculiar pleasure in contemplating simple and readily comprehensible ratios."[3] Determined to elucidate how mathematical ratio passed into the "particular pleasure" of consonant sounds, Helmholtz embarked on a study of unprecedented scope, investigating not only the nature of musical sound and its propagation but also the nature of that sound's perception in the human ear.[4] Although the physiological portion of Helmholtz's work fell subject to revision shortly after its publication, the reorientation its inclusion necessitated positioned him to achieve several major insights into the nature of harmony. And so, paradoxically, it is on the strength of its acoustical rather than physiological analysis that the physician's landmark treatise *On the Sensations of Tone as a Physiological Basis for the Theory of Music* (*Die Lehre von den Tonempfindungen als Physiologische Grundlage für die Theorie der Musik*, 1863) retains pride of place within the study of musical sound.

It is a fact far less frequently remarked on that Helmholtz's *Sensations of Tone* also marks a decisive development in the study of language. Its anomalous chapter devoted not to the sounds of musical instruments, nor yet to the singing voice, but to "the musical sounds of vowels" (*Klänge der Vocale*), bears the considerable distinction of being the first to offer a physical account of vowels' acoustic structure.[5] It responded to two intractable questions that had emerged over the preceding century as scientific problems: What distinguishes vowel sounds from all other sounds, and what distinguishes one vowel sound from the next? Seamlessly extending his analysis of musical tone to linguistic sounds, Helmholtz proposed a single term in answer to both questions: "*Klangfarbe*," or "sound-color." With his 1863 treatise, Helmholtz thus introduced "color" into the scientific discourse on vowels, making it impossible—at least in German—to discuss vocalic sound without speaking of color as well. But what sort of "color" was this? What was *Klangfarbe* in Helmholtz's conception? This chapter recalls and explicates Helmholtz's decisive resignification of *Klangfarbe* in his *Sensations of Tone*, showing how this new definition enabled the novel migration of color metaphor from musical tones to vowels.

Overtones

Helmholtz's novel definition of *Klangfarbe* emerges as the fruit of an investigation into the aural experience of music conceived as "sensations of tone" (*Tonempfindungen*). The scope of these sensations is defined explicitly at the start of the work. Helmholtz delimits them first not by any property inherent to the tones themselves, but rather by the sense organ of their detection: the ear.[6] Within the "sensations of sound" (*Schallempfindungen*) thus described, Helmholtz establishes a further distinction between "musical sounds" (*musikalische Klänge*) and "noise" (*Geräusch*).[7] This division, in contrast to the first, resides in the nature of the stimulus: "musical sounds" result from periodic motion of the air, "noise" from non-periodic motion.[8] Consequently, this division also differs from the first in that it is not absolute. Unlike sensations of taste and sound, whose distinction is guaranteed by the discrete sense organs integral to their definition, noises and musical tones "may certainly intermingle in very various degrees, and pass insensibly into one another." One may create noise by compounding multiple musical sounds, "as, for example, by simultaneously striking all the keys contained in one or two octaves of a pianoforte."[9] Since musical sounds may be compounded to create noise, Helmholtz reasons, they must be "the simpler and more regular elements of the sensations of hearing," and hence the evident starting point for study.[10]

Although the category of sound Helmholtz sets out to investigate is introduced as "musical sounds" (*musikalische Klänge*), the modifier "*musikalische*" disappears almost immediately from his text. But a sentence after the category's introduction, Helmholtz offers "the sounds of musical instruments" as examples not of "*musikalische Klänge*" but merely of "*Klänge*," proceeding to the opposition from which the chapter "*Geräusch und Klänge*" derives its name. The text offers little room for doubt that the term *Klänge* is to be understood as *musikalische Klänge*; indeed, the English translator Alexander Ellis implicitly argues as much in his decision to translate *Klänge* systematically as "musical tones."[11] Yet Helmholtz's fleeting introductory modifier "musical" is telling. Its presence attests to its absence, or at least its potential absence, from *Klänge*—acknowledging the possibility of non-musical *Klänge*. As the schema Helmholtz presents can admit of no such category, the ambiguity lurking in the language is quickly cast out. Yet the question, once identified, persists: What would such nonmusical *Klänge* be, and can they be so easily banished from an inquiry into sensations of tone?

The term "tone" (*Ton*) itself emerges to designate a specialized category of *Klänge*: a "tone" is a musical sound resulting from aerial vibrations strictly pendular in nature.[12] Helmholtz offers an illustration to clarify this distinction. Taking a taut string fixed at both ends, he notes that such a string "may first be made to vibrate as in fig. 17a, so that its appearance when displaced from its position of rest is always that of a simple half wave" (see Figure 2).[13] The string moves back and forth across this central axis, availing itself of the greatest possible distance from its position of rest. It accelerates as it approaches the center and slows as it stretches to the outer reaches of its curve. This motion, Helmholtz explains, is precisely like that of a pendulum, which accelerates to its greatest speed just as it swoops through the low point of its arc. Carried out in the string at a speed perceived as vibration, this pendular motion "gives just one tone, the deepest it can produce."[14] Born of a single sounding body set in pendular motion, a "tone" by definition corresponds to a single pitch (*Tonhöhe*), the pitch of a musical sound having long been known to reside upon the frequency of its periodic motion.[15] The application of the term *Tonhöhe*, however, remains distinct from that of *Ton*, marking but one aspect of a sound of which a great deal more might be said.

It had been observed at least as early as 1701 by the French mathematician Joseph Sauveur that the movement of an open string could involve several different arcs beyond this basic one.[16] It had also been observed, indeed far earlier, that the seemingly singular sound produced by a sonorous string belied many subtler, indissociable sounds.[17] It was not until Helmholtz's study, however, that the arcs Sauveur had identified were

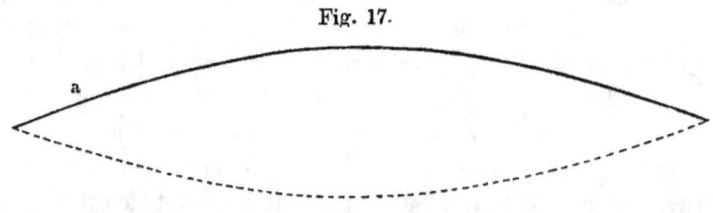

FIGURE 2. Helmholtz's illustration of a simple wave (*Tonempfindungen*, 1863)

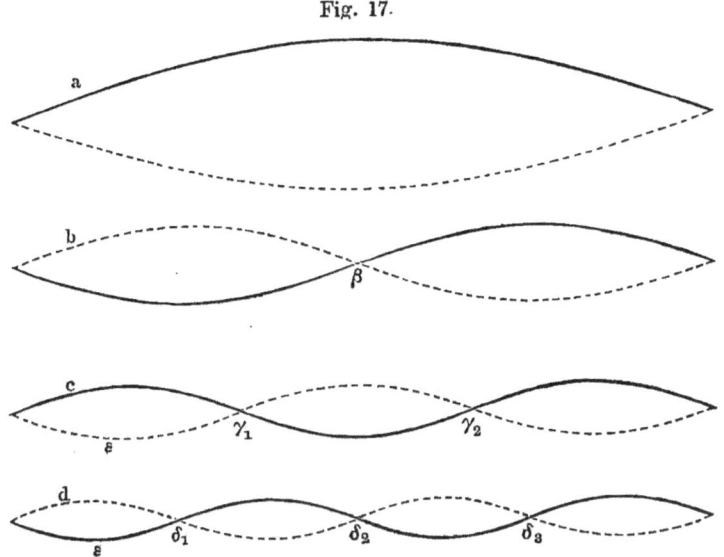

FIGURE 3. Helmholtz's diagram for the curves through which a string may simultaneously pass (*Tonempfindungen*, 1863)

demonstrated to produce multiple simultaneous sounds of discrete and verifiable pitches: or, as Helmholtz called them, "overtones" (*Obertöne*).

Helmholtz's account was enabled by two nineteenth-century developments in the realms of physics and mathematics: G. S. Ohm's aforementioned articulation, in 1843, of the mathematical equation characterizing the periodic motion of a musical tone and Joseph Fourier's demonstration, in the 1820s, of the decomposability of all periodic motion. During an investigation into the propagation of heat, Fourier uncovered a generalizable principle: under a given set of conditions, any periodic function could be decomposed into a series of periodic functions whose frequencies would divide evenly into the fundamental one.[18] Such a principle, Helmholtz was quick to perceive, must apply to the periodic motion of musical sound as described by Ohm. Although the mathematical proof behind the "Fourier series" is quite complex, the motion it describes in music is easily illustrated. One need look no further than Helmholtz's figure 17 (see Figure 3). Although the simple movement described in figure 17a is easy to transform conceptually into the aerial vibration of a musical tone, anyone who has observed the vibration of sonorous strings knows that their movement is not quite so simple. One is obliged to admit that the simplicity of the pendular account belies a far more unwieldy wiggling. Any additional movement in the string, however, must result from its passing simultaneously through other wave-curves commensurate with its total length (such as those in figures 17 b, c, and d), for no string will assume the shape of a curve whose length does not coincide, in some multiple, with its own. All the wave-curves available to the string, then, must represent perfect divisors of the one in figure 17a. Or, in Fourier's terms, the periodic motion depicted in figure 17a must be decomposable into the movement depicted in figures 17b, c, d, and so on. Thus, Fourier's theorem provided the mathematical basis for Helmholtz's argument that these waves coexist within a single string.

The proportional relations between these wave-curves, however, can also be conceived in terms entirely independent of the Fourier series. Designating the tone produced by the longest wave-curve a as the "prime tone" (*Grundton*), Helmholtz demonstrates that "[i]n the vibrational form b the string produces only the upper octave of its prime tone, in the form c the twelfth, and in the form d the second octave."[19] One may well continue to the ever higher pitches resulting from the increasingly minute wave-curves of the string. The intervals thus revealed are far from obscure: they are, in order of ascendance, the octave, a perfect fifth beyond that, a perfect fourth beyond that (or the second octave), another major third up, a minor third up, another minor third up, and a whole tone (see Figure 4).[20]

That these forms of vibration exist simultaneously may be verified, Helmholtz explains, by means of sympathetic resonance (*Phänomen des Mittönens*).[21] A phenomenon already well-known to the musicians of Helmholtz's day, sympathetic resonance is easy to observe.[22] When the strings of two violins are tuned to exact unison, and the string of one instrument is bowed, the corresponding string upon the other will begin to vibrate visibly.[23] This is because the aerial vibrations of the first string correspond in wavelength to the prime tone of the second. Hence, the second string is easily set in motion by these movements of the air, while

FIGURE 4. Helmholtz's first scale of the overtone series (*Tonempfindungen*, 1863)

the other strings upon the violins, attuned to other wavelengths, appear unmoved. Although such a string can be made to sound many tones, as the violinist's art amply demonstrates, one tone may nonetheless be identified as most natural to it. For this reason, Helmholtz refers to this tone, and this tone alone, as the string's "proper tone" (*Eigenton*).

Through sympathetic resonance, the student of sound may visually verify the presence of ambient wavelengths in the air. Raise the lid of a pianoforte, Helmholtz urges, and select the note whose presence you wish to ascertain—middle C, for example. Raise the damper on the corresponding string and place a small wood chip on it. "You will find," Helmholtz writes with assurance, "the chip put in motion, or even thrown off, when certain other strings are struck." The strings that cause the chip to move—"c, F, C, A_1b, F_1, D or C_1"—are those whose primes correspond to wave-curves evenly divisible by that of a middle C. The proper tone of middle C is present in the sounding of any of these notes, as evidenced by the movement of the chip. "We must therefore not hold it to be an illusion of the ear or to be mere imagination," Helmholtz concludes, "when in the musical tone of a single note emanating from a musical instrument, we distinguish many overtones, as I have found musicians inclined to think, even when they have heard those overtones quite distinctly with their own ears."[24] He summarizes his findings as follows:

> The ear, when its attention has been properly directed to the effect of the vibrations which strike it, does not hear merely that one tone whose pitch is determined by the period of the vibrations in [fig 17a], but in addition to this, it becomes aware of a whole series of higher tones, which we will call the sound's harmonic overtones [*die harmonischen Obertöne des Klanges*], in contradistinction to the first tone, the prime tone, as it may be called, which is the lowest and generally the loudest of all the overtones, and by the pitch of which we judge the pitch of the whole sound [*Klang*].[25]

Thus, the prime, or proper tone born of any given string is but one component of the sound emanating from it: "it" being less properly a tone than, as its other name suggests, a chord.

Adopting Ohm's sinusoidal equation for a single tone, Helmholtz uses the term *Ton* to designate only those "simple tones" (*einfache Töne*) whose movement corresponds to it: strictly pendular aerial vibrations productive of a single pitch. A tone is thus, in Helmholtz's usage, defined exclusively by the nature of its sound waves, without reference to the instruments of its production or detection. This definition is somewhat at odds with the term "tone" itself, whose earliest attestations tie it precisely to the tension of a stretched string. The German *Ton*, like the English *tone*, derives from the Greek τόνος, which means "that by which a thing is stretched" or "a stretching, tightening, straining, strain, tension."[26] As Greek music theory is based on the sounds of stretched strings, it is unsurprising that the term for "tension" should extend to designate the particular sounds determined by strings' tautness.[27]

If, in its earliest recorded form, a "tone" designated the sound of a taut string, the term gained a new application in the discourse of the Pythagoreans, who understood it not as a sound but as an interval. While the ancient study of music had long identified three basic consonances (the fourth, the fifth, and the octave), the minimal interval of a single "tone"—upon which the entire modern terminology is based—played no role in the classical calculations. The classical measurements were based on the unit of half a monochord: the octave being the "diaplasion diastema" (διπλάσιον διάστημα), or "doubled line"; the fourth, the "hemilion diastema" (ἡμιόλιον διάστημα), or "line 1½ [units] in length"; and the fifth, the "epitriton diastema" (ἐπίτριτον διάστημα), or "line 1⅓ [units] in length."[28] Not until the time of the Pythagoreans does the interval of one tone become requisite to musical terminology: the "epitriton diastema" becoming the *diapente* (διαπέντε), literally "through five [tones]," and the "hemilion diastema" the *diatessaron* (διατεσσάρων), or "through four."[29] This minimal unit has persisted, more or less recognizably, since that time, and continues to form the basis for the diatonic scale [dia (διά) + tonos (τόνος), or, "proceeding by tones"] of Western music.[30]

Although there is no doubt that the "*Ton*" of Helmholtz's title refers to the sound waves identified by Ohm rather than the Pythagoreans' minimal unit, the ancient terms persist in Helmholtz's text, as well. While not inviolable, the interval of one tone is as imperative to Helmholtz's schema of sound as is the modern measure of pitch. As the English translator Alexander Ellis notes, "Even Prof. Helmholtz himself has not succeeded in using his word *Ton* consistently for a *simple* tone only."[31] One distinction between the two terms nevertheless remains inviolate. The term *Ton*, even in its erroneous applications, remains strictly confined within the realm of music, while its modern successor, *Klang*, slips into an ambiguous zone of sounds whose musicality is less assured.

Having demonstrated the existence of overtones in the sounds of sonorous strings, Helmholtz proceeds to verify their presence in the music of other instruments. He determines not only that many—indeed, most— musical sounds contain overtones, but also that the intervals at which they occur "is precisely the same for all compound musical tones."[32] Strings, bells, flutes, brass horns, and reed instruments all produce musical sounds whose powerful prime belies an array of overtones sounding at the very same, set intervals. Thus, the intervals of the overtones composing a musical sound, be they consonant or dissonant, could not be said to arise from the instrument of their production.

What Helmholtz does find the instrument of production to determine, however, is the degree of realization of the overtones in any given instance. In verifying the various overtones present in a sonorous string, for example, Helmholtz finds the tones' upper boundary to be determined by the physical limits of the string at hand. Fine strings will yield a greater number of higher overtones than thicker strings because wave-curves cease to form when the length of string required for their production is "too short and stiff to be capable of sonorous vibration."[33] Thus "violin and the lower pianoforte strings" will yield about ten overtones, while "extremely fine wires" can easily generate sixteen to twenty.[34] The sonic difference readily perceptible to the human ear lies in this physical difference, Helmholtz explains, though "in most cases the mathematical analysis of the motions of sound is not nearly far enough advanced to determine with certainty which overtones will be present and what intensity they will possess."[35]

What strings reveal once again elucidates generalizable principles, and Helmholtz proceeds to demonstrate how the physical constitution of various instruments affects both the range and the intensity of the overtones they produce. The phenomenon is most readily evident, he suggests, in bells. "The overtones are most easily perceived when they are not in harmony with the fundamental tone," Helmholtz explains, "as in the case of bells." While the first few overtones lie at intervals consonant with the prime tone and one another (the octave, twelfth, and second octave), the intervals of incidence diminish as the overtones ascend, causing the sounds they produce to grow increasingly dissonant. Instruments with fewer, deeper overtones, such as the violin and pianoforte, will therefore sound more pleasing and unified than instruments generating many higher overtones, such as bells. "The art of the bell-founder," Helmholtz observes, "consists precisely in giving bells such a form that the deeper and stronger overtones shall be in harmony with the fundamental tone, as otherwise the bell would be unmusical, tinkling like a kettle. But the higher overtones are always out of harmony, and hence bells are unfitted for artistic music."[36]

Accounting for the curiously different forms of the sound waves generated by two bodies sounding at the same pitch with the same volume, the overtones furnished a physical basis for the ear's ability to identify individual sources of sound. Physicists' assumption that an instrument's sonic stamp lay in the form of a sound's vibration (an assumption "hitherto based simply on the fact of our knowing that the quality of the tone could not possibly depend on the periodic time of a vibration, or on its amplitude"[37]) could thus be considered demonstrated. It was no small feat. In establishing the role of the overtones in creating the differing sounds produced by various instruments, Helmholtz furnished the first known system of measurement for an exceedingly enigmatic aspect of sound. The musical sounds Helmholtz knew had, by his own account, been subject to specification in terms of just two axes: that of pitch and that of volume.[38] A tone's pitch had been shown to depend on the speed of the vibrations it provoked in the air, and its volume could be accounted for in the amplitude of those vibrations. There were a great many aspects of sound, however, of which those two equations offered no account. Evident to all human beings, yet unidentified in terms of physical acoustics, these aspects included the difference between "smooth" or "harsh" tones, the distinctions between the various vowel sounds,[39] and "that property of sound, by which we know the tone of a violin from that of a flute or of a trumpet."[40] Escaping as they did the systems of quantification known to the study of music, these aspects of sound fell, by default, into an amorphous, axis-less dimension generally referred to as "quality."

"Quality," while widely discussed, was a vague and heterogeneous notion at best. As Helmholtz observes in his 1863 study, "There has been a general inclination to credit quality with all possible peculiarities of musical tones that were not evidently due to pitch or volume."[41] Pursuing greater clarity in this obscure field, Helmholtz found that, contrary to the negative conception by which "quality" contained everything not attributable to pitch or volume, it could, in most cases, be demonstrated to be a function of both. The quality of a sound was determined by, but not reducible to, the pitch of its prime tone; its particular shading was determined by the degrees of realization the sounding instrument permitted its various overtones. The quality of a sound was thus not something other than pitch and volume; it was a complex pattern of their relations: pitches realized with varying degrees of force that, like a sonic stamp, marked all musical sounds emanating into the air with the imprint of their instrument of production. For this quality no longer qualitative but quantitative in nature, Helmholtz proposed a name unattested in his sources: "*Klangfarbe.*"

The Tone of a Breath

During his investigation, Helmholtz introduced a novel device for analyzing musical sound. The "Helmholtz resonator," as it is still known today, consists of a blown glass sphere or metal tube with openings at two opposing points (see Figure 5). The interior dimensions of the resonators are calculated to correspond to a specific wavelength, enabling their instruments to isolate and amplify a particular pitch. If one applies such a resonant cavity to one's ear while stopping the other, Helmholtz explains, "most of the tones produced in the surrounding air will be considerably damped; but if the proper tone of the resonator is sounded, it will bray into the ear most powerfully."[42] Resonant cavities had been used in sound analysis for quite some time, but the Prussian researcher's instruments possessed one crucial difference. Resonators of the past had been open at one end only and were at the other end affixed with a drum, whose

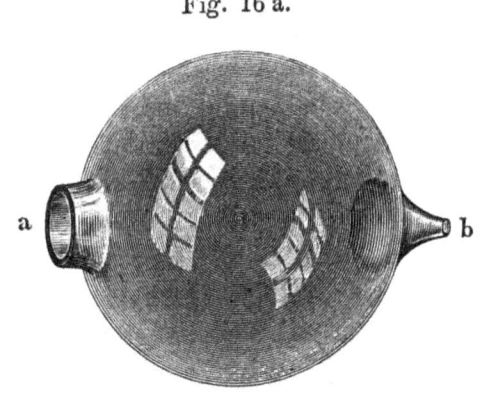

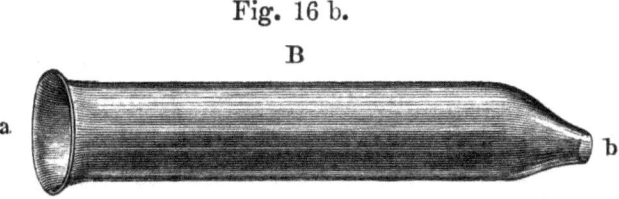

FIGURE 5. Helmholtz resonators, as illustrated in the *Tonempfindungen* (1863)

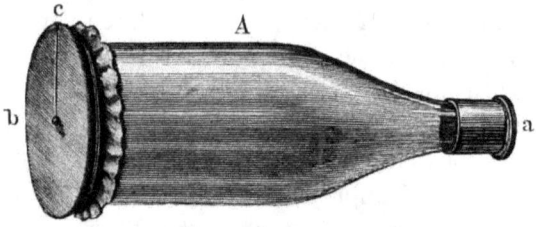

FIGURE 6. Bottle Resonator, as illustrated in the *Tonempfindungen* (1863)

movement, manifested in the bobbling of the bead fixed beside it, would indicate the presence of the cavity's proper tone (see Figure 6). Helmholtz's innovation was to remove this drum, molding the open end of the resonant chamber into a funnel instead. Fitting this funnel into the ear with a bit of soft sealing wax, Helmholtz created a resonator that functioned in much the same way as the previous device, excepting that "the observer's own tympanic membrane has been made to replace the former artificial one."[43]

While investigating the upper overtones of reed organ pipes with the aid of such resonators, Helmholtz stumbled upon a curious phenomenon. It could happen, he observed, that the proper tone of the resonator would correspond not to the prime tone played by the instrument, but to one of its overtones, in which case "the corresponding overtone is really more reinforced by the resonance chamber than the prime or other overtones, and consequently predominates extremely over all the other overtones in the series." The resultant sound, Helmholtz observes, has "consequently a peculiar character, and more or less resembles one of the vowels of the human voice."[44]

The finding was not, on the whole, unintuitive. As the English scientist and inventor Robert Willis had observed more than three decades before, "It is agreed on all hands that the constructions of the organs of speech so far resemble a reed organ-pipe, that the sound is generated by a vibratory apparatus in the larynx, answering to the reed, by which the pitch or number of vibrations in a given time is determined."[45] Although the pitch of the voice is determined by the reed-like vocal cords, Willis continues, "this sound is afterwards modified and altered in its quality, by the cavities of the mouth and nose, which answer to the pipe that organ builders attach to the reed for a similar purpose."[46] The basic structure of a vowel as one produced of a reed-like sounding body and a resonant cavity was thus plain enough and by all accounts as uncontested as Willis claimed. The nature of the resonant cavity's peculiar effect on the tone of the sounding body, however, had remained obscure.

Its unraveling had begun at least as early as 1679, when Samuel Reyher, Professor of Mathematics and Law at the University of Kiel, published a brief excursus on vowels in his study of the five books of Moses.[47] Pondering the nature of the language "written by the finger of God" into the tablets at Sinai, Reyher considered an argument recently advanced by his colleague Franciscus Mercurius van Helmont. The "true nature of the vowels," Helmont had argued, lay in their divine structure, manifest both in the letters of the Hebrew alphabet and in the human speech organs poised to produce their sounds.[48] Unconvinced by the extravagant contortions of Helmont's sectional drawings but intrigued by this question of "the true nature of the vowels," Reyher veered off on a brief tangent from the text he had set out to elucidate. "I have sometimes observed," he reflects, "that vowels differ not only in the shape of the mouth and tongue, but also as to the quality of the tone" (*vocales non tantum figura oris & linguæ, sed etiam ratione toni differre*). Moving away from the speech organs of vowel production and toward the vowel sounds themselves, Reyher observes that these tones are observable "if the voice is suppressed, and only the breath exhaled, such that it can be heard only by one or more in the immediate vicinity."[49] Reyher suggests that any whispered vowel bears within it a distinctive "tone," different from those hovering within the other vowel sounds. The tones, curiously, derive not from the voice (*voce*)—whose shared etymology with the term "vowel" (*vocalis*) indicates the closeness of their relation—but from another source entirely. It is when the vocal cords are suppressed, rather than struck, that the vowel's tone emerges most clearly, ushered in by the isolated exhalation of the breath (*si suppreßa voce & quali halitu solo pronuncientur*).

To record these tones, Reyher relates them to the "keys" (*claves*) of a musical instrument, most likely a harpsichord, summarizing his observations on a musical staff (see Figure 7).[50] As the lines above them indicate, the tones, though marked with the letters A–G familiar to the modern musician, are not transposable by octaves as the modern letters are. The vowel "E," for example, corresponds to $\bar{a}$, though not to **a**, which corresponds to the deepest of the "A" vowels; the vowel "O" corresponds to **g**, but not to $\bar{g}$, which corresponds to the vowel "Æ." Thus, the notation seems to suggest that Reyher's "tones" correspond to what might, in modern terms, be called "pitches."

Reyher's brief account marks a curious development in considering linguistic sounds. Rather than render his observations about speech

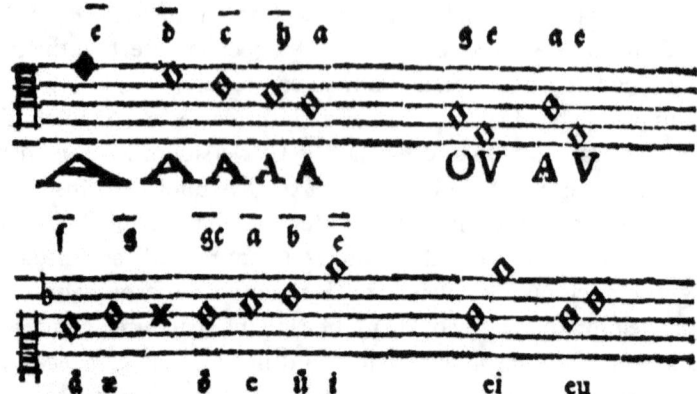

FIGURE 7. The scale of the vowel sounds as recorded by S. Reyher (*Mathesis Mosaica*, 1679)

sounds in drawings of the human speech organs, as Helmont had done, or in verbal descriptions of those organs' movements, as was exceedingly common at the time, Reyher turned instead to the musical scale.[51] The novelty of this decision may be more fully appreciated when considered in light of the history of musical and linguistic thought. In the late Antique division of knowledge that took hold in the Middle Ages, the study of language and the study of music were decidedly distinct. The first fell to the side of the trivium, home to the arts of grammar, rhetoric, and dialectics; the second, to the side of the quadrivium, beside the arts of astronomy, mathematics, and geometry.[52] The seamless ease with which Reyher moves, via the term "tone," from linguistic sound to musical note thus belies a leap of considerable proportions. The musical notation Reyher employs, to be sure, is said to derive from tiny marks noted above words to be recited (neumes), indicating and prescribing their manner of intonation.[53] But the tones the German mathematician renders in their script are not those of the singing or even speaking voice. They are tones that emerge in the event of that voice's suppression: in the speech of voiceless air resounding in the nose and mouth.

Although Reyher proceeds no further into his inquiry, the phenomenon he observed would resurface in several studies in the following century. In a phonetics dissertation submitted in Heilbronn in 1781, Christoph Friedrich Hellwag cites discussions of musical tones within the vowel sounds by not only Reyher, but also De Brosses, Nast, Heinicke, and Fulda.[54] Hellwag himself attests to his conviction that "there echoes in each of the different vowels a tone relative to the musical scale," though the inner harmony that this observation seems to him to impute to human speech, and perhaps to the human speech organs, presents too overwhelming a question to pursue.[55] Further investigation of the subtle tones would resume some twenty years later, when the physician and Lutheran minister Heinrich Gustav Flörke, in seeking to refine the German writing system for foreign readers, noted the problematic absence of any notation for the "scale of the vowels" (*Tonleiter der Vokale*).[56] How, indeed, were foreign readers to intuit the proper intonation of the German vowels, which manifested themselves in such various ways depending upon the consonants surrounding them? "When I say 'att,' for example," Flörke writes, "and in so doing allow the 'a' to make something clearly audible, the tone of the breath (*Ton des Hauches*) goes from the vowel 'a,' which we take as the fundamental tone (*Grundton*), to the major third above it— and when I pronounce the 't' at the end more forcefully, to the fourth."[57] As his terminology and title suggest, Flörke conceives of the vowel tones in terms of a musical scale, but unlike Reyher, he records those tones in the relative terms of musical intervals. The French "e fermé," for instance, is identified as "one whole tone" (*einen ganzen Ton*) higher than the low 'e' or 'ä,'"[58] but none of Flörke's vowels is fixed to a particular pitch. Noting that men, women, and children speak in markedly different registers, Flörke concludes that the vowel scale must be a transposable set of intervals, musical in their internal relations, but not fixed, as it were, in any one key. These intervals, however, prove far more difficult to discern than Flörke had initially hoped. Slipping up and down not only in relation to one another, but also in relation to themselves in different phonetic contexts, the vowel tones defy Flörke's attempt at a comprehensive writing system for their sounds. Overwhelmingly numerous, inconstant, and above all, so subtle as to escape even the attentive ear, the tones disappear from Flörke's writings shortly after they appear. "In the noisy city of Berlin," the minister concludes, "one seldom finds a moment so peaceful as to permit him, undisturbed, to attend to the tone of a breath, which is always very weak—unless he wants to use a sleepless, midnight hour to do so."[59]

Over in the quiet quadrangles of Cambridge, the young Englishman Robert Willis came upon the problem from an entirely different angle. Willis approached the question of vowel tones not by observing the sounds of his own speech but by trying to imitate them through artificial means. In a paper "On the Vowel Sounds and on Reed Organ-Pipes," presented at the Cambridge Philosophical Society in the winter of 1828–29, Willis argued that the vowels of the human voice fell in a set, linear series whose order could be demonstrated. Following the lead of two eighteenth-century inventors credited with the creation of speaking machines, Christian Kratzenstein and Wolfgang von Kempelen, Willis had affixed a reed to a sliding pipe of variable length, finding that when the reed plays one consistent note and the pipe is simultaneously made to extend in length, "the series of effects produced are characterized and distinguished from each other by that quality we call the vowel."[60] The vowels produced pass through a set series, IEAOU, which, upon completion, reverses its order and repeats itself indefinitely, "the vowels becoming less distinct in each successive cycle."[61] Recording the vowels' series and the lengths of pipe at which they occur, Willis finds not only that "the pitch of the sound produced is always that of the reed or primary pulse," but also that the lengths of pipe at which the vowels sound bear a calculable relationship to the wavelength of the sounding pitch.[62] Any vowel can be produced at any pitch, in other words, provided that the size of the resonating cavity is adjusted to a particular proportional relationship to that pitch's wavelength.[63]

Although Willis observes quite clearly that it is the pitch produced by the sounding body, and not the proper tone of the resonator, that determines the dominant pitch produced, he remains hesitant to dissociate pitch from "vowel quality," as he calls it. Upon recognizing the irrelevance of the reed's pitch to the whole instrument's ability to produce any vowel, Willis immediately argues with himself, "But this vowel quality may be detected to a certain degree in simple musical sounds: the high squeaking notes of the organ or violin, speak plainly I, the deep bass notes U, and in running rapidly backwards and forwards through the intermediate notes, we seem to hear the series U, O, A, E, I, I, E, A, O, U, &c." So it would seem, Willis maintains more on intuition than on evidence, as if "each vowel was inseparable from a peculiar pitch."[64]

As Willis notes, his was a variation upon the curious quandary Wolfgang von Kempelen had articulated nearly forty years before. Although the Hungarian scientist had recognized the same manifest reality that a vowel may be produced at any pitch and, therefore, must be structurally independent of it, he also expressed a sense of dissatisfaction with this conclusion. "It seems to me," wrote Kempelen, "that when I pronounce the different vowels on the same pitch, they possess something that suggests a change to my ear and gives me the impression of a certain melody—which, however, I know perfectly well can only be produced by the variation of higher and lower pitches."[65]

Seeking to relate the "peculiar pitch" of each vowel to the equation governing the pipe length necessary for its production on a given pitch, Willis turns to the Swiss mathematician Leonhard Euler's recent explanation of the "secondary pulses" he observed to accompany any given note.

Perhaps, Willis hypothesizes, the "peculiar pitch" of the vowel produced at any length of pipe corresponds to the "secondary pulsations" of the primary pitch sounding from the reed. For the hypothesis to hold, he reasons, "we ought to be able to shew that the note peculiar to each vowel in simple sounds, is identical with that of the secondary pulse in the compound sound."[66] Supposing "for simplicity . . . that after the third [pulsation] they become insensible," Willis assumes only one secondary pulse, whose wavelength he designates as "s." Upon investigation, he finds that, indeed, the proportion of pipe length to the sounding pitch that governs the production of vowels does seem to correspond to the "secondary pulse" of the sounding note.[67] "Hence it would appear," Willis ventures to surmise, "that the ear, in losing the consciousness of the pitch of s, is yet able to identify it by this *vowel* quality."[68] In other words, the vowel sound would seem to replace the proper tone of the resonant chamber—itself matching up with the "secondary pulse" of the note played by the reed.

Bringing the proper tone of the resonant chamber into a mathematical relation with the primary pitch sounded by the reed, Willis proposed the structure of a vowel with unprecedented precision. Evidently far from certain of his own findings, however, he no sooner stated his results than he retreated in doubt. "As far as I have tried," Willis writes, "it appears to be the case, but there is so much room for the exercise of fancy in this point, from the difficulty of fixing on the exact vowel belonging to a simple sound, that I do not mean to insist upon it."[69]

Insist upon it is precisely what Hermann von Helmholtz did, finding that, exactly as Willis's paper had suggested, each vowel—or more precisely, each resonant cavity of the mouth necessary to the pronunciation of each vowel—possessed a proper tone. Using resonators tuned to tones higher than those of his sounding reeds, Helmholtz was able to examine these tones with considerable precision. While Willis had investigated only five vowels, constantly noting the lack of clarity in their production,[70] Helmholtz advanced proper tones for eight. With spherical resonators, he was able to deduce the pitches of the resonant chambers that would produce the vowels U, O, and A, concluding that "the resonance of [a] single [over]tone is sufficient to characterize the vowels above mentioned."

Other vowels proved more elusive. Considering the shape of the mouth required for their production, Helmholtz discarded his globe-shaped resonators in favor of bottle-shaped ones. "When a bottle with a long narrow neck is used as a resonance chamber," he explains, "two simple tones are readily discovered, of which one may be regarded as the proper tone of the belly and the other as that of the neck of the bottle."[71] Pairing

FIGURE 8. Helmholtz's second scale of vowels' proper tones, produced after the bottle-resonator experiment (*Tonempfindungen*, 1863)

bottles with reeds, Helmholtz found that when the reed played a tone whose overtones coincided with the tones proper to the neck and belly of the bottle, most of the vowels no single resonator would yield might be produced.[72] He thus arrives, after much experimentation, at the arrangement pictured in Figure 8.[73] These are not the pitches at which the human voice produces the vowels in question. Rather, they indicate the tones the throat and mouth poised to pronounce those vowels would principally reinforce if such tones were played into them. Helmholtz suggests that this phenomenon may be experienced to some degree by singing a vowel into a piano whose dampers are raised and observing which strings, beside the prime sung, are set in sympathetic vibration. Or, he adds, echoing Reyher, Flörke, and his colleague F. C. Donders, by whispering vowels and listening for the pitch of the whistle thus produced.[74]

A few points in Helmholtz's account bear further comment. First, it will no doubt be objected that the pitches listed will not always coincide with an overtone of the note voiced. Helmholtz offers a simple explanation in response to this objection. While Willis had, for the sake of simplicity, supposed the presence of but one "secondary pulse,"[75] Helmholtz determines, using resonators applied to the human ear, that "the first six to eight overtones are clearly perceptible, but with very different degrees of volume according to the different forms of the cavity of the mouth."[76] Thus, there are several overtones available in any voice, only one of which need coincide with the proper tone, or tones, of the vowel it wishes to produce. To this is added the observation that the proper tones of the vowels demonstrate a certain tolerance. While the overtone that strikes most perfectly upon the proper tone of the vowel will, naturally, be most distinct, the mouth's resonant cavity will respond to a range of pitches within a certain distance from its proper tone.[77] Thus, Helmholtz concludes, "It is only when the proper tone of the cavity of the mouth falls midway between the prime tone of the note sung by the voice and its higher Octave [first overtone], or is more than a Fifth deeper than that prime tone, that the characteristic resonance will be weak."[78] Unsurprisingly, human beings tend not to speak on such pitches. The range of pitches at which humans can speak being limited, they can produce vowels at nearly any pitch they choose, as "all of these pitches of the speaking voice have the corresponding proper tones of the cavity of the mouth situated within sufficiently narrow intervals from the upper overtones of the speaking tone to create sensible resonance of one or more of these overtones, and thus characterise the vowel."[79] Finally, Helmholtz adds, the speaking voice "probably through great pressure of the vocal ligaments upon one another [. . .] possesses stronger overtones than the singing voice."[80] This explains why spoken vowels possess greater clarity than sung vowels. "Were it otherwise," Helmholtz observes, "'books of words' at concerts and operas would be unnecessary."[81]

In the Helmholtzian account, then, vowels are categorically distinguished from all other sounds not by their "peculiar pitches" or "proper tones" but by their common assertion of an interval. While most *Klänge* consist of a powerful prime accompanied by overtones decreasing in volume as they ascend and diminish, a vowel consists of a dampened prime accompanied by an overtone of rivaling, even overpowering, presence. This second tone (which need not be the second overtone) disrupts the normal, progressively diminishing balance of tones, resulting in a decidedly peculiar sound, or "color." This *Klangfarbe*, unlike all the other *Klangfarbe* investigated in Helmholtz's work, manifests itself in a distinctive sound immediately recognizable to the human ear as a vowel. Rather than sounding the musical interval that its structure would lead one to expect, the combination of reed-plus-resonator produces something entirely different, which the human ear identifies not as a musical interval but as a linguistic element. As Robert Willis quizzically observed, it is as though "the ear, in losing the consciousness of the pitch of [the resonator], is yet able to identify it by this *vowel* quality."[82] Though Willis had gone to great effort at the start of his study to assert that "Vowels are a quite different affection of sound from both pitch and quality [. . . and b]y quality, I mean that property of sound, by which we know the tone of a violin from that of a flute,"[83] in truth, his experiments lead to the collapse of that very distinction. In Helmholtz's account, the "affection of sound" constitutive of vowels is revealed to be but a particular type of *Klangfarbe*. "Vowel quality" was not other than *Klangfarbe*; it was precisely that.

Yet, as Willis's observation attests, the passage from musical tone to vowel quality is a stubbornly strange one. Indeed, it would appear to entail a "loss of consciousness" of a pronounced musical pitch—a pitch that is, nonetheless, requisite to its realization. The passage into the element of language would appear to require a passage out of the realm of music—phenomenal, physiological, or psychological in nature. To speak of the *Klänge der Vokale* ("musical sounds of vowels"), then, is to find one's self in a curious contradiction in terms. For it is only in the forgetting of its musical aspect that a vowel emerges as an element of language, yet it is only as an element of language that a vowel may be said to exist at all.

The vowel sounds investigated by Willis and Helmholtz, for all the complexity of their structure, comprise a category of sound assumed rather than demonstrated. "Vowels" are simply heard, intuitively, as such. Both scientists note that vowel sounds differ across languages, but the overarching category of vowels remains a matter of intuition, its identification hinging entirely upon the human ear. Helmholtz offers no external means of defining this category of sound, which, though named unambiguously as a linguistic one (*Vokale*), emerges under the rubric of "musical sounds," or *Klänge*. Unlike the other types of musical sound beside which vowels are treated, such as *Klänge der Saiten* (Musical Sounds of Strings), *Klänge der Streichinstrumente* (Bowed Instruments), *Klänge der Flötenpfeifen* (Flute pipes), and *Klänge der Zungenpfeifen* (Reed pipes), the category *Klänge der Vokale*—tellingly translated in an entirely different manner as "Vowel Qualities of Tone"—begs the question of its own definition. For the subsection to match its neighbors, "*Vokale*" would have to designate a type of sounding body: the instrument to which a particular *Klangfarbe* corresponds. The imprecision that such a parallel title would introduce—*Klänge der menschlichen Stimme* (Musical Sounds of Human Voices), say—suffices to indicate why Helmholtz might have preferred the sacrifice of parallel structure. Not the human voice itself, but rather a specific category of its sounds, vowels require some sort of reference to language. Although one can imagine an organizational structure by which *Klänge der menschlichen Stimme* might have been productively divided into *Sprachliche Klänge* and *Unsprachliche Klänge*, the distinction between "linguistic sounds" and "nonlinguistic sounds" was not one of which the pioneering Prussian scientist could avail himself.

No more can the scientists of today. The lack of physical means of distinguishing linguistic from nonlinguistic sound remains a fundamental problem of linguistic science. One could turn to any number of thinkers confronting this difficulty, but none is perhaps more prominent than Noam Chomsky, who points out that "a basic problem [of linguistic study] is that even the simplest elements of discourse are not detectable by procedures of segmentation and classification. They do not have the required 'beads on a string' property for such procedures to operate, and often cannot be located in some identifiable part of the physical event that corresponds to the mind-internal expression in which these elements function." Speaking beings hear some sounds as language and dismiss others as not-language, but the tools of physical science possess no such discriminatory capacity. Chomsky explains that "even the simplest units—morphemes, elementary lexical items, for that matter even phonological segments—can be identified only by their role in the generative procedures that form linguistic expressions."[84] Without the hearer conscious of language as such, linguistic sounds recede into a great mass of undifferentiated noise, and neither the science of linguistics nor that of physical acoustics has yet obtained a means of categorically, rather than approximately, distinguishing them from everything else.

If the *Klänge der Vokale* introduce the decided difficulty of rigorously defining linguistic sound, so, too, do they raise the question of the reach of the term "musical." If one takes Helmholtz at his word, the title of his chapter, *Klänge der Vokale*, should be translated as "the musical sounds of vowels." In Helmholtz's construction, "musical sounds" does not designate one category of the many sounds belonging to vowels, of which other categories might be offered (such as, for example, "the linguistic sounds of vowels"). Instead, it suggests that vowels themselves fall within the category of "Musical Sounds." Respecting the definitions outlined at the start of the *Sensations of Tone*, one would be obliged to concede that vowels are indeed musical sounds, or *Klänge*, *Klänge* having been defined as sounds resulting from periodic motion of the air.[85] From this purely acoustic perspective, however, why this particular periodic motion is perceived by the human ear as language remains entirely opaque, as does the degree to which it is perceived as "musical." Taking for granted the existence of a category of sound definable only in terms of language yet quantifiable only through measurements known to music, Helmholtz brings forth aspects of vowels of which neither the study nor the notation of language had offered any account. One might say he found music in the sounds of human speech. But one would be obliged to ask to what degree that music, in becoming speech, had ceased—at least for human beings—to sound.

From Tone to Color

Helmholtz's *Sensations of Tone* thus furnished a novel, physical account of what enables the ear to distinguish between the tones of different sounding bodies, as well as what enables it to make out vowel sounds. Helmholtz demonstrated that the key to both phenomena lay in "*Klangfarbe*," or "sound-color." The answer was, in a way, circular, seeing as it was Helmholtz's 1863 *Sensations of Tone* that established the term *Klangfarbe* in its modern sense: as a technical designator for distinctive sonic properties tied to the physical structure of sound waves. Because Helmholtz's physical explanation of *Klangfarbe* revealed it to be responsible not just for the sonic stamp linking a sound to its source but also for the differences between vowel sounds, the term *Klangfarbe* extended, following Helmholtz's usage, into the realm of linguistics. In the German discourse following the *Sensations of Tone*, it became not only possible but indeed unavoidable to speak of vowels in terms of their "sound-colors."

This extension of the term exposes a complexity in the concept of *Klangfarbe* as Helmholtz established it, revealing the term to bear two decidedly incongruent definitions. Although the *Sensations of Tone* demonstrates *Klangfarbe* to inhere in the particular balance of overtones sounding in the expression of any given tone, the text begins by identifying *Klangfarbe* in terms of its function rather than its form. The opening pages of the *Sensations of Tone* define *Klangfarbe* explicitly as "that peculiarity which distinguishes the musical tone of a violin from that of a flute or a clarinet or the human voice, when all of these instruments produce the same note at the same pitch."[86] As Helmholtz explains in a popular lecture on the material,

> Whether a violin or a flute, or a man or a dog, is close by us is a matter of interest for us to know, and our ear takes care to distinguish the peculiarities of their tones with accuracy. The means by which we can distinguish them, however, is a matter of perfect indifference. Whether the cry of the dog contains the higher octave or the twelfth of the fundamental tone has no practical interest for us, and never occupies our attention. The overtones are consequently thrown into that unanalysed mass of peculiarities of a tone which we call its *Klangfarbe*.
>
> Because the existence of overtones depends on the wave form, as I was able to state previously, we can see that *Klangfarbe* does, too.[87]

As a means of introducing his object of study, Helmholtz's progression from functional to formal definition is perfectly logical. Yet the juxtaposition of the two definitions reveals telling discrepancies between them. According to its functional definition, *Klangfarbe* is what distinguishes the sound of a human voice from that of an animal or a musical instrument; it is what forever binds the sound to the sounding body. According to its formal definition, however, *Klangfarbe* distinguishes different vowels within a single voice and—crucially—enables the identification of the same vowel across different voices. In the case of vowels, *Klangfarbe* could not be said to tie sounds to sounding bodies, seeing as, irrespective of the differences in the bodies that produced them, vowels across voices are understood to be the same. Unlike the *Klangfarbe* of musical instruments, the *Klangfarbe der Vocale* names sonic structures that transcend bodily difference, enabling diverse bodies to participate in a shared system of signification.[88]

Whether the "color" of Helmholtz's *Klangfarbe* indicates vowels or sounding bodies to the human ear, it designates sound waves' particularities: objective phenomena subject to external measurement and verification. It is curious, therefore, that Helmholtz chose to baptize these objective forms with a metaphorical name whose meaning was at odds with the structure he had revealed them to bear. As Emily I. Dolan has shown, during the eighteenth century, the color metaphor that is arguably as ancient as music itself had migrated from pitches—in the tradition of Isaac Newton's *Opticks* and Father Castel's infamous ocular harpsichord—to incidental qualities of musical tone other than pitch and volume. The idea of "color" and, indeed, specific "colors" thus came to attach to specific instruments, and the color metaphor gained a new guarantor in the understanding of instrumental timbre as accessory. Instruments' distinctive "sound colors" were conceived as an issue of performance rather than composition, as paints fleshing out a master drawing rather than determining its design.[89] In late eighteenth-century musical discourse, the color metaphor enabled novel discussion of instrumental timbres, but at the same time, "tone-color resisted rigorous analysis[. . .]. The notion of color, then, highlighted those aspects of music that were difficult, skirted reason, and trafficked with the irrational."[90]

One would imagine that Helmholtz, having submitted those unruly aspects to the laws of physical acoustics, would have jettisoned the color metaphor that highlighted their purported irrationality. He certainly could have done so, seeing as when he referred to "that unanalysed mass of peculiarities of a tone which we call its *Klangfarbe*," the "we" of his formulation included few—if any—beyond himself.[91] The truth is that the German language lacked a clear convention for designating the aspect—or, perhaps, aspects—of sound that Helmholtz studied. Helmholtz named it *Klangfarbe*, but Seebeck and Ohm, in keeping with their predecessors, had never used that term, referring instead to a "difference of (musical) sounds" (*Verschiedenheit der Klänge, Klangverschiedenheit*).[92] The 1832 German translation of Robert Willis's English-language paper—whose explicit definition of "quality" anticipates Helmholtz's definition of *Klangfarbe* with near-verbatim precision[93]—repeatedly translates this "quality" not as *Klangfarbe* but as "Klang," with a parenthetical "(*quality*)" repeatedly inserted in attestation of the confusion glimpsed by the text's anonymous translator.[94] The Dutch ophthalmologist F. C. Donders, who also published in German and counted amongst Helmholtz's closest interlocutors, employed the French loan word "das Timbre" in his 1857 paper on the differences between vowel sounds.[95]

The term "timbre" as it appears in the late eighteenth-century French musical discourse provides the closest anticipation of the concept Helmholtz's *Klangfarbe* would forge, and the lack of a corresponding German term for "timbre" had emerged as a translation problem by the turn of the nineteenth century.[96] Having initially designated a drum (< *tympănum*[97]), the word "timbre" by the mid-eighteenth-century had come to refer to impressions of musical sounds that could not be accounted for in terms of pitch or volume. The most prominent definitions were advanced by Jean-Jacques Rousseau in his entries on "Sound" (*Son*) and "Timbre" (*Tymbre*) in Denis Diderot's *Encyclopédie* of 1765, as well as his entry on "Timbre" in his own *Dictionnaire de musique* (1767).[98] Here, timbre is conceived as a single, albeit enigmatic, property of sound, readily identified by comparing different instruments including the voice:

> The difference between sounds described by timbre cannot be accounted for by a sound's pitch or volume. An oboe would be difficult to mistake for a flute: it could not soften its sound to the same degree. The sound of a flute would always have a certain *je ne sais quoi* of softness and pleasantness, while that of an oboe would have a certain dryness and harshness, which makes it impossible to confuse the two. What could we say about the different timbres of voices with the same force and pitch?[99]

Shortly after Helmholtz's *Sensations of Tone* appeared in 1863, the French definition of "timbre" expanded to include the technical acoustic sense of the "specific quality of a sound [. . .] resulting essentially from the combination of the overtones that accompany the primary note played (*Qualité spécifique d'un son[. . .] résultant essentiellement du concours des harmoniques qui accompagnent la note fondamentale jouée*)."[100]

What *timbre* gains in German translation, of course, is *Farbe*, and Helmholtz's reasons for welcoming this semantic valence remain unclear. Certainly, a compound term built out of *Klang*- follows logically from the study's terminological structure, which grounds the phenomenon in *Klänge* and thereby rules out such terms as *Ton*, *Laut*, and—clearly—*Klang* itself. And it is entirely plausible, if unverifiable, that the French flavor of the imported "das Timbre" eliminated that term from consideration. Other terminological possibilities (*Klangverschiedenheit*, etc.), however, remained. Why, at the very moment that his work furnished physical explanations that—at least ostensibly—required no reference to the human, did Helmholtz enshrine a metaphorical term whose synesthetic structure equating sound with color lacked any physical, empirically verifiable basis?

The term's presence recalls another of Helmholtz's great works, the *Physiological Treatise on Optics* (*Handbuch der Physiologischen Optik*), a study conducted over the same years as the *Sensations of Tone*.[101] The simultaneity of the two projects is evident throughout both texts, as well as in the supplementary essays and lectures Helmholtz authored in advance of their publication. Taken together, Helmholtz's collected writings on light and sound between 1852 and 1867 leave no room for doubt as to the scientist's awareness of their phenomenal similarity. Reminders of their physical kinship as waves are frequent, as are analogies between the perception of musical sound by the ear and that of color by the eye. "Just as the ear apprehends vibrations of different periodic time as tones of different pitch," Helmholtz is fond of explaining, "so does the eye perceive luminous vibrations of different periodic times as different colours."[102]

Rather than pursue the physical similarity further, however, Helmholtz consistently turns to questions of perception. Ever the disciple of the great physiologist Johannes Müller, who was his teacher, Helmholtz recalls that it is the senses, and not external phenomena, that determine the nature of sensation. Summing up a position he maintained throughout his scientific career, he explains, "Just as, on the one hand, each sensory nerve, excited by however so many influences, gives exclusively those sensations within the quality range proper to it, so, on the other hand, do the same external influences — when they impinge upon different sensory nerves — produce the most varied kinds of sensations, these always being taken from the quality range of the nerve concerned."[103] The example Helmholtz selects to illustrate this fact is not sound and light, but rather, light and heat. He writes,

> The same aether vibrations as are felt by the eye as light, are felt by the skin as heat. [. . .] Here the difference in kind of the impression is moreover so great, that physicists felt at ease with the idea that agents as apparently different as light and radiant heat are alike in kind, and in part identical, only after the complete likeness in kind of their physical behaviour has been established, by laborious experimental investigations in every direction.[104]

Such an orientation would leave the way entirely clear for Helmholtz to pursue an evident question underlying the *Optics* and *Sensations of Tone*: In what way and to what degree are sound and light "alike in kind"? Yet these questions remain surprisingly tacit in both works. Only once does Helmholtz directly correlate the two phenomena. In the second volume of the *Optics* (1860), he reviews the long history, beginning with Newton, of attempts "to divide the intervals of colour in the spectrum on the same basis as that of the division of the musical scale," assembling a table of their correspondences on the basis of wavelength.[105] The units placed in parallel are both, tellingly, "tones": the *Farbentöne* on the right bearing witness to a third, visual aspect of the ancient term, silently sounding throughout the *Sensations of Tone*.[106] The tones corresponding to a pendular vibration of the air are placed on the left; those corresponding to a particular wavelength within the solar spectrum are on the right. The range of tones included is defined by the solar spectrum, though the intervals specified within that spectrum are dictated by divisions of the musical scale. The pitches noted are fixed within specified octaves, indicated by the capitalization of the musical notation, although they are, interestingly, listed neither by wavelength nor pitch number. Instead, they are set in a chromatic scale, manifest both in the interval selected (that of a semitone) and in the alignment of the two octaves in side-by-side columns:[107]

F$^\sharp$,	end of Red.	f$^\sharp$,	Violet.
G,	Red.	g,	Ultra-violet.
G$^\sharp$,	Red.	g$^\sharp$,	Ultra-violet.
A,	Red.	a,	Ultra-violet.
A$^\sharp$,	Orange-red.	a$^\sharp$,	Ultra-violet.
B,	Orange.	b,	Ultra-violet.
c,	Yellow.		
c$^\sharp$,	Green.		
d,	Greenish blue.		
d$^\sharp$,	Cyan-blue.		
e,	Indigo blue.		
f,	Violet.		

Observing that the interval of a semitone does not seem to correspond in any meaningful way with the colors strongly distinguished as different by the eye, Helmholtz concludes that "the magnitudes of the colour intervals are not at all like the gradations of musical pitch in being dependent on vibration frequencies."[108] The "colour intervals" to which Helmholtz refers, however, unlike the musical ones beside them, are intervals based entirely on perception. Although Helmholtz turns directly to experimental refractions with prisms and then proceeds vigorously through the history of color theory in search of a physical means of measuring the magnitudes of color intervals, his chapter on "The Simple Colors" (*Die einfachen Farben*) ends, essentially, in defeat. Lacking any external means of distinguishing the colors perceived as different by the human eye, Helmholtz concludes, "It is clear that in this so-called colour harmony, no such absolutely definite relations are to be expected as are characteristic of the musical intervals."[109]

Mathematical relations intrinsic to the visible color spectrum were not the only thing that lay, frustratingly, beyond Helmholtz's reach. At the close of his lecture "On the Physiological Causes of Harmony in Music," delivered in the winter of 1857 at the University of Bonn, Professor Helmholtz gestured not toward the infinite possibilities of where further research might lead but rather toward the limits of what his own study of musical sound could hope to achieve. In a passage worth quoting in full, he mused,

> ... both harmony and dysharmony alternately urge and moderate the flow of tones, while the mind sees in their immaterial motion an image of its own perpetually streaming thoughts and moods. Just as in the rolling ocean, this movement, rhythmically repeated, and yet ever varying, rivets our attention and hurries us along. But whereas in the sea, blind physical forces alone are at work, and hence the final impression on the spectator's mind is nothing but solitude—in a musical work of art the movement follows the outflow of the artist's own emotions. Now gently gliding, now gracefully leaping, now violently stirred, penetrated, or laboriously contending with the natural expression of passion, the stream of sound, in primitive vivacity, bears over into the hearer's soul unimagined moods which the artist has overheard from his own, and finally raises him up to that repose of everlasting beauty, of which God has allowed but few of his elect favourites to be the heralds.
>
> But I have reached the confines of physical science and must close.[110]

The lecturer perceived a limit he would not transgress. His talk sought to elucidate the "physiological causes of harmony in music," a subject evidently distinct, in his mind, from that of music itself. "The essential basis for Music is *Melody*," Helmholtz states, in no uncertain terms, in the preface to the third edition of the *Sensations of Tone*.[111] And between the study of harmony and that of melody, there lay, at least for Helmholtz, an inviolable threshold. It was this same threshold that his obituarist Carl Stumpf would identify many years later at the heart of the *Sensations of Tone*. In this monumental work on "the fundamental principles of art," Stumpf recalls, the reader "is led step by step from the simplest truths of physical acoustics to their physiological conditions, until finally, deep in the center of the system, he is brought [. . .] over the threshold into the aesthetics of music. Here the author deliberately stops."[112]

It was a curious move on the part of a mind that pressed vigorously at the limits of the knowledge of its day, boldly advancing into uncharted territories of physiology, physics, and psychology. But the obscure zone distinguishing the movements of the sea from the waves of sound constitutive of, say, a symphony was one that Hermann von Helmholtz did not enter. That region he left to an "elect" of which he could not count himself a member. But if the scientist's eloquent account is apt to provoke regret at his restraint, so, too, does it argue for the justice of his deference.[113] His glimpse beyond the threshold of his expertise suffices to indicate the "heralds" whose work continues in the line of his gaze. One might easily turn to a twentieth-century stanza by Wallace Stevens, which, in its well-known meditation on the singer by the sea, seems to pick up precisely where Helmholtz left off:

> If it was only the dark voice of the sea
> That rose, or even coloured by many waves;
> If it was only the outer voice of sky
> And cloud, of the sunken coral water-walled,
> However clear, it would have been deep air,
> The heaving speech of air, a summer sound
> Repeated in a summer without end
> And sound alone. But it was more than that [. . .][114]

2 / The Interaction of Color

Color is the most relative medium in art.
—JOSEF ALBERS, *INTERACTION OF COLOR* (1963)[1]

Amongst the most frequent critiques of Hermann von Helmholtz's *Sensations of Tone* (1863) is the observation that it presents musical tones as isolated middles. The "tone," as Helmholtz defines it—whether simple or rich in overtones—bears a uniform physical structure from start to finish. Free of the accidents of performance, it is also untainted by the effects of onset and decay that later thinkers would come to consider crucial to sonic identification.[2] As Julia Kursell has observed, the great insight into musical tone that Helmholtz's laboratory experiments achieved was both enabled and limited by their isolation of sounds' periodic motion. The reduction of musical tone to the "steady, internal repetition of periodic sound waves [. . .] allowed the experimenter to gain repeated access to one experimental object, [. . .] granting the tools of formal description that acousticians were so eager to find." Yet it simultaneously constituted its object of study as something quite distinct from the object ostensibly concerned. Investigating the sounds of tuning forks and resonators in a controlled laboratory environment, "Helmholtz invented a new type of sound generation that avoided any characteristic beginnings and endings."[3]

The critique would, indeed, be difficult to contest. While an untrained ear can easily distinguish the bowing of a cello from the blowing of an oboe, the task proves considerably more demanding when the instruments' sounds have been stripped of their characteristic attack. Even musical timbres as dissimilar as a piano and a bass can be disorientingly difficult to distinguish when presented only in the midst of a sustained tone. Perhaps unsurprisingly, the same phenomenon may be observed in spoken vowels. As Robert Willis was neither the first nor the last to observe, "if any given vowel be prolonged by singing, it soon becomes impossible to distinguish what vowel it is."[4] Typically flanked by liquids, stops, aspirates, and so forth, vocalic sonorities prove elusive when distanced or removed from any consonantal frame. Defining vowels' extension in time, the constrictive movements that announce their arrivals and whisk them away also lend hallmark particularities to their sounds.

The issue comes up rather unexpectedly in Théodore Flournoy's 1893 study *Des phénomènes de synopsie* (Synoptic Phenomena), a book-length study of "mental imagery" induced by external phenomena ostensibly unrelated to sight.[5] The book analyzes the results of a large-scale survey conducted by the author, Professor of Experimental Psychology at the University of Geneva, and his research assistant Édouard Claparède between 1882 and 1892. In reviewing the 694 surveys returned, 296 of which report some type of *audition colorée* (colored hearing), Flournoy remarks that the most common association reported—appearing in 247 cases—connects colors with vowels.[6] He notes that in several instances, the visions of color (or "photisms," as Flournoy calls them) prompted by vowels appear to be affected by the surrounding phonetic environment. "For many people," Flournoy remarks,

> an isolated vowel prompts a formless photism, a sort of colored fog without clear edges; but the addition of a consonant prompts the appearance of a contour that is more or less defined (one subject says that the consonant appears to limit, vaguely, the colored surface of the vowel).[7]

When added to the vowels that prompt colored visions, consonants define those visions' expanse, translating temporal extension into spatial definition.

One comes upon similar remarks scattered across the scientific corpus. In the proceedings of the International Congress on Experimental Psychology held in London in 1892, for example, Professor Edouard Gruber offers the example of "a very talented poet"[8] who sees "*a* bright white, *e* bright yellow, *i* light blue, *o* deep black, u (French *ou*) faded black and the two sounds particular to the Romanian language: *ă* brown et *î* gray verging on black." Consonants prompt similar visions, Gruber reports, save that in the moment of hearing them, the gentleman sees two colors: the one belonging to the consonant proper and the other to the vowel required for its phonation. For example, the letter "*f*," itself red-cinnabar, appears with a thin ray of orange tinting its anterior side—an effect, he supposes, of the yellow *e* necessarily preceding it.[9]

The delicate mirroring of phonic effects in corresponding colored visions also emerges in Francis Galton's 1883 *Inquiries into Human Faculty and Its Development*, the first major work in English to treat colored hearing in a serious way. Here, Galton offers a case study of Dr. James Key of Montagu, Cape Colony (now South Africa), who has provided "a large series of coloured illustrations, accompanied by many pages of explanation" in an attempt to describe the colors he sees in conjunction with letters of the alphabet. For the letter A, Key provides four painted color swatches to indicate the specific shades of brown he associates with different pronunciations of the letter marked "A": as in "fame," "can," "charm," and "all." Although Dr. Key is to some degree able to isolate these vowel-color correspondences, Galton cautions, "It would not, for example, be possible to print words by the use of counters coloured like [Key's painted swatches], because the tint of each influences that of its neighbours."[10] The impressions of color corresponding to words in Dr. Key's perception can be localized to letters and principally to vowels, but their interactions with the colors of surrounding consonants compromise the accuracy of any attempt to enumerate their colors in isolation. "I have gone through the whole of them with care, together with his descriptions and reasons," Galton concludes, "and can quite understand his meaning, and how exceedingly complex and refined these associations are. The patterns are to him like words in poetry, which call up associations that any substituted word of a like dictionary meaning would fail to do."[11] As a word woven into the tapestry of a poem's syntax and sound patterning can be analyzed out of context to only an extremely limited degree, so can the vocalic nuances illuminating Dr. Key's experience of language be examined only very partially in isolation. Although Galton offers no other examples of the contextual effects brought to the fore in Key's case, he concludes his discussion by emphasizing that "my remarks, though based on Dr. Key's diagrams and statements as on a text, do not depend, by any means, wholly upon them, but on numerous other letters from various quarters to the same effect."[12]

Galton's observations on Dr. Key's case certainly seem more than anecdotal when placed in the context in Flournoy's more extensive study, which features an extended analysis of "Word Photisms (*Photismes des mots*)." Here, Flournoy observes that in most cases where subjects see colors in connection with words, the visions of colors appear to derive from the words' constitutive vowels, whose strength and nuance vary according to their phonetic and prosodic contexts:

> Many subjects are content to say that the word gives them the mixed impression, or successive impressions, of such and such colors, which are those of the dominant vowels. This impression is significantly stronger when the vowel is repeated in several consecutive syllables.
>   Sometimes, the color of the word or the syllable is not identical to that of the isolated vowel, as the environment of the neighboring consonants—even if they don't have their own colors themselves—exercises a modifying influence on the nuance of the adjacent vowel, or mars its clarity. It also happens that the various syllables run off, as it were, onto one another, and instead of many coexisting or successive colors, the word only evokes a single color, the result of the mixture of nuances belonging to various vowels.[13]

The sensations of color associated with words, tied to vowels in some way, seem to reflect a host of factors: sequence, repetition, consonantal context, and whatever determines vocalic "dominance"—presumably, stress.

In all these accounts, the color impressions connected with vowels are strikingly context-dependent. The "same vowel" appears different when isolated, surrounded by various consonants, or repeated in several consecutive syllables; the idea of listing word-color correspondences as one lists vowel-color correspondences is deemed "not possible [. . .] because the tint of each influences that of its neighbours."[14] These observations fix Galton, Gruber, and Flournoy's studies firmly in time, before the ideal of the isolated stimulus emerged and consistency was selected as a defining feature of synesthesia. This criterion emerged during the twentieth century and shows no sign of wavering in the twenty-first.[15] As Jamie Ward and Julia Simner explain in the 2020 overview "Synesthesia: The current state of the field,"

> the "gold standard" test for synesthesia is not a biological one, but a behavioral one. It rests on a widely established test that looks for one key behavioral feature of synesthesia, which is the fact that synesthetic experiences are relatively stable over time. So, a synesthete with colored letters will tend to associate the same letter with the same color over time (e.g., if A is synesthetically blue for any particularly synesthete, it will always tend to be blue for that person). In contrast, someone without synesthesia may not only find the idea of colored letters somewhat alien but would pair letters to colors only inconsistently, even if they were highly incentivized or trying effortfully. This difference between consistent synesthetes and inconsistent nonsynesthetes forms the "consistency test/test of genuineness," the widely used diagnostic for synesthesia.[16]

The establishment of the consistency criterion over the course of the twentieth century would seem to account, at least in part, for the absence of any continued inquiry into the interaction of colors that, in the late nineteenth century, were called "synesthetic."[17] The possibility of a sub-field devoted to the study of contextual variability would seem to be largely excluded from the study of a phenomenon defined precisely by its invariance.

This history might also explain why the interaction of color explored in these accounts has never been studied in connection with verse, despite these texts' evident proximity to poetry. From Gruber's "very talented poet" who sees a red-cinnabar *f* edged with the dawn of its yellow *e* to Galton's comparison of Key's color patterning with "words in poetry," these accounts draw an all but explicit link between poetics and the play of synesthetic colors. The connection might be laid out most plainly in Flournoy's discussion of "Word Photisms," which is worth consulting in the original French:

> Beaucoup de sujets se contentent de dire que le mot leur donne l'impression mélangée, ou successive, de telles couleurs qui sont celles de ses voyelles dominantes. Cette impression est beaucoup accrue lorsque la voyelle se répète dans plusieurs syllabes consécutives.
>
> Parfois la teinte du mot ou de la syllabe n'est pas identique à celle de la voyelle isolée, le voisinage des consonnes d'appui, même si elles n'ont pas de couleurs propres, exerçant une influence modificatrice sur la nuance de la voyelle adjacente, ou troublant sa netteté. Il arrive aussi que les diverses syllabes déteignent en quelque sorte les unes sur les autres, et qu'au lieu de plusieurs couleurs coexistantes ou successives, le mot n'évoque qu'une couleur unique, résultat du mélange des nuances appartenant aux diverses voyelles.[18]

The aspects of language identified here as determining synesthetic effects are poetic aspects of language. What Flournoy calls "the repetition of a vowel sound in several consecutive syllables," for example, scholars of poetry and poetics might recognize as *assonance*; the exceptional salience of the word-initial consonant (noted here as bearing a peculiar ability to color a whole word) is the effect poets depend on to create *alliteration*.[19] Flournoy, a professor not of poetry but of experimental psychology, does not use these terms, but it is interesting to note that even he has recourse to poetic terminology. In his effort to describe the effects of consonants on neighboring vowels, Flournoy observes that it is "*des consonnes d'appui* (the neighboring consonants)" that, "even if they don't have their own colors themselves, exercis[e] a modifying influence on the nuance of the adjacent vowel."[20] A technical term that finds no application outside of poetics, the *consonne d'appui* is, strictly speaking, the consonant preceding the principal vowel of a rhyme: the /l/s in *jaloux/loups*,[21] for example, or to give an approximation of the French phenomenon in English, the /w/s of *swear/where*. Although Flournoy's use of the term (*le voisinage des consonnes d'appui*) would seem to imply "neighboring consonants" in a more general sense, his use of the poetic term is telling. The experimental psychologist's effort to describe the aspects of language pertinent to the interactions of synesthetic colors leads him directly to the lexicon of poetics.

La coloration des voyelles

> It is therefore the word placed at the rhyme, the last word of the line that must, like a subtle magician, make everything the poet wanted appear before our eyes.
>
> C'est donc le mot placé à la rime, le dernier mot du vers qui doit, comme un magicien subtil, faire apparaître devant nos yeux tout ce qu'a voulu le poëte.
> —THÉODORE DE BANVILLE, *PETIT TRAITÉ DE POÉSIE FRANÇAISE* (1872)[22]

References to vowel color, coloring (*coloris*), brightness (*brillance, clarté*), nuance, and coloration also turn up in the French discourse on poetry roughly contemporaneous to Galton, Gruber, and Flournoy's work. The terms tend to condense particularly around discussions of assonance and rhyme, in which the same vowel sounds are repeated in close proximity, stressed as a result of their metrical position, or both. The language of color, almost without exception, qualifies vowel timbre in contradistinction to the metrical structures of caesura and syllable count, which find figuration in drawing and line. These discussions of vowel "color" and "coloration" form an integral part of the period's trope of describing poetry as painting, associated most famously with Charles Baudelaire's essay *The Painter of Modern Life* (*Peintre de la vie moderne*, 1863–69).

In his *Treatise on French Versification* (*Traité général de versification française*, 1879) for example, Louis Becq de Fouquières presents the art of versification in terms of the painter's process. Once the line drawing—the metrical structure—has been sketched out on the canvas, he explains,

> To this drawing one adds the coloration of the vowels, some strong, vibrant, and striking, others soft and half-faded; all arranged in a harmonious series for the ear, like colors for the eye.

A ce dessin vient s'ajouter la coloration des voyelles, dont les unes sont fortes, vibrantes, éclatantes, les autres douces, à demi éteintes, toutes se disposant en séries d'accord pour l'oreille, comme les couleurs pour les yeux.[23]

Becq de Fouquières slips seamlessly from vowel timbres to lustrous hues, the grooves of his thought following the etymological affinity binding the *coloration des voyelles* to the painter's *couleurs*. His analogy aligning metrical structure with drawing and vowel timbre with color recalls a very similar account of poetic composition offered by Stéphane Mallarmé in an 1866 letter to François Coppée:

I think that, the lines having been so perfectly sketched out, what we need to aim for above all is that, in the poem, words [...] reflect one another until they no longer seem to possess their own colors, but to be mere transitions of a scale.

je crois que, les lignes si parfaitement délimitées, ce à quoi nous devons viser surtout est que, dans le poëme, les mots [...] se reflètent les uns sur les autres jusqu'à paraître ne plus avoir leur couleur propre, mais n'être que les transitions d'une gamme.[24]

Words, each one endowed with its "own color," might be made to form more perfect poems if discerningly arranged, as in the deceptively simple painting that, on closer inspection, reveals an extraordinarily nuanced palette of hues.[25] In verse, the task would consist of arranging the words so that their colors interreflect to create a subtly variegated yet unified palette, the way ripples of water cast colors about so quickly that they coalesce. With the delimiting lines already drawn, the words within the verse may "reflect one another" in a reciprocal interaction that reveals them to operate outside of linear time. The formulation recalls Mallarmé's description of verse in "Crise de vers," where words "light each other up through reciprocal reflections like a virtual swooping of fire across precious stones (*s'allument de reflets réciproques comme une virtuelle traînée de feux sur des pierreries*)."[26] In the play of mutual reflections, however, not all syllables are equal. The one that marks the end of the poetic line enjoys special prominence in setting the tone. Typically a rhyme, it can also be the line-final assonance that, for example in Charles Guérin's *Sang des crépuscules* (1895), suffices to "mark the verse, as coloration, more precious, or almost more precious than rhyme (*l'assonance y suffisant à marquer le vers, comme coloration, son feu plus ou presque plus précieux que la rime*)."[27]

56 / THE INTERACTION OF COLOR

The prominence of that line-final syllable is nowhere clearer than in the variation on this theme that appears in Théodore de Banville's *Short Treatise on French Poetry* (*Petit traité de poésie française*, 1872). Here, the great *maître de Parnasse* famously asserts that

> *in a verse, one hears but the rhyme-word,* and this word alone works to produce the poet's desired effect. The role of the other words contained in the verse is thus limited to not clashing with its effect, and to harmonizing well with it, forming various internal resonances, but maintaining the same general color.

on n'entend dans un vers que le mot qui est à la rime, *et ce mot est le seul qui travaille à produire l'effet voulu par le poëte. Le rôle des autres mots contenus dans le vers se borne donc à ne pas contrarier l'effet de celui-là et à bien s'harmoniser avec lui, en formant des résonnances variées entre elles, mais de la même couleur générale.*[28]

Just as in Mallarmé's account, the words of a verse "light each other up through reciprocal reflections," affecting one another in a way that escapes linear, temporal succession, so do they "form various resonances amongst themselves" here in Banville. The succession of speech sounds forming a line can "harmonize," sounding a simultaneous key, or chord: a "color" set by the vowel timbre of the line-final rhyme.

Banville's conviction that the sound of the word placed at the rhyme bears sole responsibility for determining a line's "color" or "effect" represents a position judged extreme by nearly all of his contemporaries, but few then or now would contest the general principle that the vowel timbre systematically stressed by the metrical structure enjoys a particular prominence in the line's effect.[29] His description of the various resonances of the syllables that harmonize into the rhyme's color also recalls—or rather, anticipates—Flournoy's observation that for some subjects, "the various syllables run off, as it were, onto one another, and instead of many coexisting or successive colors, the word only evokes a single color, the result of the mixture of nuances belonging to various vowels."[30] Flournoy's observation that the induced impression of color "is significantly stronger when the vowel is repeated in several consecutive syllables" is also relevant, seeing as rhyming timbres are, by definition, repeated: not "in several consecutive syllables," but within perceptible proximity, and in a structure that causes the listener to hear them together despite their separation in time.[31]

For Flournoy's subjects, the unit in question is the word: the various syllables of a single word run off onto one another such that the word evokes only one color; "the dominant vowels" are identified as coloring a whole word. For Banville, on the other hand, the vowel accentuated by the rhyme sets the color for the entire line of verse. But if Jean-Claude Milner is correct in observing that in French, the unit of the versified line may be distinguished from the prose sequence precisely by its behavior as a single phonological word, such a translation from word to line would make linguistic sense.[32] It would not be surprising to observe a resemblance in the interactions of color reported within the space of a word and those envisioned within the length of the line.

One wonders if Mallarmé had something similar in mind when he wrote of the "verse which, of several expressions, makes a new, total word, foreign to the language and as if incantatory (*Le vers qui de plusieurs vocables refait un mot total, neuf, étranger à la langue et comme incantatoire*)." This verse is described as "negating, with a sovereign stroke, the chance remaining in terms . . . (*niant, d'un trait souverain, le hasard demeuré aux termes . . .*),"[33] an expression that has generally been understood to assert that verse can make sound and sense coincide, or seem to ("chance" representing the contingency, or arbitrariness, of the sounds a language uses to indicate things and ideas).[34] The particular capacity of verse to collapse successive speech sounds into an impression of simultaneity would allow it to make the meaning of an utterance seem to "coincide" with its sensuous qualities. For this proposal to make sense, sensuous qualities would have to have their own meanings or at least some property that could be identifiable with a semantic value. The color terms used by Becq de Fouquières, Mallarmé, and Banville to describe vowel timbres would seem to signal one such property: the *coloration des voyelles* could be identified with the semantic value of color names.

While Mallarmé's œuvre features no odes to colors—it is often described as monochromatic[35]— critics frequently refer to his sonnet "The Virgin, the Vivacious, and the Beautiful Today (*Le vierge, le vivace et le bel aujourd'hui*, 1885)" as a "symphony in white": a name inspired by Théophile Gautier's 1849 "Symphony in White Major (*Symphonie en blanc majeur*)," as well as James Whistler's "Symphonies in White (*Symphonie en blanc: I, II, III*)."[36] The reference also derives, of course, from the sonnet's white-on-white image of a swan caught in a frozen lake:

Le vierge, le vivace et le bel aujourd'hui
Va-t-il nous déchirer avec un coup d'aile ivre
Ce lac dur oublié que hante sous le givre
Le transparent glacier des vols qui n'ont pas fui!

Un cygne d'autrefois se souvient que c'est lui
Magnifique mais qui sans espoir se délivre
Pour n'avoir pas chanté la région où vivre
Quand du stérile hiver a resplendi l'ennui.

Tout son col secouera cette blanche agonie
Par l'espace infligée à l'oiseau qui le nie,
Mais non l'horreur du sol où le plumage est pris.

Fantôme qu'à ce lieu son pur éclat lui assigne,
Il s'immobilise au songe froid du mépris
Que vêt parmi l'exil inutile le Cygne.[37]

The virginal, enduring, beautiful today
Will a drunken beat of its wing break us
This hard, forgotten lake haunted under frost
By the transparent glacier of unfled flights!

A swan of old remembers it is he
Magnificent but who without hope frees himself
For never having sung a place to live
When the boredom of sterile winter was resplendent.

His whole neck will shake off this white death-throe
Inflicted by space on the bird denying it,
But not the horror of soil where the feathers are caught.

Phantom assigned to this place by pure brilliance,
He is paralysed in the cold dream of contempt
Put on in useless exile by the Swan.[38]

The sonnet's drama revolves around the agonized swan's desire to flee a frozen lake and its inability to do so. The text is composed in two distinct movements distinguished by a shift in narrative perspective. The first quatrain presents a first-person exclamation (traditionally understood to be that of the swan), which expresses the hope that "the virgin, the vivacious, and the beautiful today" will break apart the "hard forgotten haunted lake." The second quatrain and concluding tercets shift into the third person, contextualizing the opening exclamation with a narrative account. A swan suddenly recalls the hopelessness of its situation, tries unsuccessfully to shake off the agony in which it finds itself, and, shrouded in contempt, ceases all movement. Disorienting syntactic displacements proliferate throughout the text's fourteen alexandrines, creating enigmatic constructions that seem to both demand careful decipherment and defy any singular interpretation. Syntactic gymnastics aside, however, the poem's lexicon leaves little room for doubt as to how the story ends: the swan's hopes for what the day might bring are definitely dashed.

Uniformly hailing the sonnet as a tour de force of extraordinary, even "stupefying"[39] beauty, readers from Albert Thibaudet and Émilie Noulet to Bertrand Marchal have also drawn attention to its one striking formal feature: all of the sonnet's rhymes are built around the tonic vowel /i/. Mallarmé's "symphony in white" is thus also frequently described as a "symphony in *i*," reflecting the narrow range of timbres featured in its rhymes.[40] In an article indicatively titled "More on the Divine Swan (*Encore le divin Cygne*, 1948)," Jacques Duchesne-Guillemin observes, "What makes the sonnet a unique marvel is that it is simultaneously a symphony in white and a symphony in *i*."[41] Henri Morier's *Dictionnaire de poétique et de rhétorique* (1998) goes one step further, citing "'Le Vierge, le Vivace et le Bel Aujourd'hui', sonnet in I major according to Thibaudet, because of its rhymes, in which a unanimous whiteness is painted by means of synesthesia (*où se peint par synesthésie une unanime blancheur*)."[42] It is not clear, in Morier's *Dictionnaire*, if the "synesthesia" in question is presumed to be that of the reader, the author, or indeed both, but it is relevant that Mallarmé did, famously, lament the "perversity that makes the timbres of *jour* [day] and *nuit* [night], contradictorily, dark in the first case, bright in the second (*la perversité conférant à* jour *comme à* nuit, *contradictoirement, des timbres obscur ici, là clair*)."[43] Directly contrasting a quality of the vocalic timbre in *nuit* with the darkness of night, Mallarmé would seem to state all but explicitly that the vowel /i/ is, in his view, bright.

In his commentary on the line, Gérard Genette observes of the perversely bright *nuit* that

> its vocalism consists in a diphthong formed of two "bright" vowels of very proximal timbres, separated by a nuance quite comparable to the one distinguishing the yellow glow of gold from the white brilliance of silver—a dissonance that contributes significantly to the subtle luminosity of this word.
>
> *son vocalisme consiste en une diphtongue formée de deux voyelles 'claires' de timbres très proches, séparées par une nuance assez comparable à celle qui distingue l'éclat jaune de l'or de l'éclat blanc d'argent, dissonance qui entre pour beaucoup dans la luminosité subtile de ce mot.*[44]

Genette places quotation marks around Mallarmé's visual qualifier "bright" and suggests only that the "nuance" separating (presumably) /ɥ/ from /i/ is "comparable" to the one distinguishing "the yellow glow of gold from the white brilliance of silver."[45] Yet he, too, seems sensitive to "the subtle luminosity of this word." With its precise attention to the play of light and color sparked by proximal letters, Genette's remark recalls the Romanian poet's description of the thin ray of orange illuminating the anterior side of the letter *f*.

In a slightly earlier rumination on the same vowel, Paul Valéry staked out a position similar to Genette's. On a sleepless night in March 1942, he made note of "the most beautiful possible line (*le plus beau vers possible*)" in all of French poetry:

Shadows are always dark, even when cast by swans

L'ombre est noire toujours même tombant des cygnes[46]

Turning the line over in his restless mind, Valéry sensed its particular pathos to be quickened by a sharp contrast between its first and last words. He describes this contrast as "simultaneously phonic and semantic (*simultanément phonique et sémantique*)." Between the dark *L'ombre* and piercing clarity of *cygnes*, he hears a sonic contrast that calls out for comparison to the parallel, visual juxtaposition of the shadow and the swan. "There is neither any means nor any hope of doing better," Valéry concludes, returning to bed with a solemn salute to Victor Hugo, "the grim reaper of French literary production (*le Dieu faucheur de toute la fabrication française*)."[47]

Valéry does not equate the sonic contrast with the visual one, contenting himself with the mere observation of a parallel opposition at play in the phonic and semantic strata of the verse. He shows no sign of awareness that, roughly a century earlier, its author explicitly attributed both whiteness and brightness to the vowel "I." Like Mallarmé, Victor Hugo also imagined painting in vowels, leaving considerable room for wonder about just how metaphorical he imagined vowels' "colors" to be:

Wouldn't one think that vowels exist for sight almost as much as for the ear, and that they paint colors? One can see it [/them]. A and I are the white, bright vowels. O is a red vowel. E and EU are the blue vowels. U is the black vowel.

Ne penserait-on pas que les voyelles existent pour le regard presque autant que pour l'oreille et qu'elles peignent des couleurs? On le[s] voit.

A et I sont des voyelles blanches et brillantes. O est une voyelle rouge. E et EU sont des voyelles bleues. U est la voyelle noire.[48]

In these scribbled musings now preserved at the French National Library, probably dating from the late 1830s,[49] Hugo presumes vowels to exist for the ear, wondering only secondarily whether they might also exist for the eye. His reflections, therefore, begin by considering vowels as sounds rather than written signs. He poses the question of their ontological status in a general way, in the impersonal, third-person singular, suggesting that he imagines these impressions to be shared ("One sees it[/them]," rather than "I"). The community who would perceive these associations would seem to be speakers of French, though it could also extend beyond that, as the word lists Hugo compiles include, in addition to many French words, the Latin *Sirius* (the brightest star in the nighttime sky) as well as the Arabic transliteration *Aldebaran* (the brightest star in the constellation known to English speakers as Taurus).

Although Hugo begins by enumerating correspondences between vowel sounds and colors (*voyelles, couleurs*), his musings quickly turn to letters and light (*lettres, lumière*). Remarking that "almost all of the words that express the idea of light contain As and Is and sometimes both letters," Hugo draws up three lists of words signifying something light-related and containing the letter A, the letter I, or both. The lists reveal Hugo's ideas of "A" and "I" to be both capacious and capricious. The I-only list, for example, features words containing the written symbol <i> but not the phoneme /i/ (*oeil, soleil*), as well as words containing the phoneme /a/—but not the written symbol <a> (*étoile*). This would suggest written signs to be determinant, yet *matin* turns up on the A-only list despite its <i>, which is admittedly pronounced /ẽ/ rather than /i/, though so is the <i> of *étincelle*, which appears on the I-only list. Neither the I-only list nor the A-only list features any words without the written signs <i> and <a> respectively, but the A-and-I list does, notably, include words without the written symbol <i> (*rayon, rayonner*). This would suggest that for Hugo, the written sign <y>, which in French is called the *i grec* ("the Greek I"), is a species of "I"—or else that the semi-vowel /j/ is.

The letter-light associations illuminating Hugo's lexicon are plainly irreducible to a single, simple correspondence, but there are a few constellations worth drawing out of their entangled stars. The first might trace the word *cygne* from Mallarmé and Valéry through Hugo's ruminations. In the absence of the word itself—*cygne* appears nowhere in Hugo's lists—one can observe only that its <y> and /i/ both suggest that it easily could feature there—particularly when one considers Hugo's inclusion of *Sirius*, whose initial syllable is nearly identical to that of *cygne*. A second constellation could be glimpsed in the shape of the structure that opposes bright I's and A's to dark U's in Hugo's thought. Overall, Hugo's "bright" vowels are more anterior in their place of resonance than their "dark" counterparts. This structure brings Hugo's impressions into rough alignment with Valéry's, as the phonic contrast perceived by the twentieth-century poet opposes the posterior *ombre* /ɔ̃:bʁ/ to the anterior *cygne* /siɲ/. Finally, one could note that, anticipating Genette and Mallarmé, Hugo also stops to contemplate the curious brightness of the French word *nuit* (night). Hugo, however, resolves this contradiction for himself by observing that the word contains both a dark vowel (U) and a light one (I). This, he concludes, is just as it should be. After all, "The night has stars."

Le vers blanc

> *I rhyme, therefore I am . . . fear not, it's a blank*
> *—an oystershell on the lam!*
> Je rime, donc je vis . . . ne crains pas, c'est à blanc.
> —Une coquille d'huître en rupture de banc! —
> —TRISTAN CORBIÈRE, *LES AMOURS JAUNES* (1873)[50]

One wonders how often it is possible, as it has been here, to read the visual terms shared between the psychological and poetic discourses as the same terms bearing varying degrees of intensity. Could one hazard the proposition that the reports of synesthetic colors' interactions merely render explicit what the poetic discourse assumes, however subconsciously? That the discourses resist clean, categorical separation is, in any case, manifest. The psychological accounts cannot be articulated without identifying and describing poetic aspects of language, and the poetic discourse would be incoherent without readers' ability to envision vowel timbres as colors. However subconscious the translation of sound into sight may be, it is essential to the coherence of the poetic discourse and particularly to its conception of verse as a painterly art. A provocative conclusion might propose that the two discourses are, in truth, one and the same. A more prudent one would content itself with observing only that the ways vowel colors behave in the poetic texts largely correspond to the ways synesthetic colors interact in the early scientific corpus.

If the perspective of poetics casts the history of *audition colorée* in a new light, so does the perspective of nineteenth-century psychology afford a privileged vantage point on poetic history. Focused attention on terms like *couleur*, *nuance*, *coloration*, and *coloris* makes it impossible not to see that these terms enable a discourse on poetry that highlights aspects of language distinct from both signification and metrical structure: timbre, assonance, consonance, dissonance, rhyme. The language of color emerges as an index of nonmetrical principles of composition, giving rise to a vision of versification as an art of color that, *à la limite*, might be imaginable even in the absence of line. Color terms offer the means to articulate and envision poetic form without meter, yet also without the turn to graphic layout that characterizes the dominant narrative of nineteenth-century poetry in the West. In the broadest strokes of poetic history, the symbolist poets, and particularly Stéphane Mallarmé, are the ones who pivot poetry away from metrical forms and toward graphic ones. Color language, however, traces a different shift: away from metrical, linear structures and toward a vision of verse as a kind of color composition, however virtual. "Those faithful to the alexandrine, our hexameter," Mallarmé writes in "Crise de vers,"

> are loosening the childish, rigid mechanism of its length from within; the ear, freed from a gratuitous inner counter, feels the pleasure of discerning, on its own, all the possible combinations and permutations of twelve timbres.

> *Les fidèles à l'alexandrin, notre hexamètre, desserrent intérieurement ce mécanisme rigide et puéril de sa mesure; l'oreille, affranchie d'un compteur factice, connaît une jouissance à discerner, seule, toutes les combinaisons possibles, entre eux, de douze timbres.*[51]

The weakening of meter causes vowel timbres to resonate differently, attracting the ear to their subtle harmonies, nuances, and coloration. As Banville attests, rhyme emerges as a formal feature of paramount importance. Paul Verlaine put it in even stronger terms:

> Our little-accented language cannot accommodate blank verse, and neither Voltaire, Viceroy of Prussia in his time, nor Louis Bonaparte, King of Holland in his, has sufficient authority to make me hesitate for even an instant at the idea of breaking with this absolute principle. Use weak rhyme, use assonance if you like, but with no rhyme and no assonance, there is no French Verse.

> *Notre langue peu accentuée ne saurait admettre le vers blanc, et ni Voltaire, vice-roi de Prusse en son temps, ni Louis Bonaparte, roi de Hollande au sien, ne me sont des autorités suffisantes pour hésiter,*

> *fût-ce un instant à ne me point départir de ce principe absolu. Rimez faiblement, assonez si vous voulez, mais rimez ou assonez, pas de vers français sans cela.*[52]

Verlaine's *vers blanc* is a direct translation of the English "blank verse," a term coined by Robert Greene in 1588 expressly to denigrate Christopher Marlowe's unrhymed lines.[53] The term does not seem to have attracted much scrutiny. The need for it appears to have emerged from the fact that the (unrhymed) quantitative verse of antiquity was too highly regarded—and formally distinct—to furnish a comprehensible insult to the unfortunate Marlowe. As Derek Attridge reports, in late sixteenth-century England, "If one's lines did not rhyme, one was attempting quantitative verse. There was simply no word, and no concept, for blank verse."[54] Aggressively marking the negative space where rhyme seemed needed but failed to appear, Greene coined both a new term and a new concept for a kind of verse defined negatively by a lack of line-final consonance.

From this perspective, the term is almost more apt in French than in its native English, for as the tradition has abundantly shown, unrhymed English verse can still play with stress-timed rhythms, creating accented assonances and alluring alliterations. It is possible to have poetic lines in English in which the absence of rhyme does not constitute a glaring problem. But in a language without lexical stress, as Verlaine instantly realized, to draw a blank where the rhyme should be is to jeopardize the very existence of the line. Stripped of the play of vowel colors, such a line might well struggle to distinguish itself from prose. Paul Verlaine weakened the metrical structure of French verse to the point that it took but a nudge from the *verslibristes* to topple it, but rhyme, or assonance—the play and patterning of vowel timbre—he deemed its one indispensable, absolutely constitutive element. Without it, there could be no verse: one would be left not with a symphony in white, but with a blank canvas: an absence of any art at all.

3 / Mallarmé and the Tension of Timbre

Chimera, attested in our having thought of it ...
Chimère, y avoir pensé atteste ...
—STÉPHANE MALLARMÉ, "CRISIS OF VERSE" (1897)[1]

In the winter of 1894, Stéphane Mallarmé traveled to England "bearing news." "The most surprising kind." Judging from the opening lines of the lecture that was the reason for his voyage, he was fairly bursting with it. "I do indeed bring news," he declared to the audience assembled at Oxford's Taylorian Institution on the first of March: "Verse has been tampered with" (*On a touché au vers*). A fissure had emerged in the ancient unity long known indifferently as verse or as poetry, and Mallarmé, tracing it, had deduced the magnitude of its implications with astonishing prescience. Standing before the fault line that would bring untold reconfigurations, he marked the moment. He pointed. "That is where we are, right now," he observed. "The separation."[2]

The separation Mallarmé's lecture describes is binary in nature: it identifies, on the one side, "very strict, numerical, direct, with the play of its two parts, meter, from before," and on the other, "the development of that which just recently obtained the name of *prose poem*." The separation divides meter from all the prose poem has inspired. It does not place the two elements in a relation of succession; it merely separates them. For despite the qualifier "from before" (*antérieur*) beside "meter" and the "just recently" (*naguères*) that characterizes the recognition of the prose poem, what exists on either side of the divide persists into the present. As the derivatives of the prose poem flourish, "meter, from before, carries on; nearby."[3]

From a twenty-first-century perspective, the division Mallarmé describes seems readily recognizable as the one that exists today between "poetry" and "verse." Poetry, a porous and essentially undefined category, is as contested in scope and validity as were the prose poem and its derivatives in Mallarmé's day; verse, on the other hand, is just language set to meter.[4] That meter may be syllabic, accentual, tonal, quantitative, or any combination thereof, but whichever it is, it is the defining feature of the form we call verse, as it has been since antiquity. And while we are generally unwilling to accept that the world we live in is a world without poetry, we are less disconcerted at the suggestion that we might live in a world without verse. The art of versification, if not obsolete, is hardly a dominant one in the world today. No one seems terribly upset by this.

It might seem perverse, therefore, or at least unintuitive, to propose an inquiry into "verse"—the form that, more than a century ago, ceased to be synonymous with the far more lively "poetry." Verse, from the contemporary vantage point, would appear to have been just one possible form for the poetic spirit: a shell that housed a life that nonetheless continues on. Why dwell on the abandoned shell if the life has relocated elsewhere? In order, I suppose, to imagine the life that was: the life that once pulsated in the shell; the life that, indeed, made it. If that life is the same one that persists in poetry today, surely the shell has much to tell about it. This chapter investigates the form called "verse" insofar as Stéphane Mallarmé understood it at the moment it broke with "poetry." It advances two propositions: first, that for Mallarmé, verse is not defined exclusively by meter; second, that in Mallarmé's account, verse can exist in the absence of meter if it engages another aspect of language: "timbre." Finding that vocalic timbres, be they bright, dark, or colored, can awaken a tension between linguistic sensuality and signification, the chapter reveals synesthetically perceptible vowel properties to be integral to Mallarmé's conception of verse.

The Separation

The separation Mallarmé announced in his Oxford lecture drew a binary division between the "very strict, numerical, direct, with the play of its two parts, meter, from before," and "the development of that which just recently obtained the name of *prose poem*." The substantives established as mutually exclusive are thus "meter" (*le mètre*) and "the development" (*l'épanouissement*). An asymmetry is immediately apparent. These substantives are not alike in kind: "the development" refers to a subset of literary production, "meter" to a formal constraint.

In the case of Mallarmé's announcement, framed as a field report from a neighboring nation, the meter at hand is the meter of French; more precisely, it is the "very strict, numerical, direct, with the play of its two parts, meter, from before." "Very strict," because it is bound by inviolable rules of syllable placement, rhyme type, and word boundary; "numerical," because it demands a procedure of counting; "direct," which is another way of saying "linear"; "with the play of its two parts," bifurcated by a mandatory caesura, or perhaps coupled by rhyme; "from before," having dominated French verse in previous centuries. Mallarmé's punctuation and word order are significant: while "strict, numerical, direct, with the play of its two parts" precede "meter," the temporal modifier "from before" is placed after the substantive and separated from it by a comma. Thus, it is pointedly not "the previous meter" (*le mètre antérieur*), which would be both singular and specific. Mallarmé's construction suggests "meter" in a more general way, as a more capacious category: "meter, from before" (*le mètre, antérieur*). The specification "with the play of its two parts" (*à jeux conjoints*) indicates that this meter is capable of internal division. The "parts" to which Mallarmé refers are most likely the two hemistiches divided by the medial caesura of the twelve-syllable alexandrine (the verse form that dominated French versification from the sixteenth through the nineteenth centuries), indicating that Mallarmé is imagining meter in terms of the unit of the line. But it is also possible that the "two parts" refer to the lines themselves, as in French according to Mallarmé, "lines of verse go by twos or more, due to their terminal accord, that is, the mysterious law of Rhyme."[5] In either case, the meter from before is tied to a total measure derived from that of the line. On one side, then, we have meter and the line.

And what is "the development of that which recently obtained the name of *prose poem*"? Mallarmé explains its contours at some length. "[V]erse is everything, as soon as one writes," he reports, less with the air of the author than with that of the surprised onlooker. There is "versification as soon as there is a cadence."[6] Here, verse has broken with meter: although meter falls to one side, "verse" unexpectedly turns up on the other. And not just "verse," but indeed "versification"—a term that, by its conventional definition, should designate precisely the art of composing in accordance with the metrical dictates across the divide. All that remains in terms of constraint upon "verse" is "writing" (*dès qu'on écrit*) and "cadence." At first glance, the two constraints would appear to be mutually exclusive. Cadence, whether understood in the phonological sense of "vocal stress upon accented syllables, dividing a sentence into rhythmic units" or in the musical one of "the progression of chords, according to certain harmonic rules, that concludes a musical phrase"[7] would seem to pertain to the production of the voice; "writing," to that of the pen. If they cannot be jointly applied, the two constraints must be understood in parallel: in spoken language, verse exists as soon as a voice suggests a cadence; in written language, verse exists as soon as someone writes. We have a tautology. The constraint "as soon as one writes," in context, can only be understood if "to write" is read in a narrowed sense.[8] In other words: written language is verse as soon as someone writes literature. But what is the difference, for Mallarmé, between verse and literature? Is this statement not also a tautology?

If the defining feature of this particular prose is, as yet, obscure, one thing is certain: it is not to be confused with "writing" as a general category. "The prose of any sumptuous writer" falls within this domain specifically because it is "withdrawn from habitual haphazard usage"; such writing "is valid insofar as it is a broken line, playing with its timbres and even hidden rhymes."[9] Mallarmé dissolves the distinction between the broken line (*le vers rompu*) and the prose poem (*le poème en prose*); prose and verse are no longer opposed. In the absence of meter and the line, verse and prose are one and the same; between the two forms, there is no longer any distinction.

Thus, the exact date of the Taylorian lecture is important: March 1, 1894. It represents a decisive moment not just in the history of verse but also in the history of the poet's thinking about it. For just fourteen months before, Mallarmé had published a book entitled, precisely, *Vers et prose*.[10] Neatly organized into two sections, plainly labeled *Vers* and *Prose*, the book features Mallarmé's versified poems in the first half, his prose writings in the second. Although the "Prose (pour Des Esseintes)" appears in Part I and "Poèmes de Poe" in Part II, the apparent contradiction is in fact none at all. For Mallarmé's title "Prose (pour Des Esseintes)" belies a strictly versified poem; "prose" in this context refers to the Latin hymns sung in Catholic services.[11] And the poems of Edgar Allan Poe, though versified in English, appear exclusively in Mallarmé's prose translations.

By March of the following year, however, this is no longer the case. In place of the formal opposition, which relates two elements like in kind, an asymmetrical division has emerged. Within the vast realm of prose, there exists a subcategory that partakes of poetry and even of verse; it plays with cadence, timbre, and rhyme; it is distinguished from the versified poetry that preceded it by a singular absence: that of the metrical line. The separation does not divide verse from prose or verse from poetry; verse, stretched to breaking, falls on both sides of the divide.

This separation forms the basis of the title "Crisis of Verse" (*Crise de vers*), Mallarmé's watershed essay of 1897.[12] The word *crise*, in other words, bears the full freight of its Greek root (κρίσις), by which it designates "a separating"— a sense still palpable in certain English words of shared derivation ("discern," "discriminate").[13] The topic of the essay is thus the separating, or scission, of *le vers*, itself the bearer of two distinct meanings. *Le vers* is the versified line: once known in English as "a verse" and most precisely described in this context as "the metrical line" that is in the process of breaking apart. "Crise de vers," in this sense, might be translated as "the fracturing of the line." But *le vers* also bears the meaning of "verse," the genre comprised of literary works composed in metrical lines; hence the standard translation "Crisis of Verse." This "crisis" designates a decisive stage, "a sudden rupture" in the history of verse, to be sure.[14] But so too does it articulate, by means of its etymological root, a separating: of *le vers* (the line) and of *le vers* (verse).

Of Verse With Verses and Verse Without

If *le vers* (verse) need not comprise *vers* (lines), the question arises: What, if anything, makes it verse? "Verse is everything, as soon as one writes," Mallarmé declares—but only to follow that capacious definition with a number of statements that obscure its apparent extent. Verse is not limited to writing, as "versification" exists as soon as a voice expresses a cadence; everything written is not verse, only that which is "withdrawn from habitual haphazard usage." But how does some prose "withdraw" from "habitual haphazard usage"? Some prose, the passage tells us, such as "the prose of any sumptuous writer," falls within this domain specifically because it is "withdrawn from habitual haphazard usage"; such writing "is valid insofar as it is a broken line, playing with its timbres and even hidden rhymes."[15] The precise construction is significant. The verb *valoir* ("to be valid as") confers a classificatory judgment, placing this prose—let us call it "prose verse"—within the same genre as the broken line (*le vers rompu*). The conjunction *en tant que* ("insofar as it is") assumes an aspect shared between the elements conjoined. This aspect allows us to understand the first element within the more established terms of the second. "Insofar as it is," to be sure, is not "is"; Mallarmé does not fully dissolve this prose into the broken line. Such a statement would introduce the problem of the line, a precise measure for which Mallarmé has not, in this text, established any prose equivalent. What Mallarmé says is, rather, that prose verse operates as the broken line does, using an aspect proper to both of the elements conjoined by *en tant que*. This aspect is stated: "playing with its timbres and even hidden rhymes." What distinguishes this prose from all prose is, or at least can be (for we do not know if the aspect stated is singular or merely an illustrative example), the play of timbres and rhymes.

"Verse," then, it would seem, admits of at least two definitions. It may be language ordered by meter into the unit of a line, or it may be language that plays with timbre and rhyme. Language can demonstrate one or the other of these behaviors and constitute verse; it may also demonstrate both. The definitions are not mutually exclusive. Prose verse cannot avail itself of the metrical line, but metrical verses can certainly make use of timbre and rhyme. Indeed, Mallarmé contends in his 1887 essay "Solennité," they are better when they do: "This is the superiority of modern verse over ancient verse, which forms a whole but doesn't rhyme."[16] Rhyme is not necessary to metrical verse, at least not in all languages, but it is preferable.

Timbre, too, appears within the confines of meter. As the reader will recall, Mallarmé writes in "Crise de vers" that those who remain "faithful to the alexandrine, our hexameter, are loosening the childish, rigid mechanism of its length from within; the ear, freed from a gratuitous inner counter, feels the pleasure of discerning, on its own, all the possible combinations and permutations of twelve timbres."[17] Yet it seems, at least here, that timbre can suffer from the excessively "rigid and puerile mechanism" of the alexandrine, or more precisely, its "measure"—which is one meaning of the word "meter." The play of timbres becomes apparent to the ear only when that ear has been "liberated from a gratuitous inner counter." Timbre and meter would appear to be engaged in a certain rivalry, just as rhyme and meter are. But while the Mallarmé of 1887 insisted on the necessity of meter over rhyme, it is the play of timbre and rhyme that emerges as crucial for the Mallarmé of 1897.

Mallarmé's "timbre," though not explicitly defined, is established in "Crise de vers" as occurring twelve times within an alexandrine; its length, therefore, is or can be equal to that of a syllable. We might provisionally say that a "timbre," in Mallarmé's vocabulary, consists of a vowel or diphthong optionally flanked by consonants. A relation emerges: a timbre is the minimal element required to form a rhyme. Poor rhyme requires, at minimum, the matching of two vowel timbres; there is no rhyme in French that does not engage timbre. If there can be no play of rhyme without a play of timbre, our second definition of verse may be simplified further still. Verse may be language ordered by meter into the unit of a line, or verse may be language that plays with timbre.

But what, more precisely, does it mean to "play with timbre"? Mallarmé offers an extended reflection on the topic in "Crise de vers." The dating of the passage is, again, significant. Absent from the 1886 preface to René Ghil's *Traité du Verbe*, in which many key passages from "Crise de vers" first appeared, as well as the 1892 prototype for "Crise de vers" that appeared in *Vers et prose*, "In Relation to Verse (*Relativement au vers*)," Mallarmé's paragraph on timbre appears for the first time on September 1, 1895.[18] Which is to say, after the separation. It then reappears, in its definitive form, in "Crise de vers," an essay whose title, like its discussion of timbre, announces a significant development in its author's understanding of verse. The passage is well known:

> ... but, at times, in turning to aesthetics, I regret that discourse fails to express objects by means of strokes corresponding to them in coloring or bearing, which exist in the instrument of the voice, amongst languages and sometimes in one. Beside the opaque *ombre* [shade], *ténèbres* [shadows] is not very dark; what a disappointment, before the perversity that makes the timbres of *jour* [day] and *nuit* [night], contradictorily, dark in the first case, bright in the second. The wish for a term of brilliant splendor, or for a dark one, the opposite; as for the simple examples of brightness—*Only*, be aware that *verse would not exist*: it philosophically remunerates the deficiency of languages, superior complement.

> ... *mais, sur l'heure, tourné à de l'esthétique, mon sens regrette que le discours défaille à exprimer les objets par des touches y répondant en coloris ou en allure, lesquelles existent dans l'instrument de la voix, parmi les langages et quelquefois chez un. À côté d'*ombre, opaque, ténèbres *se fonce peu; quelle déception, devant la perversité conférant à* jour *comme à* nuit, *contradictoirement, des timbres obscur ici, là clair. Le souhait d'un terme de splendeur brillant, ou qu'il s'éteigne, inverse; quant à des alternatives lumineuses simples—*Seulement, *sachons n'existerait pas le vers: lui, philosophiquement rémunère le défaut des langues, complément supérieur.*[19]

The clash described here takes place between elements like in kind: the "coloring or bearing" (*coloris ou allure*) of "objects" and the coloring or bearing that "exists in the instrument of the voice, amongst languages, and sometimes within one." The specific vehicle through which this coloring or bearing appears in the voice and in language is "timbre," as evidenced by the poet's dismayed lament, "what a disappointment, before the perversity that makes the timbres of *jour* and *nuit*, contradictorily, dark in the first case, bright in the second."[20] The timbre of *nuit* is bright; the timbre of *jour* is dark.[21]

The vehicle through which coloring or bearing manifests itself in objects is more obscure. This is partially due to the fact that the "objects" of Mallarmé's formulation are not precisely objects in the conventional sense of "things in the world." The "objects" that Mallarmé cites—day and night—are more accurately "facts of nature" or even "natural occurrences" (*faits de nature*) understood from an anthropocentric perspective and structured by the semantic divisions of the terms that designate them (*jour, nuit*). Thus, they are not precisely physical objects in the world, nor are they explicitly linguistic constructs; they are indifferent to the distinction. The point bears stressing. A pre-Saussurean thinker, Mallarmé does not systematically make the threefold distinction between the signifier (the psychological imprint of a word acquired through repeated aural experience), the signified (the abstract concept corresponding to the word), and the referent (the physical object that provides a concrete example of the concept). Here, there is only "the term" (the signifier) and "the object" that refers indifferently to the linguistic construct and the referent.[22] Thus, Mallarmé may conceive of the same "connection" between, on the one hand, "signification and the form of a word"[23] and, on the other, "spectacles of the world [. . .] and the speech tasked with expressing them."[24] In what may well be the best-known passage in his entire oeuvre,[25] the passage directly preceding the reflection on *jour* and *nuit*, Mallarmé articulates the source of the "objects" to which he refers:

> Languages, imperfect in that they are many, the supreme one is lacking: thinking being writing without accessories, nor whispers, but still tacit immortal speech, the diversity, on earth, of idioms prevents anyone from uttering words which, otherwise would be found, through one, unique strike, materially truth itself. This prohibition rules precisely, in nature (one brushes up against it with a smile) so that no one has any reason to consider himself God;

> *Les langues imparfaites en cela que plusieurs, manque la suprême: penser étant écrire sans accessoires, ni chuchotement mais tacite encore l'immortelle parole, la diversité, sur terre, des idiomes empêche personne de proférer les mots qui, sinon se trouveraient, par une frappe unique, elle-même matériellement la vérité. Cette prohibition sévit expresse, dans la nature (on s'y bute avec un sourire) que ne vaille de raison pour se considérer Dieu;*[26]

The barrier encountered here arises from the human will to express thought in linguistic form. Thought, described as "writing without accessories, nor whispers,"[27] precedes any putting into language. It is in the effort to articulate "immortal speech" (*l'immortelle parole*) that the thinking being runs up against a "prohibition." That prohibition stands not against uttering words that would correspond perfectly to an objective reality but against uttering words that would materialize one's own thought.[28] Only one thinker gets to do that, Mallarmé notes with a smile: God. "This prohibition rules precisely, in nature (one brushes up against it with a smile) so that no one has any reason to consider himself God." God does not exist for Mallarmé at this point, hence the passage's initial assertion that "the supreme [language] is lacking." The supreme language, for Mallarmé, is not lost, broken, or forgotten; it is simply "lacking." It does not exist and never has—except, of course, as a "Chimera, attested in our having thought of it."[29]

In the supreme language, objects understood in Mallarmé's sense correspond perfectly with expression. This correspondence is not attested as a whole, but one catches glimmers of its possibility now and again by which to infer what it would be. These glimmers appear not just in language but in many forms of human expression, and when he spots them, Mallarmé tends to call them "poems." Hence his confession that "I never sit on a concert bench without perceiving amid the obscure sublimity the sketch of one of the poems immanent to humanity or those poems' original state, all the more comprehensible for being silent,"[30] or his account of a ballet dancer as a "poem detached from any scribal apparatus."[31] For Mallarmé, these "poems immanent to humanity" are nothing less than that by which "humanity" can be said to exist at all. Like the constellations that exist only by means of the viewer who, in the same act, both reads and writes them,[32] "poems" constitute the sign by which the human being evidences and asserts the human category.

Many arts afford glimmers of this sign, but for Mallarmé, it is ultimately language that holds the greatest potential to realize it. "It is not the elementary sonorities of brasses, strings, or woodwinds," he writes emphatically, "but undeniably intellectual speech at its apogee that must evidently, opulently, result, as the totality of the relations existing in everything, Music."[33] The greatest hope of realizing the "totality of the relations existing in everything"—and "everything," for Mallarmé, includes humanity—lies in "intellectual speech at its apogee." And "intellectual speech at its apogee" is, or at least can be, "verse":

> Thus launched out of itself, the principle that is none other than —
> Verse! drawing inward no less than releasing for its full flowering
> (the instant they shimmer and die in a rapid bloom, on something
> transparent like ether) a thousand beautiful elements, hurried,
> rush together and order themselves in accordance with their essential values. Sign! in the central gulf of a spiritual impossibility that

nothing belongs exclusively to everything, the divine numerator of our apotheosis, some supreme mold that does not exist as any object: but it borrows, to burnish a seal, all the scattered ore, unclaimed and floating like riches, and to forge them together.

Ainsi lancé de soi le principe qui n'est — que le Vers! attire non moins que dégage pour son épanouissement (l'instant qu'ils brillent et meurent dans une fleur rapide, sur quelque transparence comme d'éther) les mille éléments de beauté pressés d'accourir et de s'ordonner dans leur valeur essentielle. Signe! au gouffre central d'une spirituelle impossibilité que rien ne soit exclusivement à tout, le numérateur divin de notre apothéose, quelque suprême moule n'ayant pas lieu en tant que d'aucun objet qui existe: mais il emprunte, pour y aviver un sceau tous gisements épars, ignorés et flottants selon quelque richesse, et les forger.[34]

The "Verse" of this passage, to be sure, is verse in meter: the words whose declamation prompts it are explicitly ordered "according to an absolute meter."[35] The "drawing inward" and "releasing" of the "thousand beautiful elements" described as "hurried" suggest linguistic elements engaged in a sort of tension with time, "rushing" into an "order" dictated by "their essential values." The instant that order is attained is also the instant it perishes: "the instant they shimmer and die in a rapid bloom." But the instant, brief as it may be, is nonetheless a "Sign" furnished by the "absolute meter," attesting to "some supreme mold that does not exist as any object." The supreme mold, like the supreme language, attests to a human vision of language ordered in an "absolute" way. Gathering from haphazard, ordinary language "scattered ore, unclaimed and floating like riches," the absolute meter restores the order that is absent in words spoken without it. It will "burnish a seal"; in the terms of the passage with which we began, we might say that it "philosophically remunerates the deficiency of languages, superior complement." What is the deficiency (*défaut*)? Implicitly, the order in which the elements find themselves before they "rush," at the impetus of the absolute meter, into their "essential" order. There are, in other words, two orders—or perhaps, states: "crude or immediate here; there, essential."[36]

This passage from "Solennité," first published in February 1887, dates from before the separation; it appears in *Vers et prose*; it does not indicate that anything besides "absolute meter" could generate the vibrant tension it describes. But the "verse" that appears in "Crise de vers"—the verse that explicitly can "remunerate the deficiency of languages"—is not described in terms of meter, absolute or otherwise. That without which "*verse would not exist*" is articulated in entirely different terms. By 1897, "verse" has been reconfigured into something we have yet to grasp.

"*en coloris ou en allure*"

That without which verse would not exist is articulated in terms of a tension between the wish for a term endowed with certain properties and an encounter with a term lacking those properties, wholly or partially. While the sonic properties of *nuit* and *jour* seem to be fully opposed to the degrees of brightness inherent in the meaning of those terms, *ombre* constitutes an instance of partial correspondence, implying an object nearly as dark as the "opaque" timbre Mallarmé perceives it to bear. The properties inherent in objects and the voice thus admit of degrees; "opaque" and "not very dark" are not binary and oppositional but degrees of realization of the same quality, measured along the same axis. If the degrees of realization in terms and objects were always to correspond, verse would not exist; so would it cease to exist in the absence of the potential for correspondence. The potential for correspondence resides in the existence of the common axis: a property common to both objects and language.

That property would seem to be of capital importance. Mallarmé articulates it not as one property, but as two. The voice has the capacity to correspond to objects *en coloris ou en allure*—in "color or movement,"[37] "shading or bearing,"[38] or perhaps "coloring or pacing." The conjunction "or" (*ou*) coordinates the two distinct alternatives without establishing a disjunctive relation between them (as would, for example, "either . . . or," *ou . . . ou*); so, it seems entirely possible that the two properties could coincide.[39]

The first term, *coloris*, derived from the Italian *colorito*, began as a means of describing the art of painting and is first attested in reference to Leonardo da Vinci in the late fifteenth century. The masculine substantivization of *colorire* "to color," it shares a root with *colore* "color." *Coloris* appears in French in 1675[40] to denote the "manner of using and manipulating colors, and, *by metonymy*, the effect obtained."[41] In this metonymic usage, *coloris* differs from *couleur* in referring to an overall palette, implying an art of selection, combination, and balance. "Every artist has his style," Hippolyte Taine writes in 1865; "In the case of a painter, he has his palette (*coloris*), rich or drab, his favorite types, noble or common, his poses, his way of composing." *Coloris* concerns colors' appearance in context, disallowing isolation and abstraction: as Gabriel Séailles notes in 1911, "What makes the beauty of the palette (*coloris*) in a painting is neither the variety nor the richness of the isolated tones, but their harmony."[42] This would seem to be the sense of *coloris* that Mallarmé has in mind when he admires "the fragile powder of the palette (*la poudre fragile du coloris*)"[43] in the paintings of Berthe Morisot, and it orients the term's appearance in "Crise de vers" as well. For it is, we recall, "by means of strokes corresponding to them in coloring or bearing" (*par des touches y répondant en coloris ou en allure*) that the poet wishes language might align with objects. The term *touches*, translated in its more abstract sense as "touches"[44] and "marks,"[45] also means, quite concretely, "brush strokes."[46] Of course, *touches* are "piano keys," as well, and the *coloris* of "Crise de vers" appears not on a canvas but "in the instrument of the voice." The term's first reading, then, would call upon its metaphorical extension into the realm of music, by which it designates "the effect resulting from the use of instruments, the sounds, the timbres."[47] Thus, we might say that *coloris* refers to the qualities of the voice that it shares with musical instruments: its sounds and timbres.

This sense of *coloris* is widely attested in musical discourse of the late nineteenth century, which illuminates Mallarmé's usage considerably.[48] In Richard Wagner's 1860 *Lettre sur la musique*, for example, the German composer praises Italian virtuosos for bringing to the underwhelming melodies of Italian opera "an elegance of coloring (*grâce de coloris*), a mellifluousness of sound previously unknown to the German masters and absent from their instrumental melodies."[49] A quality particular to the voice yet imitable to some degree by an orchestra, Wagner's *coloris* names an aspect of musical sound distinct from melody yet intimately related to it. One suspects that *coloris* is Wagner's French translation of *Klangfarbe* in the pre-Helmholtzian sense he was accustomed to using, and as such, it is an excellent translation. In French vocal manuals of the period, *coloris* qualifies the singing, speaking, and reading voice, indicating a changefulness linked to vowel pronunciation. The celebrated baritone Jean-Baptiste Faure's 1886 *La voix et le chant* provides a particularly instructive example. In a section titled "On Coloring (*Du Coloris*)," Faure describes *coloris* as a singer's ability to "vary the timbre of his voice." This variation is explained as "the singer's palette, which is as rich as the painter's in terms of light and shadow and broken and bright colors, but also possesses varieties of rhythm and timbre whose combinations may be multiplied ad infinitum."[50] *Coloris* inheres particularly in vowels. It is "in the diversity of vowel timbres, open and closed, nasal and oral, that one of the most precious elements of *coloris* must be sought, and without which song is but a succession of monotonous sounds."[51] A vehicle of sonic variety, *coloris* also brings emotional nuance: "there are certain emotions that can only be obtained, certain feelings that can only be expressed through the magical effects of coloring (*coloris*)."[52] Like the *coloris* which, in Mallarmé, exists "in the instrument of the voice, amongst languages, and sometimes in one," the *coloris* of the vocal arts vacillates between music and language, singing voice and signifying vowel.

The other property noted beside *coloris* is *allure*. First attested in French in 1170 as *aleure*, the term first designated "speed of movement, walking," and is a derivative of the verb *aller* ("to go"). Used primarily to describe the gaits of horses—walking, trotting, galloping—the term can also be used in reference to the gaits of other creatures, including humans, as well as the progress of the sun. English translations in this sense might include "speed," "rate," "cadence," or better still, "pace." The term *allure*, when used figuratively, can also refer to the general aura of people or things, as well the overall pace or rhythm of a work of art; hence Sainte-Beuve's 1828 observation, regarding Du Bellay's poetry, "One is struck by the freedom of its movement (*la libre allure*), amongst other merits, and in some manner or other the rolling *fluidity* of the poetic sentence, which *unfolds* and *winds* its way effortlessly through the twists of rhyme."[53] The metaphorical extensions of the term are not limited to works of art, however; Paul Valéry, in 1931, will explain, "Proceeding in this manner will assure the *steady advancement* of our establishment, which we might call the rhythm of its operations (*allure de régime*)."[54] In twentieth-century phonetics, the term serves as the technical designator for the speed or rhythm of speech: "the rhythm (*allure*) *of the utterance* (sometimes referred to as movement) [. . .] whether it is slow [. . .] or rapid [. . .] or staccato [. . .] may be invoked to explain particular, exceptional phonetic behaviors."[55] Perhaps it is time to reconsider our translation of *allure*. While the English "pace" or "pacing" bears the advantage of the walking movement at the origin of the French term, it lacks any capacity to suggest the "staccato" rhythm of the technical designator. The best term available, though hardly a perfect translation, would seem to be "rhythm": a term that, in its Greek derivation, designated "a particular manner of flowing."[56]

The two properties Mallarmé identifies as common to objects and language are thus quite distinct. Although we cannot say with certainty what they are in "objects," we can say with considerable precision what they are in the voice. The first, coloring, refers to its sounds and timbres; the second, rhythm, refers to the pacing and accentual distribution of utterances. Regarding the category to which Mallarmé's examples pertain, we have little choice but to say "coloring," for while "brightness" is not precisely "coloring," it is "rhythm" even less.

Thus, the answer to the question "What is that without which verse would not exist?" is dual in nature. There are two answers. Mallarmé explains one of them in considerable detail: it is the tension that arises between one's desire for a term with a particular coloring and one's encounter with a term lacking that coloring. The desired coloring is the one inherent in the object named and inheres in meaning; the encountered coloring is that of the timbre in the term pronounced and inheres in sound. This is the answer afforded by *coloris*. Let us call it the *tension of timbre*.

The second answer lies in the term *allure*. Considered beside the numerous examples provided to illustrate "coloring," the lack of explanation with regard to "rhythm" suggests that the author assumes the matter to be self-evident. He does not explain it. We know of its presence only because of the inclusion of "allure" in the expression "en coloris ou en allure." And because, in the line directly following the passage under consideration, Mallarmé names it. Concluding his reflection on the desire necessary to verse to make the coloring of meaning correspond with the coloring of sound, he writes, "Strange mystery; and, from no lesser intentions, meter appeared in incubatory times."[57] The second answer is meter.

Meter also generates a tension in language; meter also awakens a human desire to see fragments of language "order themselves in accordance with their essential values."[58] Those values, in the case of meter, are not colored, but rhythmic—they have to do with speech sounds' succession in time. If the tension of timbre may be defined as the tension that arises from a discrepancy between one's desire for a term of a particular hue and one's encounter with a term of a different color, metrical tension might be described as the tension that arises between one's desire for an expression with a particular rhythm and an encounter with an expression lacking that temporal structure.

Before drafting his Taylorian lecture over the winter of 1893–94, the only aspect of language Mallarmé recognizes as capable of stamping the forger's seal upon an utterance to make it verse is meter. From March 1, 1894, onward, however, "verse" admits of two definitions. It may be language ordered by meter into a line, or it may be language that engages the tension of timbre.[59]

A Theory of Verse

Let us return, once more, to the passage. Can we really say that there are two, and only two, answers to the question "What is that without which verse would not exist?" The difficulty, to begin with, is one of syntax. The verb of the italicized warning appears in the conditional: "*verse would not exist.*" It seems to partake of a hypothetical if-then structure, such as one typically finds in the form "If X __, then Y___." But the first clause is missing. X, therefore, remains an enigma. We infer from the context that the missing clause concerns the wish articulated at the beginning of the sentence: "The wish for a term of brilliant splendor, or for a dark one, the opposite." The missing clause, we hypothesize, would be "If that wish were realized." Thus, "If we had a term of brilliant splendor, or for a dark one, the opposite, *verse would not exist.*"

This seems reasonable enough. But taken literally, it would imply that meter is not capable of creating verse on its own. In this reading, verse resides on one aspect of language and one aspect alone: the tension of timbre. This is manifestly false.

Might we, then, read the missing clause in a different sense? Perhaps by taking into account the component of the sentence that we have thus far ignored: "as for the simple examples of brightness"? This phrase, which refers to the desired "term of brilliant splendor" and its dark opposite, reduces those entities to illustrations of a general idea. We have assumed this idea to be the tension of timbre. But the categories to which the examples pertain are multiple: they are "simple examples of brightness," of which other examples might be, and indeed have been, offered; but the principle of "brightness," according to our current understanding, is itself but an example of the larger category of "coloring." This categorization, however, was made only reluctantly; "brightness" was said to partake of "coloring" only because it could not be assimilated into "rhythm."

But might not "coloring" and "rhythm," too, partake of a larger category, a category into which "brightness" might more comfortably fall? Just as we read the "term of brilliant splendor" and its opposite as indications of a general principle, so might we also read "coloring or rhythm" as examples pertaining to a shared category. By this reading, that without which verse would not exist might be understood as a single principle, of which rhythm, coloring, and brightness are three examples. They are not even, necessarily, the only possible examples. Nothing in Mallarmé's syntax, when thus understood, precludes the possibility of yet other linguistic phenomena capable of instantiating the principle they enact in verse.

So what is the principle? It would have to partake of what is common to the tension installed in language by meter and timbre. Let us return to the two passages that describe these experiences: "Solennité" and "Crise de vers."

The force that drives the passage on meter is the listener's perception—and expectation—of an order to be realized: the "thousand beautiful elements," we read, "rush together and order themselves in accordance with their essential values." We understand this "order" to be that of the "absolute meter"; it operates according to the elements' "essential values." Referred to as the "divine numerator of our apotheosis," this order partakes of a system based on number. Placed in parallel with—even, arguably, granted the appositive of—"some supreme mold that does not exist as any object," it also partakes, unmistakably, of the supreme language. This supreme order exists in a state of tension with another force: it "draws in" and "releases"; the elements are "hurried"; they "rush." In moving to the meter, the earthly language reveals the presence of other constraints against which it must work. We infer these constraints to be the ones that govern language in non-meter: the rhythm and word order governed less by sound and more by syntax. The particularity of the experience of meter seems to lie not only in an awareness of the realized metrical order but also in a heightened awareness of this other, unrealized order: the one dictated by sense. The second order, although ever present in nonmetrical speech, is usually unconscious because unchallenged; meter, whether it actually disrupts this order or not, introduces the possibility of disruption. And it is the possibility, not the violation, that creates the tension constitutive of verse. Metrical verse awakens the speaking being's awareness of the arbitrary rhythms of everyday speech: the pauses and groupings that have been uttered so often as to seem necessary, inviolable, and absolute. Meter, in furnishing another order, exposes the contingency of the one that was already there.

The same might be said of the passage on timbre. It, too, asserts the existence of an order intrinsic to language: an order that stands at odds with the order inherent in everyday usage. It, too, resides in a human expectation of the linguistic element. Only someone who expects a particular timbre can be "disappointed" "before the perversity that makes the timbres of *jour* and *nuit*, contradictorily, dark in the first case, bright in the second." This perversity reigns in non-verse, but no one particularly notices because no one thinks to expect otherwise. What distinguishes the experience of timbre in Mallarmé's account is merely the heightened perception of an order intrinsic to linguistic sound: an order that differs from the order governing non-verse. In offering a glint of this order, timbre reveals the arbitrary nature of the one governing everyday speech.

What distinguishes verse from non-verse, then, would appear to be nothing more than an idea of order: an awareness of the arbitrary principles governing everyday speech, coupled with a desire to replace these principles with non-arbitrary ones. Both the awareness and the desire are generated by the emergence of the non-arbitrary order, internal to language, that holds the potential to disrupt the mechanisms governing non-verse. For Mallarmé, this other order is singular and absolute: it is the order of the supreme language. Its singularity is implied by the singularity of the "supreme mold" in the passage on meter,[60] and by that of "the supreme [language]" in the passage on timbre.[61] Mallarmé simply assumes that the "essential values" of the elements will be universally perceived and uncontested, just as he assumes his readers will hear *jour* as dark and *nuit* as light. The idea that some fortunate soul might perceive the timbre of *jour* as something other than dark does not appear to cross his mind, any more than the possibility that someone might think of days as dark. Because there is only one supreme language, the values accorded its timbres are universal and not specific to the phonology of any single language. Thus, the supreme language, for Mallarmé, is in no way particular to French. It inheres "amongst languages"; it is "absolute."[62] The principle of verse based on a relation to the supreme language therefore defines not only French verse but all verse.[63]

For Mallarmé, then, verse exists as soon as a speaking being is sensitive to the (non-)existence of the supreme language: as soon as that being, expecting it, can be "disappointed" by the sounds that come in its stead. This seems to be the fundamental difference distinguishing verse from non-verse: the tension installed in language by its non-correspondence with the supreme one. This tension is premised merely on an idea of the supreme language in language. It depends, therefore, on a "Chimera, attested in our having thought of it."

The poet can attain the supreme language, in a way, in the metrical line. The metrical verse in "Solennité" does achieve its "full flowering," and the "thousand beautiful elements" do, at that instant, align to form a "Sign!" Whether the poet can attain the supreme language through the tension of timbre is less clear. Mallarmé does not offer us any such gratifying moments of alignment when it comes to timbre; the closest he comes to providing an example of fulfilled correspondence is the rather lackluster example of "*ombre*, opaque." It is not even clear, in the case of timbre, over what unit the poet would make the timbres of sense correspond with those of sound. In the case of meter, the unit was the line, but after the separation, the line has been withdrawn. A timbre inheres in a single syllable, as we know from Mallarmé's mention of the "twelve timbres" of the alexandrine; a single timbre can color an entire word, even one of multiple syllables (*ténèbres*). But the unit over which the poet's timbres could attain a perfect correspondence of sound and sense, conquering the "perversity" that misassigned them, remains completely obscure.

In what sense, then, can the play of timbre be said to constitute verse? For verse, in Mallarmé, negates chance. That is its role. As Gérard Genette, amongst many, many others, observed over half a century ago, Mallarmé "assigns to poetic language the specific task of suppressing, or more precisely giving the illusion of suppressing the arbitrariness of the linguistic sign."[64] In the poet's own words, it is "the verse that, from many expressions, refashions a total, new word, foreign to the language and as if incantatory [...] negating, in a sovereign sweep, the chance remaining in terms...."[65] If the tension of timbre does not do this, what does it do?

Mallarmé tells us it "remunerates the deficiency in languages."[66] The formulation merits a moment's reflection. For despite the resemblance by which *rémunérer* has, for centuries, been misspelled in both French and English as *rénumérer* ("renumerate"), the verb bears no reference to number and, thus, no reference to meter. And despite the superficial similarity by which it might be taken as synonymous with "giving the impression of suppressing the arbitrary nature of the linguistic sign," to "remunerate the deficiency in languages" is not to "eliminate chance," nor even to "negate" it.

To read the expression *rémunère le défaut des langues* as synonymous with *nier le hasard*, we would have to understand *le défaut des langues* as "chance" and *rémunère* as "negate." The word *défaut*, however, suggests an absence, not a presence; the word is defined as "the absence of a thing or person whose presence is necessary or desirable (generally, for the formation of a coherent whole)."[67] Chance is not absent in languages, but present; its presence is not necessary or desirable—on the contrary, it inspires "regret." The equation *le défaut des langues* = *le hasard* is therefore imprecise. That which is "absent" but whose presence would be desirable is not *le hasard*, but *la suprême*. It is not chance that is lacking in languages; it is the supreme language.

The question, then, is what distinguishes *rémunérer l'absence de la langue suprême* from *nier le hasard*. The verb *rémunérer* is primarily an economic one; it means "to pay someone a sum in exchange for work or services rendered."[68] In the medieval period, it carried a strong religious connotation, as *le rémunérateur* was another name for God: he who rewards Christian virtue.[69] In both economic and religious usage, the structure of the verb involves two steps, two parties, and two elements: an initial transaction, in which party one renders a gift, service, or work (element one) to party two, and a second transaction, in which party two compensates party one, typically but not exclusively by means of a financial or spiritual reward (element two). Whether the transactions be religious or economic, an element of faith is required from party one: that party two will carry out the second transaction.

Mallarmé's sentence conforms to a derivative use of the verb, by which element two serves as grammatical subject and "remunerates" the direct object, element one, in the sense of "constitutes the remuneration of,"[70] or, more plainly, "makes up for." In this usage, the parties disappear, causing the transaction to take place between elements alone. The giver, be it the economic power that pays or the God that rewards, has been eliminated; so, too, has the laborer or believer. Mallarmé's verb enacts a very simple equation that takes place entirely within language: verse makes up for the absence of the supreme language.

While this formulation does entail a principle of equivalence and a gesture of compensation, its structure does not emphasize or even necessarily entail a "negation." The action entailed in *rémunérer* is distinguishable from that of, say, *annuler* (to cancel) or *supprimer* (to suppress, eliminate, delete). Paying someone for services rendered is not the same as canceling the whole transaction. Accounts are settled in both cases, but in the second, nothing will have taken place; in the first, something will. And that which will have taken place is a *rémunération* of language unto itself. Mallarmé's selection of verb to articulate what verse offers "in return" reveals the impossibility of the initial offering: the prefix *re-* belies the absence of any such verb as *munérer*. The supreme language was never offered because the supreme language never was. The remuneration is the second transaction to an absent first. The element of faith, therefore, has been eliminated. Unlike the economic equation as well as the religious one, the remunerative equation that produces verse relies not on faith in a "supreme one" but on the supreme one's absence.[71]

There has been a separation of *le vers*. The line, ordered by meter, gives the impression of having negated chance. This is the "antique verse" whose worship Mallarmé maintains in his preface to the *Coup de dés*; it is the *vers* of the quotation previously cited, which might be better translated not as "verse," but indeed, as "*the line* which from many expressions makes a total, new word [...] negating, in a sovereign sweep, the chance that remains in terms. . . . "[72] But the line, for Mallarmé, is no longer synonymous with "verse." The line is but one instance of the greater principle whose defining feature is its capacity to expose the supreme language in language: not necessarily to give the impression of having attained it. Thus, there can be such a thing as a "free verse" (*vers libre*); verse can exist in the absence of the line, "playing with its timbres, and even hidden rhymes." This verse cannot suppress, eliminate, or negate chance. Severed from the line, it can only point to the supreme language that it is not, but which we, in noticing, affirm to be.

4 / The Colors of the Universal Alphabet

> *The matter came up, one day in my seventh year, as I was using a heap of old alphabet blocks to build a tower. I casually remarked [. . .] that their colors were all wrong.*
>
> —VLADIMIR NABOKOV, SPEAK, MEMORY (1947)[1]

At a meeting of the American Oriental Society held in New York City in 1861, Yale Professor of Sanskrit W. D. Whitney offered a spirited assessment of his German colleague Karl Richard Lepsius's *Standard Alphabet for Reducing Unwritten Languages and Foreign Graphic Systems to a Uniform Orthography in European Letters*.[2] Lepsius's alphabet had appeared simultaneously in English and German editions in 1855, and a significantly revised and expanded second edition, again in both languages, was on its way to the printers as Whitney was delivering his remarks.[3] Lepsius's alphabet was but one of several competing transcription models to emerge in the mid-nineteenth century, with notable rivals including Max Müller's "Proposals for a Missionary Alphabet" (1854); Alexander Ellis's *The Alphabet of Nature* (1845); Isaac Pitman's *Stenographic Sound-Hand* (1837); Alexander Melville Bell's *Visible Speech: The Science of Universal Alphabetics* (1867); and, of course, the International Phonetic Alphabet that made its debut appearance in Paul Passy's *Les Sons du français* (1887).[4] These "universal alphabets" were developed with various aims: establishing efficient shorthand, standardizing regional pronunciation, and grappling with the many non-European languages of overseas empires. But collectively, what they sought to provide was a single set of symbols capable of transcribing all possible sounds of human speech. Such "alphabets" thus differed from the graphic writing systems from which they took their name, as the language to which they were meant to correspond in the first instance could not properly be said to be one. What universal alphabets of the nineteenth century sought to describe was not a single idiom or yet all existing or even extant tongues, but a hypothetical extent of sound bound only by the physical limits of the human speech apparatus. The range of sound to which they were meant to answer was thus anatomically circumscribed but acoustically infinite, confronting the alphabets' architects with the daunting task of imagining and accommodating sonic distinctions proper to languages long since forgotten and yet to be heard.

At the 1861 meeting in New York, Whitney threw his considerable scholarly heft behind Lepsius's alphabet, praising it for meeting the complex challenges of the genre "in a higher degree than any other which has hitherto been put forth."[5] But Whitney's praise came with qualifications. He took particular exception to Lepsius's vowel system, singling it out as "more unsatisfactory and open to criticism than any other part of his work."[6] For reasons that Whitney could not fathom and which clearly incensed him, the eminent Egyptologist and distinguished member of the Berlin Academy had allowed himself to be

> seduced into drawing out a fantastic analogy between the vowel sounds and the colors, which has not the slightest substantial ground, neither teaches nor illustrates anything, and can only stand in the way of a clear and objective view of the actual phonetic relations of the subject.[7]

The intensity of Whitney's irritation may account for his decidedly erroneous reproduction of Lepsius's vowel triangle (see Figure 9),[8] which appears in the early pages of the *Standard Alphabet* (see Figure 10)[9] and is put into relation, via footnote, with a color "pyramid" (see Figure 11).[10] Lepsius establishes the analogy by means of the two triangles' corners. "There are three primary vowels, as there are three primary colours," he explains, and just as the mixing of primary colors yields infinite nuances of hue, so does the mixing of the three primary vowel sounds result in diverse vowel timbres.[11] In both triangles, each of the four interior members is to be understood less as a discrete point than as a continuum of gradations between extremes: expanses of sound or color within which infinite

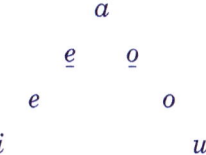

FIGURE 9. W. D. Whitney's 1861 reproduction of K. R. Lepsius's vowel triangle

86 / THE COLORS OF THE UNIVERSAL ALPHABET

$$\begin{array}{cccccccc} & & a & & & & a & \\ & e & ö & o & & e & _{d.}ö & o \\ i & & ü & & u & i & _{d.}ü & u \end{array}$$

FIGURE 10. K. R. Lepsius's vowel triangle as printed in his *Standard Alphabet* and *Das allgemeine linguistische Alphabet* (1855)

$$\begin{array}{ccc} & red, & \\ orange, & brown, & violet, \\ yellow, & green, & blue. \end{array}$$

$$\begin{array}{ccc} & roth & \\ orange & braun & violet \\ gelb & grün & blau \end{array}$$

FIGURE 11. K. R. Lepsius's color pyramid as printed in his *Standard Alphabet* and *Das allgemeine linguistische Alphabet* (1855)

nuances can be imagined without having to be named. Thus, the central vowel ö, for example, is likened to brown, "which equally arises from a mixture of the three prime colors."[12]

Each model admits a single exception: a mobile member hovering ambiguously in the pyramid's interior. Amongst the vowels, this exceptional entity is "the *indistinct vowel-sound* from which [. . .] the other vowels, as it were, issued and grew into individuality, and to which the unaccented vowels of our aged European languages often return."[13] This originary vowel, whose phonetic contours Lepsius suggests by means of the unstressed es of the French *sabre*, the English *velvet*, and the German *lieben*, "comes among the clear sounding vowels next to ö, being itself a mixture of all the others, but it is capable of various shades (*ist vielgestaltig*) and sometimes approaches nearer to *a*, or to *i*, and *u*." This chameleonic vowel Lepsius marks with the symbol "ę" and likens to gray: the "colour" that, paradoxically, "does not belong to the circle of individual colours (*Er ist der grauen Farbe zu vergleichen, die gleichfalls nicht in den Kreis der eigentlichen Farben gehört)*."[14]

Whitney's objection to the vowel-color analogy lay in its departure from the physiological basis established as the condition of possibility for a universal alphabet. He held that substituting a color triangle for the human speech apparatus

> is not merely a leaving out of sight one's physiological basis, but a trampling it under foot and rejecting it for a foundation of cloud; that it is a backsliding into the old reprehensible method in phonetics, of describing and naming things from subjective comparison, instead of from actual analysis and determination of character; and that the whole color analogy is quite unworthy of a place in our author's phonetic manual.[15]

The criticism, apparently unbeknownst to the critic, lay bare the paradoxical premise of the project—for who could offer an objective account of the phonetic relations between as-yet-unimagined sounds of no empirical existence at all?

Not long after Whitney's critique appeared in print, Lepsius himself responded to his colleague's criticism in the pages of the very same *Journal of the American Oriental Society*. He renounced the vowel-color analogy completely. "I give up this comparison [...] wholly to your criticism," he wrote. "It has no real concrete value, and I have made no manner of application of it." Lepsius accounts for his introduction of the parallel on the grounds that the "simple and very apposite analogy of the triangle of colors saved me any further explanation of my [vocalic] arrangement with those readers who were not so familiar with its physiological foundation as I myself could not but be." But he made no real attempt to disperse the "foundation of cloud" on which his analogy was accused of residing, preferring to disown it "in order to free myself from the reproach of a fanciful theory, which is so abhorrent to me that I should be sorry to bear even the appearance of it."[16]

The retraction is a curious one. If the vowel pyramid was built on the physiological foundation Whitney perceived it to lack, one might well wonder (as, indeed, Whitney did[17]) why Lepsius did not explain it. One might also wonder at the strange ambivalence of his renunciation concerning the charges brought. He states that the vowel-color analogy "has no concrete value," only to reassert it as "very apposite" and cite its instructional utility; he renounces it not because he concedes that it *is* "a fanciful theory" but because to be accused of such "is so abhorrent to me that I should be sorry to bear even the appearance of it." The eminent academician maintains a strange but studied interval between his convictions and his retraction, leaving room for wonder as to why he should have been so anxious to distance himself from charges of fancy he might have easily dispersed.

To begin with, he might have explained that the triangular organization of vocalic sound could be traced at least as far back as Christoph Friedrich Hellwag's 1781 *Dissertatio de formatione loquelae*, which featured a vocalic triangle explained as an abstract representation of vowels' place of resonance within the mouth. In Hellwag's model, *i* is imagined high in the back of the mouth, *u* hovers just behind the alveolar ridge, and *a* sinks low over the relaxed tongue (see Figure 12).[18] Lepsius might also have pointed out that experiments with paints and pigments had led color theorists of the eighteenth century to furnish triangular and pyramidal color models situating red, blue, and yellow at their angles, citing Johann Heinrich Lambert's "Color pyramid" of 1772 (see Figure 13),[19] Tobias Mayer's color triangle of 1758 (see Figure 14),[20] or August-Ludewig Pfannenschmid's adaptation of Lambert's pyramid (see Figure 15) in the more practically oriented and widely circulated *Attempt at Instructions for Mixing All Colors from Blue, Yellow, and Red According to the Enclosed Triangle* (*Versuch einer Anleitung zum Mischen aller Farben aus Blau, Gelb und Roth nach beiliegendem Triangel*, 1781).[21] Identifying red, blue, and yellow as "prime" or "primary" colors because unobtainable by means of mixed pigments, Lambert, Mayer, and Pfannenschmid sought to derive all other colors from the proper proportions of these three.[22]

Of course, Lepsius might also have abbreviated his account of the vowel-color analogy's history by pointing out that his teacher at the University of Göttingen, Jacob Grimm, had already placed the vowel and color triangles in an analogous relation in the 1840 edition of his *Deutsche Grammatik*. Here, in an effort to furnish a vocalic model valid for all Indo-European languages, Grimm presents a vowel triangle, footnoting it, just as Lepsius would do, with the explanation that "expressed in colors, A is white, I red, U black, E yellow, O blue. Orange and violet seem like resplendent diphtongues (ei, iu): ái would be rose, áu sky blue (*in farben augedrückt ist A weiß, I roth, U schwarz, E gelb, O blau. orange und violet scheinen prächtige diphthongen (ei, iu): ái wäre rosa, áu himmelblau*)" (see Figure 16).[23]

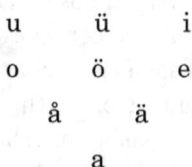

FIGURE 12. C. F. Hellwag's vowel triangle (1781)

FIGURE 13. J. H. Lambert's color pyramid (1772)

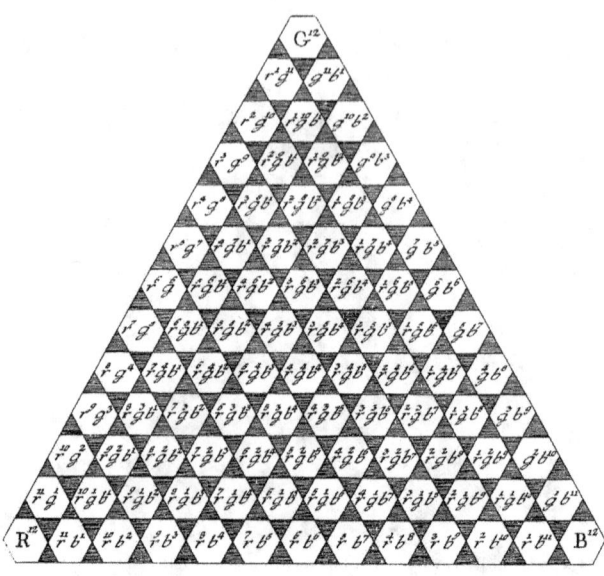

FIGURE 14. T. Mayer's diagram proposing ideal proportions for mixing all colors from red, blue, and yellow (1758)

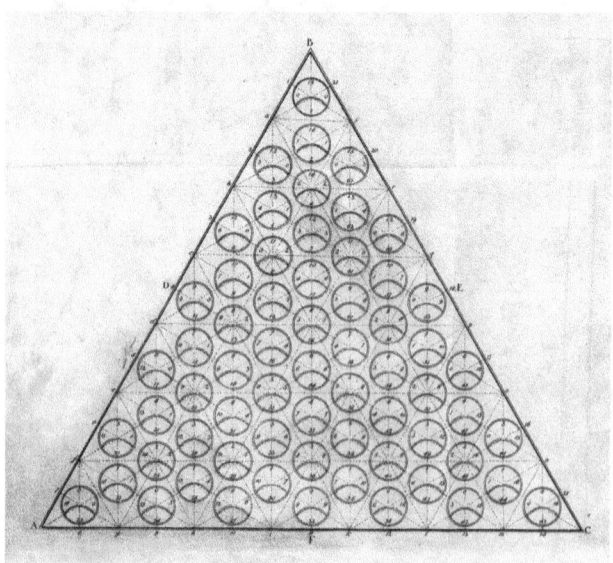

FIGURE 15. A. L. Pfannenschmid's instructions for mixing all colors from red, blue, and yellow (1781)

```
        A
    E       O
  I           U
```

FIGURE 16. Vowel triangle proposed by Jacob Grimm in the 1840 edition of the *Deutsche Grammatik*

The origins of Lepsius's vowel-color analogy are thus easy enough to trace through the annals of German linguistics and color theory, and it may well be the case that this distinctly Teutonic lineage accounts, at least in part, for Whitney's bewilderment. The analogy's instructional utility relies on readers' prior acquaintance with the color triangle, an acquaintance evidently absent from the experience of the American-born professor, as his indignant footnote attests: "the triangle of colors, it is to be presumed, was hardly, if at all, more familiar to our author's readers than that which it was brought in to illustrate."[24] Rather than clarifying the relationships that obtain between vowel sounds, the color triangle, for Whitney, merely introduced a new and confounding element.

One could stop here, concluding that the "fantastic analogy" so bewildering to the American linguist was an eminently explicable cultural product: the coincidence of a color theory built around a triangular schema and a conception of vocalic sound adhering to the same geometrical shape. The "foundation of cloud" forming the basis for the analogy would be, if not dispersed, at least displaced into the eighteenth century. But this turns out to be just half the story.

"Colored Hearing and Similar Phenomena"

At the International Congress on Experimental Psychology held in London in 1892, Professor Edouard Gruber of Romania delivered a paper on "Colored Hearing and Similar Phenomena," presenting an array of cases in which individuals experienced sensations of color prompted by unintuitive stimuli: musical sounds, voices, numbers, and, overwhelmingly, vowels. Gruber concluded by stressing that the interest of these strange sensations, which were far less rare than one might initially expect, was not purely theoretical, as those who possessed such visions often applied them to practical ends. In his recent *Inquiries Into Human Faculty and Its Development* (1883), for example, the eminent English psychologist Sir Francis Galton had presented the case of a woman whose colored sensations helped her spot spelling errors in certain English words and foreign languages.[25] As it happened, Galton himself was in attendance at Gruber's talk and spoke up in the ensuing discussion to mention that he had also "recently seen a paragraph in the life, by Eber [sic], of the late Dr. Lepsius the Egyptologist, from which it appeared that Lepsius connected colour with sounds and used those colours as a guide in his philological inquiries."[26]

The passage to which Galton refers occurs on page 76 of Georg Moritz Ebers' *Richard Lepsius, ein Lebensbild*, which had appeared in German in 1885 and in English translation in 1887. In recounting the twenty-two-year-old student's *Wanderjahren* in Paris, Ebers quotes a diary entry from November 4, 1833: "'O,' he writes one time in his diary, 'seems to me brown, a, light blue, e, colorless, a clear faint color, i, bright yellow.'"[27] The full entry, now held in the Deutsches Literaturarchiv in Marbach, reveals Ebers's omission of *u*, which appears directly after "o" in Lepsius's diary and is noted as "dark-red (*dunkel-roth*)."[28] But the diary offers little further indication of what might have sparked Lepsius's reflections. The short, isolated entry is flanked by notes from fairly distant days on very distant topics, such as climbing through the apartment window after mislaying the key (October 27) and tutoring a middle-aged Frenchman in German (November 10). But the date of the entry does provide one piece of illuminating context, as Ebers points out.[29] In the autumn of 1833, Lepsius had already completed his archaeological and philological studies in Prussia, but he had yet to begin the Egyptological research for which he would henceforth be known. His primary occupation was the writing of an essay entitled "Paleography as a Means of Etymological Research (*Paläographie als Mittel für die Sprachforschung*)," a text often cited as the earliest iteration of the interests that would culminate in his *Standard Alphabet*.[30]

The paleography paper, which Lepsius dedicated to his teachers Jacob and Wilhelm Grimm, is a searching study of how the sonorous contours of language might be imagined on the basis of extant writings. Lepsius devotes a significant portion of the work to the problem of vowels, which lack written symbols in many of the earliest scripts and yet would seem to have been required by the mechanics of phonation. "The remark that neither Sanskrit nor Hebrew originally wrote the vowels," he writes,

> leads us to the necessary conclusion that originally one and the same sign denoted consonant and vowel, but that only a single vowel was known, which took shape after every consonant. From this indeterminate or, if you will, indifferent original vowel, which most naturally corresponded to the short *a*, *i* and *u* separated out over time, from which the remaining midtones and mixtures (*Mitteltöne und Mischungen*) then reemerged.[31]

Imagining the emergence of the basic vowel triangle that inaugurates the *Standard Alphabet*'s presentation of "The System of Vowels," this section of the paleography paper similarly presents *a, i,* and *u* as the primary vowels, imagining all other vocalic sounds as intermediates between these three. In the 1855 text, the indeterminate, originary vowel is marked with the symbol "ę," distinguishing it from the *a* that may be opposed to *i* and *u*, but there can be little doubt that the "indeterminate or, if you will, indifferent original vowel," of the paleography paper is the *Standard Alphabet*'s "*indistinct vowel-sound* from which, according to the opinion of some scholars, the other vowels, as it were, issued and grew into individuality, and to which the unaccented vowels of our aged European languages often return."[32] In the *Standard Alphabet*, this "originary vowel" is said to be capable of assuming various "shades" and is likened, contradictorily, to "the color gray," "which also does not belong to the series of individual colours."[33] The same contradiction may be observed in the Paris diary, where "e" is described as "colorless, a clear faint color (*farblos, eine helle, matte Farbe*)." In both the paleography paper and the *Standard Alphabet*, this indeterminate vowel sound figures as both origin and end: it is the amorphous, originary vocalic sound that divides itself into the complex vocalism of a language, as well as the sound to which "the unaccented vowels of our aged European languages often return."

In the paleography paper, Lepsius measures the perfection of a language by the diversity of its vowels: "vocalism," we read, is "the most beautiful part of the sensuous body of language," and at its height, it will offer a "beautiful play of colors in its sounds and inflections (*das schöne Farbenspiel der Laute und Flexionen*)." Over time, however, these hues will "gradually dull and recede into a uniform gray (*sich allmählig abstumpfen und in ein gleichförmiges Grau sich verlieren sehen*)."[34] As Lepsius considers how the "initially sparse vocalism" of Ancient Rome developed into the rich, vibrant nuances of French and Italian, he compares "the colorful play of vowels in language (*den bunten Spiele der Vokale in der Sprache*)" with the "splendid colors of the flora and fauna (*der Farbenpracht der Kräuter und Blumen*)" in South Europe; he delights in the diverse vocalism of the later German and older Greek dialects, wondering in dismay, "Where has it disappeared again in Modern Greek, in New High German? There everything has dissolved into *i*, here into *e*, only ruins of the old splendor."[35] Lepsius's aesthetic assessments of various languages could certainly bear further scrutiny, as could his methods for discerning their degrees of vocalic diversity. Of relevance here, however, is that the sounds of opposable vowels are described consistently as colors: the later German dialects bear "the most varied play of colors in [the] simple and compound vowel sounds"; it is "the colorful play of vowels in language" that characterizes modern Italian. The absence of this diversity is "dull" and, more precisely, "gray." This "gray" vocalism is less a particular vowel, of course, than a mercurial mess of undifferentiated vocalic sound.

It would be tempting, once again, to conclude here with a closing observation that the vowel-color analogy of the *Standard Alphabet* was not merely a cultural product born of coincident color and vowel triangles, but also an unsuspected public record of its author's privately recorded synesthesia. Yet such a conclusion, like the first, would be partial at best—because, as the attentive reader will have observed, the colors likened to vowels in the *Standard Alphabet* and the colors associated with them in the Paris diary are not quite the same. If one assumes, for the sake of argument, that the diary's vowels are the vowels of German imagined phonetically and endeavors to place them within Lepsius's vowel pyramid, one meets with only moderate success. The "colorless" *e* with its "clear, faint color" can certainly pass for the "*indistinct vowel-sound*" Lepsius compares to gray, and the "bright yellow" *i* matches up nicely with the bottom left corner of the color pyramid. A willful reader could even, by a stretch, imagine that the "o" described in the diary as "brown" might have signaled a sound closer to "ö," making it a near-match. But no amount of cheating or abusive reading can make a light-blue *a* red and a dark-red *u* blue. At best, one could observe that in terms of brightness alone, *u* remains comparatively dark, whether "dark red" or "blue," and that the same holds for the luminous value of "red" and "light blue." One could also observe that although the vowels understood to form the primary vowel triangle—a, i, and u—do not correspond to the same colors in the two texts, they do, in both cases, correspond to the hues that Lepsius understood to be "primary."

One is obliged to concede that the "foundation of cloud" Whitney so vehemently protested would seem to comprise at least two components: an existing framework for understanding color relations and a synesthetic capacity to relate that framework to vocalic sound. If, in hindsight, the framework seems largely contingent on cultural and historical circumstance, the synesthetic capacity that draws vowels and colors into an analogous relation seems far less so. This may well be most evident in the spirited arguments lodged against the vowel-color analogy. In his 1874 commentary on Jacob Grimm's vowel-color parallel, for example, Alexander J. Ellis expresses a frustrated perplexity reminiscent of W. D. Whitney's: "It is singular," the distinguished English phonetician writes, "that Grimm compares this vowel triad to a colour triad of a curious description, and the means (e, o), inserted between the extremes (i, a) and (a, u) to other colours, after an analogy which I find it hard to follow." Befuddled by Grimm's account of the interaction of colors as well as his reasons for proposing such an analogy in the first place, Ellis condemns the model in no uncertain terms. "These are mere fancies," he declares, "unfounded in physics, based upon nothing but subjective feeling, and yielding no result." Fortunately, he consoles himself and his reader, "The quantitative theory which we now possess is entirely physical, depending upon pitch and resonance."[36]

No sooner does Ellis banish Grimm's spurious vowel-color analogy into a pre-scientific past, however, than he advances one of his own. "If we adopt the vibrational or undulatory theory of light," he continues, "then there is this analogy between colour and pitch." Replacing Grimm's unstated basis with wavelength, a physical property common to vowel sounds and colors, albeit in different directions, Ellis charts vowels along a simple line representing pitch frequency, placing them in relation to a color continuum. The simplicity of Ellis's analogy is enabled by the linearity of his color model and his reduction of vowels to the primary pitch characteristic of their formation (or, in the parlance of the twenty-first-century linguist, F_1). Matching up these pitch and color wavelengths, Ellis finds that "the physical analogies of vowel and light are (i) blue, (a) green, (u) red," then continues to observe, "I believe that these are even subjectively more correct than Grimm's."[37] All while advancing a physical property as the basis for a more legitimate analogy, Ellis blithely observes this analogy to be "subjectively more correct"—betraying his own perception of a potential fittingness between colors and vowels. The relation between the analogy based in physics and Ellis's subjective perception, moreover, seems anything but arbitrary. One cannot help suspecting that the physical facts of which Ellis is convinced hold sway over the analogies he feels, "subjectively," to be correct. But if such is the case, the reverse equation would impose itself, as well: one would be obliged to ask whether the analogies Ellis senses, subjectively, to be correct hold significant if unconscious sway over his assessment of physical facts. Had Ellis sensed Grimm's vowel-color combinations to be "subjectively correct," would he have felt compelled to draw up new combinations by isolating different aspects of color and vocalic sound?[38] Whatever the case may be, when Ellis contends that, like Grimm, Lepsius "misses the actual analogies between musical pitch and optical colour,"[39] the source of his conviction in the validity of "the actual analogies" is decidedly dubious.

A similar critique could be made of none other than Whitney himself, who, after denouncing the grave error of Lepsius's color-vowel pyramid, reveals that his own conception of vowels also permits—indeed, may well require—a color analogy. As the linguistic historian Robert W. Albright has observed, after reading Whitney's impassioned criticism of Lepsius's vowel-color pyramid, "it is somewhat astonishing to find Whitney employing a color analogy three pages afterwards as an argument for the more theoretical problem of the origin of vowel sounds."[40] In addressing the question of vowel origin—which Lepsius, like many of his contemporaries, imagined as a process of increasing diversification from one undifferentiated vowel sound—Whitney objects, "When an untaught race begin to learn to paint, they do not use neutral tints, but the brightest and most startling colors"—from which it apparently follows that early speech "no more began its vowel system with the neutral vowel than its consonant system with sibilants and spirants."[41] The basis for Whitney's assertions concerning the painting practices of "untaught races" is wholly unclear, but his argument's reliance on the very analogy he so vehemently rejected is not. As Albright rightly observes, "One cannot help wondering how [Whitney] would reconcile his use of analogy in explaining the origin of vowels with his protest against Lepsius using a similar analogy in illustrating the vowel pyramid."[42]

Indeed, one could press the issue further to observe that Whitney's analogy is not just similar to Lepsius's; it is from a certain angle identical. Like his German colleague, Whitney associates the "neutral" originary vowel with "neutral tints" and opposable vowels with "their distinctive qualities" to "the brightest and most startling colors."[43] In both models, colors are associated less with vowels' physical, sonic properties than with their opposability. If for Lepsius the originary vowel is "capable of various shades," "sometimes approach[ing] nearer to *a*, or to *i*, and *u*,"[44] it is "gray" and not because it is colorless but because it is chameleonic. The same sound, or more narrowly defined variation thereof, ceases to be "gray" as soon as it can be opposed to another vowel in the language—even if, from the perspective of physical acoustics, it is unchanged. For Whitney, the originary vowel is "neutral" because its "distinctive character" is "the absence of character": "it is the neutral, the indefinite, the uncharacterized vowel."[45] The "distinctive qualities" of the opposable vowels that Whitney evokes are thus less physical properties per se than they are physical properties that have revealed themselves to be linguistically decisive. In the language of both linguists, recourse to color analogy is tied quite precisely to the moment at which an amorphous expanse of vocalic sound suddenly divides against itself, creating a contrast whose detection is crucial to comprehension. This "moment" may be imagined as a point of origin of all vocalic systems, the moment the linguist perceives a vocalic nuance to be decisive to meaning-making in a foreign tongue, or the moment an infant first grasps that vocalic sounds may and indeed must be distinguished. Whatever the case may be, the moment vocalic sound betrays its decisive divisions is the moment it demands description in terms of hue, flashing before the imagination in "the brightest and most startling colors," each endowed with its own "distinctive qualities."

"Distinctive Phonic Properties"

If the synesthetic colors of Lepsius's 1833 musings fail to match up with the colors he proposes in the *Standard Alphabet* of 1855, the two sets of correspondences defy reading in the model of consistent, point-to-point correspondence that has provided the dominant paradigm for understanding synesthesia in the twentieth and twenty-first centuries. What Lepsius's texts suggest is less a consistent sensory correspondence between vocalic sounds and colored hues than *opposability* as the fundamental basis for vowel-color analogy. The nineteenth-century Egyptologist's vowel-color pyramid, viewed from this angle, might be seen to anticipate another vocalic model: one that would emerge nearly a century later at the core of another system aspiring to submit all linguistic sounds to a single set of symbols.

Like the nineteenth-century science of phonetics that had furnished so many universal alphabets, the twentieth-century science of phonology also sought to account for all possible linguistic sounds by means of a single system. Instead of assuming the letter as the basis for the dominant one sound–one symbol model, however, phonology distinguished itself by conceiving of each letter as a combination of multiple aspects, or "distinctive phonic properties" (*distinktiven Schalleigenschaften*). Exiled in Vienna on the eve of the Anschluss in the spring of 1938, the former Prince Nikolai Sergeyevich Trubetzkoy sought to forge this new paradigm in a manuscript now known as the *Grundzüge der Phonologie* (*The Principles of Phonology*, 1939). Here, Trubetzkoy contends that a unit deemed discrete in the succession of speech sounds (a letter) might also be conceived as a combination of multiple, simultaneously occurring properties. The German /k/, for example, might be described by means of four qualities: the complete occlusion of air that distinguishes it from the German "ch" (/x/), the blocking of the nasal cavity that distinguishes it from "ng" (/ŋ/), the tense tongue and relaxed larynx that oppose it to "g" (/g/), and the participation of the back of the tongue that distinguishes it from fellow plosives /p/ and /t/.[46] While the sound of the German /k/ could certainly be described in greater detail, Trubetzkoy argues, these four properties alone suffice to distinguish it from all other letters in the language. If one seeks to transcribe all the sounds imperative to language, he contends, one need only discern and enumerate those sonic properties capable of distinguishing one phoneme from another. Suspecting such properties to be much more limited in number than the phonemes to which their various combinations give rise, Trubetzkoy proposes that instead of attempting to arrange countless letters in artful anticipation of the nuances of untold idioms, linguists might more expediently account for the vast range of potentially linguistic sound by identifying and enumerating letters' constitutive properties. In Trubetzkoy's phonology, then, the letter disintegrates into dimensions of potential oppositions whose axes delimit and describe the soundscape of all languages—or, one might equally say, of language.

These axes initially appear to map the physical dimensions of the mouth, as Trubetzkoy first articulates them with reference to the mechanics of phonation. Any given vowel, for example, may be described by means of its coordinates along three axes: aperture (*Öffnungsgrad*), localization (*Lokalisierung*), and resonance (*Resonanz*). Thus /a/ might be identified as a vowel of "maximal aperture" as its phonation requires the greatest opening of the jaw, "posterior localization" in reflection of its primary place of resonance within the mouth, and "pure resonance" in reflection of the fact that it is not nasalized. No sooner does Trubetzkoy introduce these axes, however, than he questions the accuracy of the terms he has used. In the case of both aperture and localization, he remarks, "the same acoustic effects can also be achieved with the articulating organs in a different position," signaling the imprecision of his "inexact" anatomical shorthand. "Since the linguist, after all, is ultimately interested in the acoustic effect," he reasons, "it would perhaps be advisable to replace the expression 'properties based on degree of aperture' with 'properties based on degrees of sonority' or 'properties based on degrees of saturation' (*Schallfüllegradeigenschaften oder Sättigungsgradeigenschaften*)."[47] Proposing two possible terms to replace the anatomical "aperture," Trubetzkoy advances a synonymy between "abundance of sound" (*Schallfülle*) and degrees of "saturation" (*Sättigung*). The second term is a more general one meaning "abundance," and appears already in classical Latin appeared to qualify colors (*saturātus*)—as indeed it continues to do in both English and German to this day.[48] Replacing various angles of aperture of the jaw with an axis of sonic saturation, Trubetzkoy terminologically instantiates an analogy between abundance of sound and saturation of hue.

Tied as it is to the aperture of the jaw, Trubetzkoy's axis of saturation recalls a description of vocalic color recounted in Galton's 1883 *Inquiries*

THE COLORS OF THE UNIVERSAL ALPHABET / 99

into Human Understanding and Its Development. In the very same section evoked in connection with Lepsius at the 1892 International Congress of Experimental Psychology, Galton describes the case of Dr. James Key of Montagu, who, as the reader will recall, reported seeing different shades of brown in connection different pronunciations of the vowel A: in "fame," "can," "charm," and "all."[49] Key even provided Galton with painted samples to indicate the particular shades that correspond to variations on the vowel, which are reproduced in the work's closing pages (see Figure 17).[50] The accompanying remarks quoted by Galton amplify Trubetzkoy's subtle analogy tying color saturation to aperture: "Shades of brown," Key observes, "accompany to my mind the various degrees of openness in pronouncing A." Galton cites no other examples, though he

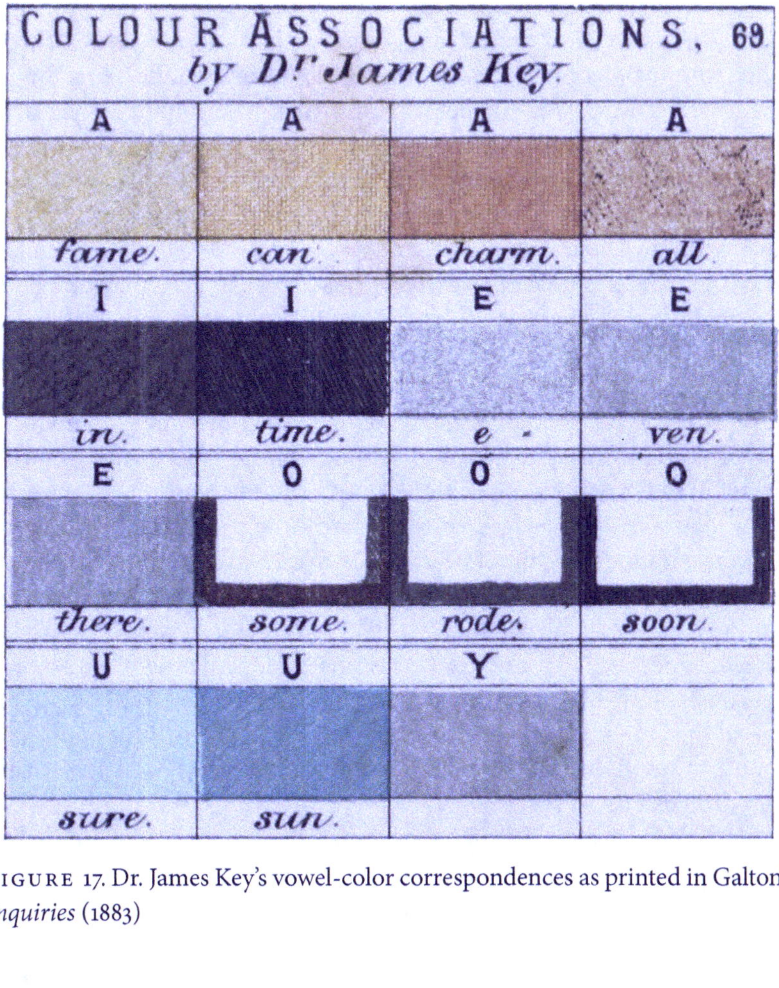

COLOUR ASSOCIATIONS, 69 by Dr. James Key.			
A	A	A	A
fame.	can.	charm.	all.
I	I	E	E
in.	time.	e.	very.
E	O	O	O
there.	some.	rode.	soon.
U	U	Y	
sure.	sun.		

FIGURE 17. Dr. James Key's vowel-color correspondences as printed in Galton's *Inquiries* (1883)

does indicate having received "numerous other letters from various other quarters to the same effect."[51]

But let us return to Vienna, 1938, and N. S. Trubetzkoy. Turning to vocalic qualities correlating with the primary place of resonance in the mouth, Trubetzkoy again ponders terminological alternatives to the spatio-anatomical "Properties of Localization." Once again, he proposes two options, both of which are translated into English by Christine A. M. Baltaxe as "timbre": *Klangfarbe*, "sound-color," and *Eigenton*, "proper tone."[52] As their interchangeability indicates, the two terms are considered synonymous, or potentially so: either could designate the aspect of vocalic sound generally linked to its primary place of resonance. The terms also share a dual reference to musical and visual spectra: *Klangfarbe* evoking an explicitly musical referent conceived by means of color metaphor, *Eigenton* echoing with all the capacious and chameleonic senses of "tone." But brightness and luminosity come most prominently to the fore in Trubetzkoy's discussion of vowel timbre, which is subdivided into two distinct properties linked to lip roundedness and tongue position. "Acoustically," Trubetzkoy observes, "the rounded vowels are darker (*dunkler*) than the unrounded, and the front vowels brighter (*heller*) than the back vowels." From the anatomical perspective of phonation, then, there are two properties of timbre, yet all eight combinations result in "a *maximally dark* and a *maximally bright* class of timbre, which may be designated as *extreme* classes since there may be one or two *medial* classes between them." It would seem as though Trubetzkoy wishes to unify the two anatomically identifiable qualities of timbre into a single acoustic one articulable in terms of brightness. If only roundedness is distinctive in a language, he points out, it becomes synonymous with the brightness/darkness opposition, and the same may be said for the isolated front/back opposition. If both roundedness and tongue position figure in a language's vowel system, "the properties of timbre of the vowel phonemes cannot be divided," from which it follows that "one should actually not speak of back rounded and front unrounded vowels, but only of maximally dark and maximally bright vowels."[53] As in the case of "aperture," Trubetzkoy's attempts at articulating "localization" in acoustic terms lead directly to synesthetic metaphor. With images of poised lips, tongues, and teeth disallowed, the language of vision seems almost to impose itself, bespeaking a translation of degrees across sensory dimensions.

Many terminological vacillations remain in the published but entirely unedited *Principles of Phonology*, whose writing was abruptly cut short in the spring of 1938. Trubetzkoy had been working with renewed urgency to finish his manuscript in the early days of that year, aware that his published positions on race and assimilation had attracted unwelcome attention from the Secret State Police of the Third Reich now preparing to annex Austria.[54] He had about twenty pages left to write and a full revision to undertake when representatives of the Gestapo arrived at his Vienna apartment, confiscating much of his work and prompting an acute attack of chest pains that took him to the hospital. Although Trubetzkoy returned home briefly, his health continued to fail, and he succumbed to a heart attack on June 25, 1938, at the age of 48.

Trubetzkoy's untimely death left the *Principles of Phonology* unfinished, with its twin axes of saturation and brightness lingering in a field of competing terms and models for defining vowels' distinctive phonic properties. The field that might have been abandoned, however, was not, thanks largely to the friend to whom Trubetzkoy had intended to dedicate his work. Roman Ossipovitch Jakobson ensured that the *Principles of Phonology* made it into print in Prague in 1939, unfinished and unedited as it might be. Jakobson also continued Trubetzkoy's work in defining distinctive sonic properties, or "distinctive features," as he would come to codify them in the field of structural linguistics he would soon lead. Jakobson was explicit in his view that distinctive features' differential nature made them particularly available for synesthetic conjunctions. As he explained in a lecture attended by Claude Lévi-Strauss at the *École libre de hautes études* in New York in 1943,

> although performing a significant function, distinctive features are themselves devoid of meaning [...] and this void seeks to be filled. [...] By virtue of the neuropsychological laws of synesthesia, phonic oppositions are positioned to evoke relations with musical, chromatic, olfactory, and tactile sensations.[55]

Jakobson's suspicion that phonic oppositions invite synesthetic conjunctions may be traced back to the work he completed during his wartime exile in the Nordic countries: *Child Language, Aphasia, and Phonological Universals* (*Kindersprache, Aphasie und allgemeine Lautgesetze*, 1941).[56] The work's proximity to Trubetzkoy's *Principles of Phonology* is readily apparent not only in its date of publication but also in Jakobson's inclusion of its first articulation, "The Sound Laws of Child Language (*Les Lois phoniques du langage enfantin*)," as an appendix to the French translation of Trubetzkoy's *Grundzüge*.[57]

In his historic attempt to lay out the universal sequence by which infants acquire speech and people with aphasia lose it, Jakobson employs metaphorical terms to designate the first fundamental vocalic oppositions to emerge in all languages. The distinctive phonic oppositions analyzed synchronically by Trubetzkoy appear here in a developmental narrative extending over time: the key oppositions characterizing particular vowels emerging in a set order as infants develop the capacity to speak. By way of Carl Stumpf, Jakobson integrates and develops the visual model implicit in Trubetzkoy's terminology. For the axis of the first vocalic opposition, which distinguishes the maximal aperture of *A* from the minimal *I*, Jakobson uses the term *"Farbigkeit"* ("color," or perhaps "chromatism")—realizing the color analogy latent in Trubetzkoy's *Sättigung* (saturation). For the axis established by the second vocalic opposition, *I-U*, Jakobson employs Trubetzkoy's proposed term for the opposition he identified anatomically as pertaining to the vowel's *Lokalizierung*, or primary place of resonance in the mouth: *Helligkeit* (brightness).

Already here, Jakobson links these metaphors to synesthesia, pointing out that "cases of pronounced coloured hearing [. . .] show the close connection of the vowels *o* and *u* with the specifically dark colours, and of *e* and *i*, on the other hand, with specifically light colours."[58] Such individuals, he continues, also demonstrate a "distinct inclination [. . .] to connect the more chromatic vowels with the variegated colours, especially *a* with red."[59] To illustrate his point, Jakobson offers the example of "S. P. (a Czech woman—32 years old, very musical, and also a talented painter)," who hears colors in vowels (and bears an uncanny resemblance to Svatava Pirkova, Jakobson's wife). Organizing the colors of S. P.'s description into his triangular model of vowel sound, Jakobson draws up, by all appearances unwittingly, a near-exact mirror image of Karl Richard Lepsius's vowel-color pyramid (see Figure 18).[60] Abused and abandoned as it was by the phoneticians of the nineteenth century, the fantastic analogy did not die. It returned unscathed to illuminate the universal vocalism that, for whatever reason, calls out persistently for its company.

a rot
o rotblau   *e* hellgrün
u dunkelblau *i* kanariengelb[119]

FIGURE 18. "S. P."'s vowel-color associations as recorded in Roman Jakobson's *Kindersprache* (1941).

5 / L'être imaginaire: Saussure's Colored Vowels

In 1983, the Swiss scholar Mireille Cifali happened upon a radio lecture by Édouard Claparède, a Genevan psychologist whose correspondence with Sigmund Freud had occasioned her archival visit. Claparède's lecture, broadcast February 5, 1936, concerned a book he had assisted in researching over forty years earlier: Théodore Flournoy's *Des phénomènes de synopsie* (1893), a compilation of "extraordinary sensations" submitted by individuals who had experienced "representations essentially relating to the domain of sight, prompted (at least apparently) by sensations or ideas outside of the ordinary laws of perception and association."[1] The book, in other words, recounted the experiences of people who saw things that, according to "the ordinary laws of perception and association," were not there.

Apparently compelled to defend these reports' reliability in his broadcast, Claparède noted the "detailed responses from experts of scrupulous conscience, whose good faith could hardly be called into question (such as Ferdinand de Saussure). C.f. Flournoy, p. 51."[2] Intrigued at the surprising reference to the founding figure of structural linguistics, Cifali contacted Flournoy's grandson Olivier, who located the late author's copy to find that the name "Ferdinand de Saussure" had indeed been jotted into the margin beside a long quotation that the printed text, for its part, attributed only to "an eminent linguist, Mr. X."[3]

Saussure's was not the only name thus jotted in. Flournoy's copy revealed the identities of several subjects who had elected to remain anonymous for reasons not difficult to discern. As Marco Mazzeo, one of the text's most acute commentators, usefully summarizes:

> between the end of the nineteenth century and the beginning of the twentieth, synesthesia was a controversial affair [...] prompting serious accusations between philosophers, scientists, and art critics. Those unconvinced of the reality of the phenomenon would attack their adversaries without the slightest hesitation, reproaching them—in the best case—for being too impressionable, and accusing them of charlatanism in the worst.[4]

Given Saussure's well-documented reluctance to publish even his most developed work—whether on general linguistics or the anagrams of antiquity—it is scarcely surprising that he should have refrained from attaching his name to passing observations on so contentious a topic.

The quotation itself, nearly three pages in length, offers an exquisitely detailed description of "the color of vowels." *A*, it recounts, is "whitish, verging on yellow," like "a paper (yellowed by time) stretched in a frame"; *I* is like mercury, "silver or quicksilver"; *ou* evokes the same sensation as "a beautiful, gray velvet, or a very soft, gray drape, very faded in tone."[5] Although the sensuous materiality of these descriptions contrasts rather sharply with the abstract, even algebraic minimalism characteristic of Ferdinand de Saussure's published prose, the authorship of the quotation, once revealed, could hardly be disputed. As Flournoy's longtime colleague at the University of Geneva, Saussure was certainly a plausible candidate for the "eminent linguist" elsewhere identified in the text as "male, aged thirty-five."[6] And even the most suspicious scholar would be obliged to concede that the quotation itself is marked by distinctively Saussurean terminology (*substance, valeur*).

I say "would be" rather than "was" because the text on vowel colors has not garnered much scholarly attention. Somewhat surprisingly, it has never been republished in the "Documents" section of the *Cahiers Ferdinand de Saussure*, where various fragments of Saussureana regularly appear, and the pages of that journal in the two decades following its discovery betray no trace of its existence.[7] This scholarly silence could be attributable to the limited circulation of the newly founded journal of Freudian studies in which Cifali's discovery was published. But it more likely reflects a certain exhaustion on the part of Saussurean scholars with anything that might have appeared to undermine the authority of the *Cours de linguistique générale*. Given the rumors of madness to which Saussure's anagram studies had recently given rise, it is not difficult to imagine why Saussureans of the 1980s might have been reluctant to take on the vowel-color text.[8] Beyond its suggestion that Saussure was subject to the sort of unverifiable visions that compelled established professionals like Édouard Claparède to defend their work in public broadcasts, the text would also appear to present an inherent connection between elements of language and things in the world, obliging its commentator to reconcile that connection with the arbitrary sign foundational to the *Cours*.[9]

Although the past few decades have seen a number of scholars endeavor to resolve that apparent contradiction, their analyses have consistently approached the vowel-color text through the lens of synchronic linguistics, attempting to protect the integrity of that science by demonstrating the vowel-color text's compatibility with its foundational principles as advanced in the *Cours*.[10] But it is far from evident that the tools of synchronic analysis, which are designed to elucidate the differential relationships internal to a single language at a given moment in time, are the scholarly tools best suited to the task of the vowel-color text's exegesis. Adopting a more hermeneutic approach, this chapter takes up the text's own preoccupation with the role of writing in its author's sensations of vowel colors, tracing the implicit relationship between orthography, phonetics, and linguistic evolution in Saussure's thought. Identifying the diachronic perspective to which Saussure's color sensations appear to be tied, the chapter turns to the linguist's oft-neglected publications in Indo-European linguistics in order to show how his synesthetic perceptions of vowels might have illuminated his groundbreaking *Thesis on the Primitive Vowel System of the Indo-European Languages* (*Mémoire sur le système primitif des voyelles dans les langues indo-européennes*, 1879).

Imaginary Beings

In response to the query, "What colors do you see in the vowels a, é, i, o, u, ou ?" ("Quelle couleur trouvez-vous aux voyelles . . ."[11]), Saussure begins by noting a problem with the question. "I don't think I can answer the question (on the color of vowels) in the terms in which it has been put," he begins, as "it doesn't seem to be the vowel as such—as it exists for the ear, that is—that calls forth a certain corresponding visual sensation."[12] This "sensation," he reflects, seems to bear some relationship to orthography:

> In French we write the same vowel four different ways in terr*ain*, pl*ein*, mat*in*, chi*en*. Now when this vowel is written *ain*, I see it in

pale yellow like an incompletely baked brick; when it is written *ein*, it strikes me as a network of purplish veins; when it is written *in*, I no longer know at all what color sensation it evokes in my mind, and am inclined to believe that it doesn't evoke any; finally if it is written *en* (which only happens after a preceding *i*), the whole of the group *ien* recalls for me a tangle of hemp ropes that are still fresh, not having yet taken on the off-white tint of used rope.[13]

Saussure concludes that if "the same vowel" can evoke "pale yellow," "purplish veins," "still-fresh hemp ropes," and no color at all, depending on how it is spelled, the "vowel as such" cannot be the stimulus for his color sensations, or at least not all of it. He continues on to suggest that this stimulus might more accurately be described as "a vowel as it is contained in [its] graphic expression."[14] This vowel, it bears noting, does not require phonation to produce its effects; it need only be conceived in the mind of the reader confronted with its written form. "These color attributes," Saussure explains, "do not attach, in other words, to acoustic values, but to orthographic ones, which I unwittingly make into substances. The being $\begin{bmatrix} vowel & x \\ letter & x \end{bmatrix}$ is characterized by this or that look, hue, feel (*tel aspect, telle teinte, tel toucher*)."[15] The name "colored hearing" (*audition colorée*), then, is imprecise.[16] The activity in question is not hearing, but reading.

Reading is not reducible to seeing, of course, and as Saussure takes care to note, whatever prompts the color sensations cannot be explained merely with reference to sight. It is not "seeing a certain letter or group of letters that calls forth this sensation," he insists; instead, "it is the vowel as it is contained in this graphic expression; it is the imaginary being formed by this first association of ideas which, through another association, appears to me as endowed with a certain *consistency* and a certain *color* [. . .]."[17] One might well pause to wonder what sort of "vowel" lurks within the term as it appears in Saussure's text at this juncture. Reducible to neither an audible sound nor a graphic expression, it would appear to be, like the well-known signifier or "acoustic image" of the *Cours*, "not the material sound, the purely physical thing, but the psychological imprint of that sound, the impression imparted by sensory evidence."[18] This vowel would be a memory, an aggregate of an oft-repeated sound, which would differ from the sound itself in one crucial respect. While a realized sound coincides necessarily with a physical form, a psychological imprint retains the memory of the signifying sound only. Thus, while a realized sound may be said to bear the properties of the material form it assumes, the psychological imprint is differentially defined and, therefore, bereft of qualities. It is a value: an abstract component of a system, like a knight in a chess game, whose consequence resides in its role within the system rather than its material form.[19] The *Cours* articulates this principle in no uncertain terms. The linguistic signifier, we read, "is in no way phonic; it is incorporeal, constituted not by its material substance but by the differences that separate its acoustic image from all others." And what is true for the signifier holds for "all the material elements of language, including phonemes": "What characterizes them is not, as one might think, their own positive qualities, but simply the fact that they do not become confused with one another. Phonemes are above all oppositional, relative, and negative entities."[20]

But if the "vowel" of the expression $\begin{bmatrix} vowel & x \\ letter & x \end{bmatrix}$ is the differential phoneme that it would appear to be, how can the "imaginary being" of which it forms a part be "characterized by a certain aspect, hue, and feel"? Two possibilities present themselves. The positive qualities could be attached exclusively to the letters associated with the vowel and bear no relationship to that vowel at all. Because Saussure states that merely "seeing a certain letter or group of letters" does not suffice to prompt the colored sensations, however, this first possibility must be cast out. The second possibility would be that the properties come to inhere in the vowel itself as it takes shape in the reader's mind. In the passage from "letter or group of letters" to "vowel," it would have to become something other than a differential phoneme: something immaterial and incorporeal, yet also in possession of "its own positive properties." This paradoxical condition, it seems, is what compels Saussure to describe the prompt for his color sensations not as a "vowel" but as an "imaginary being" (*être imaginaire*).

This imaginary being would seem to be less the differential phoneme of synchronic linguistics than the *littera* of Ancient Rome. The minimal unit of language, the Roman *littera* was said to possess three aspects, or realizations: *figura*, the written form; *potestas*, the spoken form; and *nomen*, the name by which it may be designated in teaching.[21] *L'être imaginaire* Saussure describes is very much the ancient *littera*—an abstraction that, in his native French, one might call a *lettre imaginaire*.

Traces

> *A word's pronunciation is determined not by its spelling, but by its history.*
> —COURS DE LINGUISTIQUE GÉNÉRALE[22]

Upon taking a slightly closer look at the four "imaginary beings" with which Saussure begins—$\begin{bmatrix}\tilde{\varepsilon}\\-ain\end{bmatrix}\begin{bmatrix}\tilde{\varepsilon}\\-ein\end{bmatrix}\begin{bmatrix}\tilde{\varepsilon}\\-in\end{bmatrix}$, and $\begin{bmatrix}\tilde{\varepsilon}\\-ien\end{bmatrix}$—one might note, as indeed Saussure does, that one of these is not quite like the others. In the case of "chien," the visual sensation of "a tangle of hemp ropes" is called up by the group of letters <ien>—which is to say, a different group of letters from the ones Saussure knows to transcribe the vowel /ɛ̃/ (<en>).[23] The color of this imaginary being thus appears to derive not just from the orthography of the vowel, but also from the orthographic environment that surrounds it—or, perhaps, from the phonological environment that orthography was devised to reflect. For in Saussure's account, the exceptional inclusion of the letter *i* within the fourth imaginary being seems to correspond not to a graphic specificity but to a phonological one. What makes the *i* of *chien* categorically different from the *l* of *plein* or the *t* of *matin* is not its physical shape but its phonological necessity. Without it, the <en> that follows would be not /ɛ̃/ but /ɑ̃/, as in "*en français.*" The *i*, then, might be less the letter <i> than the semi-vowel /j/ that it transcribes, which acts as a sort of timbral coefficient, signaling the exceptional quality of the vowel to come. Although the semi-vowel is appreciably distinct from "the vowel as such," it is decisive in determining that vowel's timbre as well as, it would seem, its color.

The implications of this proposition are not trivial. For if one concedes that, despite appearances, the *i* of the imaginary being $\begin{bmatrix}\tilde{\varepsilon}\\-ien\end{bmatrix}$ is not, a letter but a phonological signal, one is obliged to ask if all the letters of all the imaginary beings are not phonological signals as well. Might the groups of letters <in>, <ain>, and <ein> also indicate phonological structures in excess of what may be articulated by the isolated phoneme, "the vowel as such"? But then, what sort of "phonological structures" would these be? After all, by Saussure's own account, "-ain," "-in," "-ein," and "-[i]en" all transcribe precisely "the same vowel." From the perspective of phonology, the fact is indisputable: regardless of any variations in pronunciation, <ain>, <in>, <ein>, and <[i]en> all correspond to a single phoneme of modern French, defined by its capacity to be opposed to all the other phonemes of the language. Therefore, any difference in the aural contours of these vowels in Saussure's mind must be phonetic, not phonological.

Although phonetics and phonology both study the sounds of language, the fundamental procedures of the two fields are entirely distinct. Phonetics endeavors to describe linguistic sounds as precisely as possible, availing itself of both anatomical and acoustic vocabulary. Phonology, on the other hand, studies linguistic sounds only insofar as they are decisive in meaning, and it defines the minimal units of language in differential terms.[24] Thus, a phoneticist may establish equivalences between the speech sounds of different languages based on their properties, but a phonologist, by definition, cannot. Defining a phoneme exclusively through its opposability to other sounds within a given system, the phonologist may equate that phoneme with elements within that same system alone. An analogous element of another system, however similar in qualitative terms, can never be considered its equivalent from the perspective of phonology.[25]

A number of points in the vowel-color text would suggest that Saussure is indeed considering vowels from a phonetic perspective. When he writes that the French vowel transcribed "*ou*" and the German one marked "ᴜ" are "the same vowel,"[26] for example, he reveals the phonetic perspective from which he is considering the two speech sounds at that moment. And this phonetic perspective, as the *Cours* explicitly states, is the perspective not of the synchronic linguist but of the diachronic one: "Phonetics, all of phonetics, is the primary object of diachronic linguistics; the evolution of sounds is incompatible with the notion of a static state; to compare phonemes or groups of phonemes with what they were previously is to establish a diachrony."[27] If a linguist is to study the relationships that obtain between different languages, this linguist must have recourse to a metalanguage by which the terms of distinct idioms may be put into meaningful relation—something that phonology, by definition, cannot provide.[28]

Thus, the distinctions signaled by the letters <ain>, <in>, <ein>, and <[i]en> might reflect phonetic qualities of the phoneme /ɛ̃/: qualities that might be of consequence for phonology, or might not. The letter <n>, for example, might be understood to signal the nasal quality of the vowel /ɛ̃/, a quality reflective of the nasal consonant /n/ that was, at some point, pronounced after the vowel. Without its <n>, the final vowel of *terrain* would seem to be /ɛ/, as in *quai* [kɛ]; the final vowel of *matin* would rhyme with *parti* [paʁti]. Just as the letter <i> signals the particular timbre of the "-en" in "chien," so does the letter <n> signal the nasal quality of whatever vowel precedes it.[29] Read thus, the letters integral to the imaginary beings would indicate particular phonetic aspects of a single phoneme. They would constitute the physical traces of a former phonetic environment that, though obsolete, continues to echo in the timbre of the vowel.

So the reason for the difference of hue corresponding to "the same vowel" in Saussure's account might not lie in orthography as such but rather in the diachronic evolution to which it attests. And from a diachronic perspective, the final vowels of *terrain, plein, matin,* and *chien* are hardly "the same." *Terrain* derives from **terrānum*, a popular form of the classical Latin *terrēnum*, and bears the Latinate suffix *-ain*; *plein* derives from the classical Latin *plēnum*; *matin* from *mātūtīnum*; and *chien* from *cānem*.[30] The synchronic coincidence of sounds within the single phoneme /ẽ/ might, therefore, be said by the diachronic linguist to belie very different phonetic conditions: conditions that may no longer be of phonological consequence, or indeed even perceptible to the speaker of Modern French, but which nonetheless continue to leave their trace in orthography. This would explain not only why Saussure finds that spellings inflect his color perceptions, but also why he feels the need to specify that it is "only the vowels in words that, for me, have sufficiently defined colors."[31] Vowels in words, unlike isolated vowels, are inscribed in a lineage of linguistic evolution, bearing within them invisible laws of inflection and language change.

Saussure's color perceptions, therefore, would seem to be tied to vowels' transformations over time: to the diachronic evolution absent from the synchronic perspective that perceives vowels in purely differential terms. But we have come to a contradiction. The "synchronic perspective" from which a phoneme is differentially defined is, as the *Cours* famously instructs, the perspective of the speaking subject.[32] Yet the sensations of color in Saussure's report are experienced by a speaking subject: it is from Saussure's perspective alone that the sensations of color can be said to exist at all. Thus, the colors would seem to guide us toward a point in Saussure's thinking at which synchrony and diachrony meet: a point at which the synchronic perspective of the speaking being betrays latent knowledge of vowels' evolution over time.

Saussure's consciousness of the diachronic evolution of vowels was, of course, anything but "latent." During his lifetime, the great Genevan linguist numbered among the world's most authoritative scholars on precisely this subject, having established his professional reputation with a pioneering study of the primitive vowel system of the Indo-European languages. Yet Saussure draws no explicit connection between the colors of the vowels he describes and his intimate acquaintance with those vowels' transformations over time. Between the reading being who sees colors in vowels and the professional linguist who studies them, there would appear to be an absolute divide. One could further observe that even from the synchronic perspective of the reader, the various spellings of /ɛ̃/ correspond to vowels that, while homophonic, behave differently. The adjective *plein* [plɛ̃] has the derived form *plénitude* [pl**en**-], for example, whereas *matin* [matɛ̃] has the derived form *matinée* [mat**in**-]. To say **plinitude* or **maténée* would be to announce one's self as a deviant speaker, as most speakers of French would readily recognize, though few would be able to explain why. The imaginary being might well reflect a vowel's voyages through distant tongues, but it might also relate to the laws of apophony that govern variations in vowel timbre within a single one. *L'être imaginaire*, in other words, would seem to bear witness to a reading subject's subconscious knowledge of the laws of both apophony and language change—laws of which that reader is, of course, the unwitting bearer. Followed closely, the colors of the imaginary being might betray subtle indications of where it has been as well as, perhaps, what it will become.

The Colors of Vowels

One of the evident questions prompted by the vowel-color text concerns its unique status. If its author saw colors in vowels, is it plausible that he left traces of this perception nowhere else? The question might be posed in other terms. If Saussure the subject saw colors in vowels, did Saussure the linguist never let on?

One logical place to begin such an inquiry would be Saussure's *Mémoire sur le système primitif des voyelles dans les langues indo-européennes*—a text that, unlike the *Cours*, reflects Saussure's own rhetorical choices.[33] Upon reopening this unrelentingly rigorous inquiry into Indo-European vocalism, one cannot help being struck by its recurring references to the "hues" (*teintes*) and "colors" (*couleurs*) of vowels. The opposition of the vowels ε and α in Ancient Greek, for example, is said to exist between "the two hues ε and α (*les deux teintes ε et α*)."[34] In tracing the behavior of a particularly chameleonic "mute vowel," Saussure observes that "forms like ἐρε-τμόν, κἐρα-μος, ἄρο-τρον, ἀρι-θμός indicate that the mute vowel can assume four different colors (*quatre couleurs différentes*), without revealing what causes it to take on one rather than another."[35] Where a modern linguist would use the term "timbre" to designate the difference of sound quality distinguishing one vowel from the next, Saussure consistently refers to a vowel's "hue" (*teinte*), "coloration" (*coloration*), or "color" (*couleur*). These terms are ones that the science of linguistics has read for more than a century as metaphors, understanding that the "hue" or "color" of a vowel is something that is heard. In light of the vowel-color text, however, one wonders how Saussure understood these terms, which are overwhelmingly absent from his sources.[36]

Saussure's tendency to describe vocalic timbres in color terms may be traced back before his encounter with these sources, to an early effort he penned at the age of sixteen: "Attempt to Reduce the Words of Greek, Latin, and German to a Small Number of Roots" (*Essai pour réduire les mots du grec, du latin & de l'allemand à un petit nombre de racines*, 1874).[37] Saussure's "Essai" advances the theory that languages apparently distinct (German, Latin, Greek) can all be demonstrated to contain words deriving from "nine primitive words" or "roots." These nine roots, Saussure proposes, are each composed of a single vowel flanked by consonants (see Figure 19). The consonants, represented by the letters "K," "P," and "T" reflect wide ranges of sound whose defining feature is their place of phonation. As Saussure explains on the opening page of his essay, "K," "P," and "T" are less specific speech sounds than shorthand notation for classes of sounds that exist in all the languages under consideration: gutturals (K), labials (P), and dentals (T).[38] The vowel, marked "A," denotes all the vowel sounds of these languages and yet none in particular. While consonants from different languages may be classed and equated, Saussure argues, "the vowel, changeable element, which takes on the hues of all the skies it travels under (*qui prend la teinte de tous les ciels sous lesquels elle voyage*), or disappears entirely, cannot possibly provide a reliable index."[39] Just as a

1° les *Gutturales* :
    K, Γ, X, Ξ   - en grec
    C, G, H   - en latin
    K, G, H, Ch   - en allemand

2° les *Labiales* :
    Π, B, Φ, Ψ, M
    P, B, F, B, M
    P, B, F, V, W, M

3° les *Dentales* :
    T, Δ, Θ, Z, Σ, N
    T, D, J, S, N
    T, D, Th, Z, S, N

FIGURE 19. The nine primitive roots as advanced by Saussure in his 1874 "Essai"

stream glinting amber at sunset may well seem gray in an overcast dawn, so may a vowel that manifests itself as ε in Greek turn up in Latin as *a* and in German as *o*. The elements Saussure's analogy draws into relation are not merely vowels and reflective surfaces but, more specifically, "the hues of all the skies" (*la teinte de tous les ciels*) that a surface may reflect, and the timbres of the sounds that slip in between the consonants of all languages. The "hue" of Saussure's formulation thus forms part of an analogy, but it also constitutes a pun *avant la lettre*, simultaneously evoking celestial colors and vocalic timbres as *teintes*.[40]

One might well wonder wherein the identity of such a chameleonic "vowel" inheres. If a given vowel can appear as ε, as *a*, and as *o*—and, for that matter, disappear entirely—in what way can it be said to be one and the same vowel? After all, by its conventional definition, a vowel is defined precisely by its timbre: "timbre" is the quality of sound by which *a* may be distinguished from *e* or *o*.[41] The question of how to establish equivalence and difference between the vowel sounds goes unaddressed in the "Essai," whose ambitions are limited to establishing nine primitive roots, consonantally defined. For the purposes of the 1874 text, the undifferentiated "vowel" intuited to be required by the mechanics of phonation need never be set in opposition to any other vowel sound. Thus, Saussure devotes nothing more to it than a place-holding symbol, "A." Like the V of contemporary linguistic notation, which marks not the sound /v/ but the presence of a vowel, Saussure's "A" is algebraic rather than phonetic in nature, marking an unknown value x within a given linguistic expression.[42]

The infinitely variable "A" that "takes on the hues of all the skies it travels under" reemerges, in a way, in the *Mémoire*, which Saussure published less than five years later. As the opening lines of that text announce, its object of study is in no way straightforward: "The immediate object of this opuscule," Saussure writes, "is to study the multiple forms in which what one calls the Indo-European *a* manifests itself."[43] The object of study, "what one calls the Indo-European *a*," is identified not as a discrete and homogeneous entity but rather as something, or perhaps some things, that have been designated by a single name: "*a*." Whether singular or plural in nature, this *a* "manifests itself" (or, perhaps, its selves) in "multiple forms."

This *a* that might have appeared to be singular in nature is quickly established as comprising several discrete entities. Saussure cites the origin of this "*a*" in the foundational text of Indo-European linguistics, Franz Bopp's 1833 *Comparative Grammar*, which observes that "compared with the European languages' three vowels *a e o*, Aryan showed uniformly *a*."[44] Bopp's *a* constitutes a more circumscribed entity than the "A" of

Saussure's 1874 "Essai," however, as it is already opposed to two other vowels, marked "*i*" and "*u*." The next significant scholar of *a*, Georg Curtius, "br[oke] with the received notion that the mother language possessed only the three vowels *a i u*" to observe that "*e* appeared in the same place in all the languages of Europe, and that, consequently, it could not have developed independently in each."[45] Both Saussure's reference to "the mother language" (*la langue mère*) and the imputation of causality conveyed in his "consequently" require a moment's explanation. Both expressions signal the *Mémoire*'s belonging to the nineteenth-century science of Indo-European linguistics. Unlike the "Saussurean linguistics" that took the *Cours* as its founding document, Indo-European linguistics sought to articulate the relationships linking the languages of Europe with those of South Asia and the Middle East and, by means of these relationships, to identify the languages' points of divergence in time. The particularity of the Indo-European project is most swiftly grasped by means of its two fundamental axioms, identified by Jean-Claude Milner.[46] The first is that observable similarities between different languages admit of etiology. For the Indo-Europeanist, homophonies between languages are not products of chance but effects of a cause (hence Saussure's, or perhaps Curtius's, "consequently"). The second axiom is that this cause is a language. The cause-language, referred to by its seekers as "Indo-European," is singular and unattested: although it can be reconstructed on the basis of extant languages, it cannot be directly observed through any material artifact.[47] Indo-European, therefore, "is not simply a dead language, similar to Latin, which is no longer spoken, but which could always be restored to speaking subjects: Indo-European can never be in the position of being presumed the mother tongue of any subjects, even dead ones."[48] "The mother language," in other words, by its very nature, can never coincide with any mother tongue.

Saussure's object of study, "what one calls the Indo-European *a*," ostensibly partakes of this curious cause-language: it is a hypothetical vowel belonging to a constructed idiom, "at once the origin and the echo of an ensemble of observed forms."[49] In Saussure's thesis, however, this *a* is not "a" hypothetical vowel, as in Bopp's *Comparative Grammar*, but "four different terms." The novelty of Saussure's thesis lay in its argument that the vowel system of Indo-European possessed not one *a* but "four species of *a*," which Saussure marks with the symbols A, A_2, a, and a_2.[50] Contrary to what graphic convention might lead one to expect, A, A_2, a, and a_2 do not denote distinct timbres, but four distinct—if unattested—vowels of unknown timbre, whose existence may be inferred from the overall behavior of the vowels in the Indo-European languages. Saussure is explicit on this point. "When we wish to speak of the *sound* a or of the *a* in general, and not of the Indo-European vowel that we designate *a*," he writes in his first go at the problem, published in 1877, "we will use the ordinary character instead of the italicized one."[51] The algebraic *a*s are thus clearly distinguished from "the *sound* a" as well as from "the a in general," which comprises all that has fallen under the name of "*a*": "an aggregate without any organic unity."[52]

The four Indo-European *a*s whose distinct lineages Saussure seeks to demonstrate possess no set timbres. Like the *A* of the "Essai," these *a*s assume different hues throughout the *Mémoire*. In tracking the behavior of the third Indo-European *a*, for example, Saussure notes that "what we will call *a* [...] *appears in Slavic in the form of o*, but no matter: such an *o* is adequate to the Lithuanian and Germanic *a*; the color *o* has nothing to do with it (*ce que nous appellerons l'*a[...] *apparaît en slave sous la forme de o, mais peu importe: un tel o est adéquat à l'*a *du lithuanien et du germanique; la couleur o ne fait rien à l'affaire*)."[53] While *a* is a hypothetical vowel of Indo-European—and therefore presumably possesses a timbre, albeit an unknown one—it may "appear" in attested languages "in the form of *o*," a vowel which may be considered "adequate to the Lithuanian and Germanic *a*." Saussure's Indo-European *a* thus appears to be dual in nature: referring at once to a vowel of unknown timbre in the proto-tongue, and to a set of attested Indo-European vowels whose link to that proto-vowel resides in something other than timbre. This "something" is never explicitly defined and extremely elusive in nature. One may argue for its existence on the basis of a vowel's occurrence within a word that appears in different forms within a single language (e.g., *sing sang sung song*), as well as a vowel's occurrence in a word's analogs in other languages (e.g., ἀστέρι, *stella*, *étoile*, *star*). These analogs are established not only on the bases of meaning and part of speech (as are synonyms within a single language, for example) but also—often primarily—on the basis of their phonetic resemblance.

Establishing the defining features by which the Indo-European descendants of *A*, A_2, *a*, and a_2 may be distinguished is a central task of the *Mémoire*. One might illustrate its method through any number of examples. In Ancient Greek and the early Italic languages, for instance, Saussure notes an alternation between *e* and *o* that is "absolutely regular (ἔτεκον: τέτοκα, τόκος. tego: toga)."[54] In none of these languages, however, does *a* alternate with *e*.[55] "Then how could the *a* and the *o* of the southern languages both be the product of one and the same primitive *a*?" Saussure inquires. "By what miracle would this ancient *a* have been colored *o, and never a*, precisely in every instance in which it was accompanied by an *e*?—Conclusion: the dualism: *a* and *o* of the classical languages is originary."[56] Thus, the *e*s and *o*s of the early Greek and Italic languages are established within a single lineage distinct from that of *a*.

Despite its italicization, this "*a*" represents not the *a* of the hypothetical Indo-European A, A_2, a, and a_2, but rather the *a* of Classical Latin and the α of Ancient Greek. It therefore signals a second system of vowel representation at work in the *Mémoire*, which transcribes the attested Indo-European vowels. These vowels also merit a moment's scrutiny, as it is they, and not the algebraic *a*s, that appear to bear, or be, "colors." But to which vowels does Saussure refer when he notes "the two hues ε and α," or when he argues that a_2 has been "colored *o*"? Considering these quotations in context, one might be tempted to conclude that ε, α, and *o* refer to the phonemes of the Ancient Greek and Italic tongues. There is no lack of clarity in Saussure's text about the languages under consideration; the "hues" or "colors" of these vowels thus refer, or attach, to the speech sounds of those languages. A closer look at Saussure's formulations, however, suggests that this conclusion may be premature. Which *o* is it, after all: the Latin one or the Greek one? And when Saussure observes that "the vowel that developed before [the nasal sonant] took on, in multiple idioms, the color of the *e*,"[57] what sort of *e*, specifically, does he have in mind?

The question is not trivial. As anyone literate in more than a single language knows well, what is marked <e> in one tongue may bear little relation to what is marked by the very same character in another. And even if both languages were to be transliterated into a single phonetic alphabet, what was marked <e> in one language would still not be entirely commensurate with what was marked <e> in the next. The transcription enabled by a process of phonetic approximation, however precise, would merely mask the definitional incommensurability of the phonemes of different languages. It would suggest that the <e> of one language is identical to the <e> of the next, which might or might not be true in phonetic terms but would never be so phonologically.

The *e* whose "color" may be "taken" by the phonemes of "multiple idioms," then, is a phonetic category: an aggregate similar in nature to the "Gutturals," "Labials," and "Dentals" under whose headings Saussure classed the consonants of German, Latin, and Greek in his 1874 "Essai." Just as the symbols "K," "P," and "T" enable the author of the "Essai" to equate these languages' consonants, so do the "colors" ε, α, and *o* create pan-linguistic categories through which Saussure may equate the vowels of the Indo-European languages with one another. The two systems, however, differ in two significant respects. First, the consonantal classes of the

"Essai" were presumed to constitute the distinctive element that could be traced back to the nine "primitive roots." The vocalic color classes of the *Mémoire*, however, do not identify the distinctive element by which a vowel's diachronic lineage may be traced. That element is marked A, A_2, a, or a_2. Second, whereas the categories marked "K," "P," and "T," in the "Essai" are defined by their place of phonation, what distinguishes "the color *i*" from, say, "the color *u*" is entirely unclear. Saussure simply assumes an unstated division separating "the color *a*" from "the color *o*." These italicized vowels indicate sounds whose contours the reader is presumed to understand, although the sounds themselves cannot precisely be said to be the sounds of any earthly tongue. Strictly speaking, they are constructed vowels, phonetically conceived and yet as impossible to observe directly as Indo-European itself.

Saussure's *Mémoire* thus presents not two systems of vowel notation but three:

— the vocalic variables of Indo-European, marked A, A_2, a, and a_2
— the phonologically defined vowels of particular languages, rendered in their own alphabets (Latin, Greek) or approximately transliterated into Roman characters (e.g., the Indic languages)
— the phonetically defined vowels that may be identified in multiple idioms and are marked with the Roman characters *a*, *e*, *i*, *o*, *u*, and *y*, as well as occasionally, the Greek characters α, ε, ι, ο, and υ[58]

The three representational systems, though distinct, may interact. The algebraic variables of system one, for example, are said to be "reflected" by the phonemes represented in the symbols of system two (the speech sounds of attested languages), which themselves are often grouped into the broad phonetic categories of system three. Saussure explains in his 1877 article, for example, that "there is a kind of Indo-European *a* reflected in Sanskrit by *i* or *u* before liquids, and in the classical languages by *a* or *o* before the same consonants."[59] The symbolic variable, the "Indo-European *a*," may be "reflected" in Sanscrit by the vowels "i" and "u," and in Latin and Greek by the vowels "a" and "o." The first *a* is a variable that possesses no secure aural attributes; *i*, *u*, *a*, and *o* represent phonemes of Sanskrit, Latin, and Greek. The equation of the *a*s and *o*s of "the classical languages," however, points to a conception of those vowels in the phonetic terms of system three. The three systems of representation, then, might be considered as three alphabets aimed at the description of any given vowel. The first alphabet notes the vowel's diachronic lineage, the second, its phonemic status in a given language at a given moment in time, and the third, its phonetic "color."

But there is one more alphabet. Early in the *Mémoire*, Saussure introduces a class of sounds he calls "*coefficients sonantiques*" or "resonant coefficients." The coefficients, as their name suggests, are phonetically stable entities (in the manner of the gutturals, dentals, and labials of the "Essai") that condition the behavior of neighboring vocalic variables (A, A_2, a, and a_2). Like these hypothetical vowels, the resonant coefficients are posited as "primordial phonemes" of Indo-European and count among their number liquids (r, l), nasals (m, n), and two hypothetical phonemes marked "A" and "ọ". What makes these sounds collectively form a class is that they function both as consonants and as "sonants": phonemes that form the primary support for a syllable.[60] When they appear as "consonants" sounding with a neighboring vowel, the *coefficients sonantiques* condition the quality of that vowel's sound; when that vowel is absent, they become "sonants," independently furnishing the basis for a syllable.

Saussure easily relates the liquid and nasal sonants to existing phonemic structures in Sanskrit, Greek, Lithuanian, and other languages still, explaining how the Greek αρ, αλ, ρα, and λα, for example, may be understood as traces of a primordial resonant coefficient ŗ.[61] But for "A" and "ọ," Saussure does not point to any attested phonemes to advance his argument that these elements existed in the proto-tongue. This is because, at the time of writing, there were no known speech sounds to which "A" and "ọ" could be demonstrated to correspond. Saussure merely hypothesized their existence on the basis of the entire Indo-European vowel system, whose behavior led him to infer that there must have been two elements that, at some point, disappeared: two "coefficients" that conditioned neighboring vowels' behavior, causing those vowels to assume different hues than they otherwise would have.[62]

Saussure based his exceedingly tenuous argument on the existence of particular long vowels that seemed in several languages to demonstrate a systematic relationship to their short counterparts: a and $\bar{a}$, o and $\bar{o}$. Suspecting that it must be possible to trace these vowels' lineage using a single set of terms, he advanced the hypothesis that, in certain instances, $\bar{a}$ might be understood as a contraction of either a_1+A or a_2+A and $\bar{o}$ as a contraction of $a_1+\text{ọ}$ or $a_2+\text{ọ}$.[63] The first letter in each expression (a_1, a_2) represents a hypothetical vowel of Indo-European, and the second (A, ọ) is a hypothetical *coefficient sonantique*. These second letters are, thus, paradoxically, both variables and coefficients: hypothetical phonemes of the primordial tongue, as well as phonetically stable entities with a defining feature comparable to the articulatory features defining the liquid and nasal sonants. In the case of "A" and "ọ," that defining feature appears as nothing more than a propensity toward coloring neighboring vowels with a particular hue. For "A" and "Ǫ," it bears stressing, do not mark the phonemes *a* and *o*, nor do they represent "the hue α" and "the color *o*." Algebraic variables representing conjectured phonemes in a constructed language, "A" and "Ǫ" stand for purely theoretical speech sounds whose phonetic qualities are entirely obscure. In the absence of any positive, empirical evidence, all Saussure can cite in support of his bold proposition is a scarcely discernible pattern of vocalic lengths and colors silently sounding throughout the extant Indo-European tongues. Perceiving that pattern as no one before him had done, Saussure argued that it could only be explained by means of two vanished elements: two phonemes, which might not survive in any material form but which might still be glimpsed in the colors of the vowels beside which they once stood.

The Laryngeal Theory

Two years after Ferdinand de Saussure died in 1913, a Czech linguist by the name of Bedřich Hrozný deciphered an ancient cuneiform language that had recently been rediscovered by archaeologists in Anatolia. The language, now known as Hittite, was found to bear striking similarities to the older Indo-European languages, but it presented two puzzling phonemes that could not be convincingly placed within the established lineage of their speech sounds. The unknown elements remained a mystery for over a decade until Polish linguist Jerzy Kuryłowicz observed that they behaved precisely in the manner of the unattested *coefficients sonantiques* of Saussure's theory.[64] "A" and "Ǫ," in other words, were demonstrated to correspond to phonemes in an attested language.

The discovery validated Saussure's theoretical speculations, posthumously transforming him into the founding figure of what is now known as "the laryngeal theory."[65] But it is interesting to note that Saussure's system of *coefficients sonantiques* differs from the laryngeal theory it anticipates in one telling aspect. While the theory Saussure posited in 1879 identifies two unattested resonant coefficients, students of laryngeal theory today typically learn that there are not two such sounds but three. "$*h_1$," "$*h_2$," and "$*h_3$," as they are conventionally noted, mark three distinct sounds. $*h_2$, the "a-colouring laryngeal," draws its lineage from the hypothesized sound Saussure marked in his thesis with the symbol "A," and $*h_3$, the "o-colouring laryngeal," corresponds to the sound Saussure marked "Ǫ." But the first of the three laryngeals recognized by twenty-first-century linguists, $*h_1$, bears no trace in Saussure's study of the primitive vowel system of the Indo-European languages. One has to wonder: Why would Saussure have missed it?

Although $*h_1$ is similar to $*h_2$ and $*h_3$ in the decisive role it plays in determining vowel length, it differs from the other two laryngeal types in that it exercises no effect on vowel timbre, or "color": hence its designation as the "non-colouring" or "neutral laryngeal."[66] Otherwise put, $*h_2$ and $*h_3$ may disappear from a language and still linger in the lengths and timbres of its vowels, but $*h_1$ will leave its trace in vowel length alone. Thus, if a reader with a particularly acute sensitivity to vowel color were to study the vocalic system of the Indo-European languages, he might well catch a glimpse of $*h_2$ or $*h_3$ reflected in the vowels beside which they once stood. But the neutral laryngeal, $*h_1$, would be much more likely to escape his notice.

Conclusion: Remarks on "Synesthesia"

> *In the technical terminology of print-making, the word* remarque, *in French, refers to an engraved vignette in the margin of a plate before the artist has erased some accident or corrected it. [...] The remarks that follow are to be taken at face value: as so many guide posts in the margins of a project ...*
> —HUBERT DAMISCH, "REMARKS ON ABSTRACTION"[1]

The history of synesthesia has the advantage of a clear start date: 1812.[2] Its unsuspecting founding document is a doctoral dissertation titled *A Natural History of Two Albinos: The Author Himself and His Sister*, which was published at the University of Erlangen by the twenty-six-year-old medical student Georg Ludwig Tobias Sachs. Deep in his study of albinism, Sachs veers off on a three-page tangent devoted to "obscure representations of different colors" that recur in his mind in connection with things ostensibly unrelated to sight: numbers, days of the week, historical epochs, letters of the alphabet, musical intervals, timbres of musical instruments, and so forth. The phenomenon, he observes, is probably not related to albinism, seeing as he "recently found a trace of it in a very famous man" and, indeed, has "no doubt at all that these features also express themselves and can be described in other humans."[3] But Sachs wishes to describe his experiences nonetheless, justifying the digression on the grounds that his observations, although unrelated to his topic, are more precise and consistent (*tam distincte tamque constanter*) than any he has come across.

These two qualities, specificity and consistency, comprise "a hallmark of the contemporary literature of synesthesia," as Jörg Jewanski and his research team, the twenty-first century's leading authorities on the topic, point out. Sachs's associations are said to be "intimate and recurring" (*tam intime tamque constanter*) and also so specific as to seem, in the reading of Jewanski et al., "almost impossible to put into words." The serial nature of the stimuli Sachs cites offers another "resonance [...] with the contemporary literature." Sachs observes that his obscure representations of color are prompted particularly by things that form a simple series (*simplicem quandam seriem faciunt*), which, as Jewanski et al. point out, "is true of most contemporary cases."[4] Finally, the researchers note that "Sachs's colors themselves are said to appear in 'dark space,'" a reporting that fits into an existing data set of synesthetes who report experiencing their colors on an "'inner screen' (or mind's eye)," rather than externalized before their open eyes.

Sachs's account is thus deemed "the first convincing account of synaesthesia"[5] because it answers to much of the modern paradigm. Notably, it does not answer to all of that paradigm. Modern synesthesia typically requires that the induced sensations be involuntary or "automatic"[6] rather than sought after through willed reflection; Sachs, however, specifies that his notions of color "cannot be conceived of, or only scarcely and with difficulty, without a certain attention."[7] Both the prompt for Sachs's colors and the ontological status of the colors themselves are less clear-cut than the contemporary science might desire, as his "obscure representations of colors" veer quite near to the visions of color anyone might summon to the mind's eye. The indistinction, anathema to the modern construct but hardly unique to Sachs's case, comes up already in American psychologist William O. Krohn's 1892 review of the topic. "What is the real difference between perceptions through a sensation and one[s] through an 'automatic association?'" the author asks. He concludes that the difference is not one of kind, only of degree. "In adult life we have no such thing as pure sensation," Krohn reflects; "Every perception of a thing or quality is the sensation plus remembered sensations,—generally, organically or physiologically remembered—at least the process is a sub-conscious one."[8]

One wonders whether another aspect of Sachs's text contributes to the evaluation of his case as "convincing"—namely, the conditions that gave rise to its writing. A student of medicine, Sachs was composing an academic dissertation explicitly intended to establish his scientific legitimacy. That his account should more readily and fully answer to a modern scientific model might speak more to the historical extent of certain paradigms of medical thinking—and conventions of scientific writing—than to the novel emergence of a previously unrecorded sensory experience.

The absence of records like Sachs's prior to 1812 is one of the central paradoxes confronting Jewanski et al. "Synesthesia is likely as old as mankind," the researchers write. "Hence, there is no reason why there should not be many cases of synesthesia before the nineteenth century, although we have no sources of information about them."[9] This, by the team's admission, is a strange state of affairs. If, on the one hand, "the high prevalence of synaesthesia, together with its postulated genetic contribution, suggests that it has been around for much of human history," one has to wonder why "it was not until 1812 that the first convincing description of synaesthesia appeared."[10] It seems surprising that scholars should have left no trace of this "highly prevalent" sensory experience on the tablets and texts recording millennia of collective knowledge amassed before 1812. One would imagine that, at the very least, the phenomenon would have come up in the discourse on the senses inaugurated in the fourth century BC by Aristotle's *De Anima*—if not in the famous discussion that appears in Book II of the original text, then surely in the two millennia of commentaries and critiques that its proposals inspired.

One might also anticipate that the essays collected by classical scholars Shane Butler and Alex Purves in *Synesthesia and the Ancient Senses* (2013) would furnish the older examples that Jewanski and his team—not classicists, after all—have been unable to locate. But such is not the case. Rather than examine how "synesthesia" understood in its modern, clinical sense might have found expression in Ancient Greece and Rome, Butler and Purves define their object of study as "the sensory blending experienced by all readers, synaesthetes or not."[11] The two definitions of synesthesia are strictly defined, and their difference is studiously maintained. The editors refer to "both kinds of synaesthesia," accepting the modern scientific construct as fact ("synesthetes or not") and hazarding no comment as to how their use of the term might relate to it. The volume, they explain, explores a wide variety of readerly synesthesias while leaving the scientific concept untouched because like Jewanski et al., Butler and Purves have been unable to identify the modern condition in the ancient corpus:

> *Synaesthesia and the Ancient Senses* takes the complex resonances of its title's term to heart, offering a collection that is synaesthetic in a variety of ways. (Indeed, the only sense of *synaesthesia* we shall mostly neglect is the clinical one, regarding which, in the absence of any ancient discussion in which we can identify the same condition, we can only play the tricky game of guessing whether this or that poet was a "genuine" synaesthete).[12]

The editors then turn, as one does in literary studies, to "the modern poet most often associated with synesthesia [understood in the nonclinical sense]: Charles Baudelaire," whose 1857 sonnet "Correspondances," interlaced with the Sappho verses on which it may well have drawn, ushers readers into a rich collection of essays analyzing sensory correspondences of the ancient world.[13]

The paradox presented by Jewanski et al. thus remains unresolved. Jewanski, confronting the conundrum directly, identifies three factors contributing to his failure to locate earlier reports of synesthesia. The first is the hidden nature of the historical accounts, which tend to appear in private letters or diaries, or—as in the case of Sachs—in works on seemingly unrelated topics. The second factor, in truth a variation on the first, is the absence of the types of sources that contemporary research tools have been adapted to find: medical, psychological, and physiological journals, most of which were founded after 1848. The third and final explanation is terminological. What is now called "synesthesia" acquired this name only in the latter half of the nineteenth century. Writing in an era in which the "search term" and "keyword" provide crucial identifiers, Jewanski scarcely needs to point out that "it is difficult to find something which has no name."[14] All three explanations may be swept aside in light of Butler and Purves's observation of "the absence of any ancient discussion in which we can identify the same condition," as the limitations Jewanski cites would not apply to classicists of their philological sophistication. But it is striking to note that all three explanations point to systemic biases in the research techniques of the twenty-first century. Driven by speed-seeking technologies premised on an assumption of progress, these techniques bespeak an attrition of the patience, creativity, and readerly acuity characteristic of the humanities' highest achievements. The methodological reflection invites the question of whether the last two centuries' great surge of knowledge about synesthesia should be interpreted as evidence of scientific advancement or, indeed, as an impoverishment of access to the knowledge of the past.

The paradox, in any case, remains. Other explanations for it are implicit in Jewanski's work. One is that the phenomenon, although widespread, was simply considered unworthy of comment by those living before the nineteenth century. The world was experienced in a particular way by a discrete subset of humans, but this experience was hidden from the historical record much in the same way that it is "hidden" from most of us today. "We are all likely to know several synaesthetes amongst our personal acquaintances," Jewanski observes, "but most of us don't know who they are."[15] Unless obliged by extraordinary circumstances—such as the presentation of a scientific questionnaire—those who experience the world in a synesthetic way are unlikely to comment on their manner of sensing, which for them is in no way strange or aberrant. From this perspective, the novel development that brought synesthesia into the written record in the nineteenth century had nothing to do with a change in human sensory experience, only a change in the formulation of scientific

CONCLUSION: REMARKS ON "SYNESTHESIA" / 125

questions. For synesthesia to be recorded, a firm and widespread conception of "normal" sensory experience had to be established, prompting phenomena falling beyond its range to attract scrutiny. Viewed from this angle, the "emergence of synesthesia" in the nineteenth century would reflect the development of new, restrictive norms for conceptualizing sensory perception. It would be a question not of the "emergence of synesthesia," in other words, but one of the emergence of "synesthesia."

Perhaps a more accurate formulation would suggest that while experiencing the world in a synesthetic way is likely as old as humanity itself, "synesthesia" in its clinical sense has been defined in such a way as to prevent inquiry into synesthetic ways of perceiving before 1812. Viewed from this angle, one axiom fundamental to the rise of "synesthesia" immediately emerges as decisive: "synesthesia" does not admit of degrees. In the twenty-first century, one either "is" a synesthete or one is not (witness Butler and Purves's formulation). One can "have" synesthesia or "not have" synesthesia, but one cannot "sort-of-have" synesthesia.[16] It would be difficult to overstate the importance of this axiom to the definition of "synesthesia" as a discrete object susceptible to modern scientific investigation.

The imperative of distinguishing "genuine" synesthetes from people who mistakenly believe they experience the world in synesthetic ways (not to mention those who deliberately deceive scientific investigators) is not particularly pronounced in the nineteenth-century corpus. *Audition colorée* and related phenomena were often announced by the labels *fausse*, *pseudo-*, *quasi-*, and the like, with scientists' primary concern being the ability to distinguish them from the sensations understood to be shared by all.[17] So stigmatized were these abnormal experiences that the specter of false reporters did not present itself.[18] On the contrary, investigators of the nineteenth century seem at pains to elicit any report of synesthetic perception at all: willed, obscure, indistinct, imagined, or otherwise.

However, as scientific inquiry into synesthetic perceptions began to gain credibility during the 1890s, the need to protect "genuine" synesthesia from false, questionable, or mistaken reports began to assert itself. A skeptical review published in March 1900 in the *Revue philosophique* offers an indicative illustration of the distrust scientists faced. Members of the public, contends one M. Daubresse, cannot be expected to offer reliable reports of *audition colorée* because

> either they listen inattentively to what they are being asked, fail to understand, and say nothing, their thoughts occupied elsewhere; or they draw up eclectic, false links between things and give as supporting

evidence whatever their imagination comes up with instead of what they actually observed.[19]

The binary distinction between "genuine" synesthesia and discounted synesthetic perceptions seems to have taken hold between roughly 1900 and 1925; in any case, its terms dominate the scientific literature by 1929.[20] The division is now firmly established across disciplines. Even those who contest the hierarchy accept the binary, treating the contemporary neuroscientific construction as pan-chronic fact rather than the product of interested axioms.[21] Very recently, this binary has begun to show hairline fractures in the sciences—fractures that notably coincide with the advent of brain-scanning technologies. The availability of mental imaging, relieving researchers of the burden of relying on subjects' reports, would appear to have resulted in a burgeoning scientific openness to the possibility of a more porous border between "genuine" and "non-synesthetes."[22] The same cannot be said of the humanities, where the term "synesthesia," when evoked, tends to be revindicated only though ginger distinction from a clinical definition assumed to be authoritative.[23] So it bears stressing that the assumption of a categorical distinction between "genuine" synesthesia and perceptions or locutions that seem synesthetic is just that: an interested axiom that was useful, indeed crucial, to establishing "synesthesia" as a legitimate object of modern science.

Seeing Light

What might earlier writings on synesthetic perceptions look like? It is instructive to return, for a moment, to Sachs. The passages of his dissertation that have proven foundational to the history of synesthesia—notably also the only passages that have been translated into English—contain lists of correspondences. To the literary reader, this might well be their most striking formal feature. In enumerating the ways that Sachs's account resonates with the contemporary literature on synesthesia, Jewanski et al. draw extensively on the content of the account without commenting on its form—an oversight indicative, one suspects, of the fact that this form has become so well established in the modern scientific paradigm as to escape notice. Modern synesthetes may—and notoriously do—report wildly divergent associations from one another, but in the twenty-first century, their reports will generally be presented in a predictable, uniform way. They proceed through a commonly known series in the conventional order, whether the days of the week, notes of the scale, or letters of the alphabet, and they list corresponding elements

CONCLUSION: REMARKS ON "SYNESTHESIA" / 127

belonging to a single, identifiable set.²⁴ It is a format within which an isolated association gains legibility and credibility through its presentation as part of a series, and one that almost seems to anticipate being collated into the graphs, charts, and tables in which it reaches the scholarly public. But what if observations of synesthetic associations were organized differently, or not organized at all? Is there any reason that a synesthetic sensation noted in isolation or in combination with another kind of impression should be cast out of consideration?

In this connection, it seems noteworthy that the lists of correspondences presented in §157–59 of Sachs's dissertation are not the only passages in the work to ponder extraordinary visions. Not thirty pages earlier, in §113, the author recounts how, when he was a boy, the sounds of a violin-like instrument would cause his eyes to create their own light. He himself has forgotten the experience he is able to recall only by means of his parents' recollection:

> But we have heard from our albinos' parents that the son, when he was a boy of eight or eleven, sometimes hid in a corner at dusk, having wholly immersed himself in bringing out and combining the hoarse tones of a certain musical instrument (of his own rough and crude making, similar to a large tetrachord), while at the same time a lot of bright light emanated from his eyes.—Does not, perhaps, a certain sympathy exist between the sense of hearing and seeing? There is no doubt that the senses are interconnected in various ways.
>
> *Ast audivimus e parentibus nostrorum leucaethipum, filium, cum octo ac undecim annorum puer esset, inter crepusculum quandoque in instrumenti cuiusdam musici, tetrachordo maiori similis, et ab eo ipso rude dureque fabricati, raucis sonis educendis et coniungendis plane abditum, in angulo quodam latuisse, unaque multum vividumque lumen oculis sparsisse. Qua quidem vario modo sensus inter se connecti, nullum est dubium.*²⁵

Despite its nonconformity with the format in which modern synesthetic perceptions have come to be recorded, the passage recounts a sensory experience whose resemblance to those perceptions would be difficult to deny. In the absence of external light, the boy's eyes seem to make it; it is the tones of a musical instrument that, by all appearances, prompt its production. The locution is a curious one: *multum vividumque lumen oculis sparsisse*. In the ablative case, the boy's eyes (*oculis*) may be read as instrument or agent;²⁶ whichever they are, they spread, strew, or scatter a great deal of bright light (*sparsisse*, the perfect, active infinitive of *spargo*, *spargere* means "to strew, throw here and there, cast, hurl, throw about, scatter, sprinkle"; the verb generally appears in the agricultural context of sowing seeds or grain[27]). One wonders whether Sachs's choice of verb reflects the particle theory of light dominant in early nineteenth-century Europe, by which light was conceived not as waves emanating through the ether but as particles, or "corpuscles," as Newton had famously put it, advancing in rays.[28] In any case, it is clear that this light differs from the external light originating out in the world. This light finds its source in the boy himself: it scatters, or perhaps emanates, radiates from his eyes. One thinks of the *rayon violet*, the violet ray, emanating from the enigmatic eyes that close Rimbaud's sonnet.[29]

But Sachs's story might gleam more significantly through another text. Charles Baudelaire's 1861 essay "Richard Wagner ou Tannhäuser à Paris," along with the sonnet "Correspondances" evoked therein, has long been established as foundational to the synesthetic aesthetics of French symbolism.[30] The essay begins by considering a single piece from the Wagner concert Baudelaire attended at the Théâtre-Italien in the winter of 1830: the *Lohengrin* prelude. Baudelaire says little of the music itself, focusing instead on the visions and sensations it prompted in him. These he presents as "the inevitable translation that my imagination made of this [. . .] piece, when I heard it for the first time, my eyes closed, and I felt raised up from the earth, so to speak (*la traduction inévitable que mon imagination fit [de ce] morceau, lorsque je l'entendis pour la première fois, les yeux fermés, et que je me sentis pour ainsi dire enlevé de terre*)." He recalls his listening self with eyes closed, the helpless plaything of a music that compels his imagination's response. It is not an active, authorial "*je*" but a slightly distanced "*mon imagination*" that translates the music into a series of impressions, visions, and sensations; furthermore, this imagination is no free agent. It may produce but one possible translation. The translation is "inevitable," or even, as an earlier draft had it, "forced (*forcée*)."[31] Baudelaire puts it into the following words:

> Je me souviens que, dès les premières mesures, je subis une de ces impressions heureuses que presque tous les hommes imaginatifs ont connues, par le rêve, dans le sommeil. Je me sentis délivré *des liens de la pesanteur*, et je retrouvai par le souvenir l'extraordinaire *volupté* qui circule dans *les lieux hauts* (notons en passant que je ne connaissais pas le programme cité tout à l'heure). Ensuite je me peignis involontairement l'état délicieux d'un homme en proie à une grande rêverie dans une solitude absolue, mais une solitude avec *un immense horizon* et une *large lumière diffuse* ; l'immensité sans autre décor

qu'elle-même. Bientôt j'éprouvai la sensation d'une clarté plus vive, *d'une intensité de lumière* croissant avec une telle rapidité, que les nuances fournies par le dictionnaire ne suffiraient pas à exprimer *ce surcroît toujours renaissant d'ardeur et de blancheur.* Alors je conçus pleinement l'idée d'une âme se mouvant dans un milieu lumineux, d'une extase *faite de volupté et de connaissance,* en planant au-dessus et bien loin du monde naturel.[32]

I remember that from the very first bars, I was subject to one of those happy impressions that almost all imaginative men have known, through dreams, in sleep. I felt myself released from the *bonds of gravity,* and I rediscovered in memory that extraordinary *thrill of pleasure* that dwells in *high places* (be it noted in passing that I was as yet ignorant of the programme quoted a moment ago). Next, I found myself involuntarily picturing the delicious state of a man in the grip of a profound reverie, in an absolute solitude, a solitude with an *immense horizon* and a *wide diffusion of light; an immensity with no other décor but itself.* Soon, I experienced the sensation of a *brightness* more vivid, an *intensity of light* growing so swiftly that all the nuances of the dictionary would be insufficient to express *this ever-renewing increase of incandescent whiteness.* Then, I fully conceived of the idea of a soul moving about in a luminous medium, of an ecstasy *of pleasure and knowledge,* soaring high above the natural world.[33]

Like the sleepwalker whose movements defy attribution to a conscious subject, the "je" of the passage seems to exist in a suspended state beyond or outside of conscious control. This state, however pleasurable, is imposed rather than attained (*je me sentis pour ainsi dire enlevé de terre, je subis, Je me sentis délivré,* etc.); it is likened to the condition of sleeping or dreaming (*par le rêve, dans le sommeil*), and later, of having ingested opium (*Il semble parfois, en écoutant cette musique ardente et despotique, qu'on retrouve peintes sur le fond des ténèbres, déchiré par la rêverie, les vertigineuses conceptions de l'opium*). The listener finds himself subjected to the involuntary "painting" of his imagination (*la traduction inévitable que mon imagination fit, je me peignis involontairement*), characterized by, amongst other things, "a broad, diffuse light." The light grows ever stronger, developing from a diffuse presence into a "sensation" of a brighter light whose intensity increases so rapidly that words prove insufficient to express its "ever-renewing increase of incandescent whiteness."[34] And here, suddenly, the listener becomes active: he "conceives the idea of a soul moving in a luminous milieu." This idea is immediately identified with transcendence, "soaring far away and above the natural world."

The text's many commentators, situating the passage within Baudelaire's arguments in this essay and beyond, have read it as an interested fiction: less a faithful description of musical experience than a piece of rhetoric calculated to produce a variety of effects. Margaret Miner, for example, interprets these impressions as part of Baudelaire's broader campaign to demonstrate that "movement across the distance that separates listening from writing—or music from literature—is practically effortless";[35] Susan Bernstein points out that the state of subjection in which Baudelaire presents his listening self forms part of his larger strategy of casting Wagner as an aesthetic despot.[36] From the perspective of the passage's literary reception, the question of its accuracy or insight would appear hopelessly naïve and well beside the point. But what if one were to read Baudelaire's text as a probing and precise meditation as well as a calculated ploy? The two, after all, are not mutually exclusive. One could begin by bracketing the distrust in Miner's keen observation that Baudelaire "claims to describe impressions imposed on him by the music at the intimate level where physical sensation is not clearly distinguishable from mental activity" and observe that this indistinction between "physical sensation" and "mental activity" situates Baudelaire's visions quite precisely in a realm of sensory experience that characterizes synesthetic visions. One could also observe that Baudelaire's emphasis on his subjugation to the visions and his characterization of these visions as involuntary strikes one of the defining chords of the modern synesthesia corpus. And one could also note that Baudelaire's sensation of light is coincident with a sensation of space, and that when he observes a strange likeness between the visions brought on by the music and those induced by opium, those visions are "painted on a background of shadows (*peintes sur le fond des ténèbres*)"[37]—a formulation reminiscent of Sachs's description of his own color visions "in dark space (*in obscuro spatio*)."[38] But perhaps most crucially, one could draw attention to the decisive break in the passage where the passive listener subjected to the sensation of light is replaced, in a flash, with an active *je* who "fully conceive[s] the idea of a soul." Between the imposed, involuntary visions and the idea of a soul, there lies a decisive introduction of an intelligent will capable of conceiving ideas—or, perhaps, one could hazard the gloss: interpreting sensations.

Baudelaire's explicit aim in this section of the Wagner essay is to demonstrate that "true music brings analogous ideas into different minds (*la véritable musique suggère des idées analogues dans des cerveaux différents*),"[39] and he offers two other accounts of the *Lohengrin* prelude to illustrate his point. The first, drawn from the program distributed at the Théâtre-Italien concert but purportedly unknown to Baudelaire until after the writing of his own account, is by Wagner himself; the second, by Franz Liszt, is drawn from the program that accompanied the 1850 premiere of the full opera at Weimar. Baudelaire unites his account with Wagner's and Liszt's on the grounds that all three mention, amongst other things, "the sensation [. . .] of *an intense light* that dazzles *the eyes and the soul to the point of swooning* (la sensation [. . .] d'*une lumière intense qui réjouit les yeux et l'âme jusqu'à la pâmoison*)."[40] Baudelaire's separation of "the eyes" from "the soul" in this formulation is striking, as one might have presumed the language of eyes, vision, and light throughout the essay to figure the soul rather than designate something distinguishable from it. Indeed, all three accounts of the *Lohengrin* prelude appear to use the language of light to translate a musical intensity that induces an ecstatic state of transcendence. Wagner's text unambiguously figures the divine as the light emanating from the Holy Grail around which his opera's plot revolves: his program notes for the prelude propose a pious believer who "sees a strange apparition gradually take shape, forming a body, a face," and "finding *the luminous apparition* coming ever closer [. . .] *he sinks into ecstatic adoration, as if the whole world had suddenly disappeared.*"[41] Liszt's account explores an extended analogy by which the prelude is likened to an evolving image of light striking the sacred temple; when he suggests that "we are made to see the temple of incorruptible wood glimmering before our eyes,"[42] the eyes in question certainly seem less sensory organs than metaphorical windows to the soul.

But there are also aspects of the texts, and Baudelaire's presentation of them, that indicate his separation of eyes from soul may be more significant and precise than has been appreciated. In his own account, as we have seen, the soul "conceived" by the listener only at the prelude's conclusion appears to be prompted by the sensation of light that continues around and beyond it and that, in any case, defies full identification with it. In further commentary on his memory of the concert, Baudelaire distinguishes a "material" experience from a "spiritual" one, observing that "No musician excels as Wagner does in *painting* space and depth, both material and spiritual (Aucun musicien n'excelle, comme Wagner, à *peindre* l'espace et la profondeur, matériels et spirituels)."[43] He draws a similar distinction in his observation that all three accounts note a "*spiritual and physical bliss (béatitude spirituelle et physique)*."[44] And when Liszt describes how "the sacred painting is drawn up before our profane eyes (le tableau sacré s'y dessine à nos yeux profanes),"[45] the *tableau* he describes is, in truth, an abstract mélange of color and light. The temple is pointedly not presented in its "real and imposing structure (son imposante et réelle structure)," but is rather conjured by a composer who, "as if carefully steering our feeble senses (comme ménageant nos faibles sens)," "shows it first of all reflected in *some azure wave* or mirrored by *some irridescent cloud* (nous le montre d'abord reflété dans *quelque onde azurée* ou reproduit par *quelque nuage irisé*)." Liszt renders the image "drawn before our profane eyes" in the colors of orchestration:

> Le motif est ensuite repris par les instruments à vent les plus doux; les cors et les bassons, en s'y joignant, préparent l'entrée des trompettes et des trombones, qui répètent la mélodie pour la quatrième fois, *avec un éclat éblouissant de coloris*, comme si dans cet instant unique l'édifice saint *avait brillé* devant *nos yeux aveuglés, dans toute sa magnificence lumineuse et radiante*.

> The motif is then taken up by the mellowest of the wind instruments; the horns and the bassoons join in to prepare for the entrance of the trumpets and the trombones which repeat the melody for the fourth time, *with a dazzling burst of color*, as if at this unique moment the holy edifice had *blazed forth* before *our blinded eyes, in all its luminous, radiant magnificence.*[46]

The translation of orchestral sound into brilliant vision hinges on the provocative counterfactual "as if (*comme si*)": to listen to the music is to feel "as if" the gleaming temple façade were blinding us with its brilliance; it is "as if" Wagner were "carefully steering our feeble senses." It is significant that in Baudelaire's formulation, the locution "our senses (*nos sens*)" is rendered in a plural that does not imply one collective sense (as in "our sense of hearing," *notre sens d'ouïe*), but rather, as in English, a multiplicity of different senses.[47]

The temple so central to Liszt's account, however vague its rendering, facilitates Baudelaire's transition to his own sonnet, "Correspondances," with its opening declaration that "The pillars of Nature's temple are alive / And sometimes yield perplexing messages (*La nature est un temple où de vivant piliers/Laissent parfois sortir de confuses paroles*)."[48] The poem's first stanza echoes the romantic trope of reading pleasing natural forms as signs of a divine design, or as Baudelaire puts it, "the Earth and its shows as a glimpse, a correspondence of Heaven (*la terre et ses spectacles comme un aperçu, comme une correspondance du Ciel*)."[49] This vertical correspondence is made all but explicit in the introduction to the sonnet that Baudelaire provides in the Wagner essay, where he contends that what would be truly surprising would be that sound *could not* suggest color, that colors *could not* give the idea of a melody, and that sound and color would be *unfit* to translate ideas: things having always been expressed by means of reciprocal analogy, from the day God created the world as a complex and indivisible totality.[50]

The designer of the sensory correspondences drawn out in the sonnet would be, explicitly, "God," creator of "a complex and indivisible totality." With or without the designer, however, the world of the sonnet situates man, or perhaps, one (*l'homme*) at its center, and it is by means of that one and that one alone that "sounds, scents, and colors correspond (*les parfums, les couleurs et les sons se répondent*)." As Leo Bersani points out,

> the metaphysical suggestiveness of the first four verses is *simply dropped* in the second and third stanzas. We move from vertical transcendence to horizontal unity [. . .] that is, stimuli ordinarily associated with one of our senses can produce sensations "belonging" to another sense. Baudelaire asserts, and in the third stanza illustrates, the reality of these analogies.[51]

Just as, in his account of listening to Wagner's music, Baudelaire describes a light that delights "the eyes *and* the soul to the point of swooning (*les yeux et l'âme jusqu'à la pâmoison*),"[52] so does he conclude his famous sonnet with a separation of senses from spirit. The fresh scents, soft as the strains of oboes or green as prairies, "chantent les transports de l'esprit *et* des sens (sing the raptures of the spirit *and* the senses)."[53] The body in which Baudelaire's *correspondances* take place is host to a spirit, but so, too, is it the locus of "senses," whose transports seem anything but unrelated to "synesthesia" in the modern sense.

If the methodological necessity of maintaining Baudelaire's and Sachs's texts in separate corpora—and separate histories—seems questionable, so too does the distancing of Baudelaire's *correspondances* from the Wagnerian compositions that inspire their citation. This second division, internal to literary studies, would conceive of Baudelaire's correspondences as fundamentally unrelated, indeed antithetical, to Wagnerian aesthetics. As Susan Bernstein points out, "Baudelaire inscribes in the essay his own poem, 'Correspondances,' as a translation of Wagner's music"; yet Bernstein, *contra* Baudelaire, opposes Wagner's compositional principles to the *correspondances* foundational to Baudelaire's vision.[54] In *A New History of French Literature*, a collected volume that has long been required reading across French graduate programs in the United States, Richard Sieburth similarly distances Baudelaire's correspondences from the orchestration of the senses that Wagner envisions in the Total Work of Art, or *Gesamtkunstwerk*. "Baudelaire's influential confusion of synaesthesia with Wagner's concept of the *Gesamtkunstwerk*," Sieburth observes, probably explains why symbolists from Rimbaud to Huysmans (mis-)understood their works exploring sensory connections as "Wagnerian in inspiration."[55] Baudelaire's perception of a likeness between Wagner's art and his own is, by Sieburth's account, an unfortunate "confusion." The French poet's "theory of the intertranslatability of different senses and media" (Sieburth's gloss for "synesthesia") would be foundational to symbolism but unrelated to the "genuine synesthesia" it persistently calls to mind, as well as to the Wagnerian aesthetics that prompt its invocation. But this is not the only possible configuration of "synesthesia," "Correspondances," and the aesthetic vision of the *Gesamtkunstwerk*. The vantage point from which these three nineteenth-century inventions form part of the same story is close at hand. It requires but one more voyage: this time, to Zürich.

Gesamtkunstwerk

> It seems to me that when I pronounce the different vowels on the same pitch, they possess something that suggests a change to my ear and gives me the impression of a certain melody...
> —WOLFGANG VON KEMPELEN, *THE MECHANISM OF HUMAN SPEECH*[56]

Exiled in Switzerland for his role in inciting Dresden's May uprising of 1848, Richard Wagner turned his mind to developing a type of music that would bring the emotive expression of the speaking voice—with its urgent intonations and impassioned emphases—into more effective alignment with the crests and abysses through which he imagined the progress of musical tones. The immediate cause for Wagner's reflections was his intense dissatisfaction with the contemporary German practice of performing French and Italian operas with translated librettos or—equally vexing—composing new works with the same fundamental disregard for the language in which they would be sung. In Wagner's view, the marvelous expressivity of human speech ought to contribute to the affective power of the dramatic whole. Yet German opera, in its reliance on Italian and, increasingly, French models, had developed a divided tradition in which the libretto's relation to the musical score roughly approximated that of a label pasted below a landscape painting.[57] Retrospectively recalling the situation in an 1861 letter to Frédéric Villot, Wagner laments that Italian operas designed to showcase vocal virtuosity had come to be sung in Germany "in a language whose genius is diametrically opposed to that of Italian," while French operas were routinely staged "in hasty, slapdash translations cheaply arranged through literary maneuvering, almost always with complete disregard for the relationship of the spoken phrase to the music, and with errors of prosody to make your hair stand on end."[58]

The problem, he declared, was fundamentally one of "*Klangfarbe.*" The term appears in Wagner's theoretical texts to distinguish the particular sound of the human voice from that of all other musical instruments. "Our ear," the disgruntled composer observes, "detecting the great distinction between the sensuous tone-colour [*sinnlichen Klangfarbe*] of the instruments and that of the human voice, instinctively severs the one from the other."[59] Whether the decisive distinction between the voice and the orchestra lies in the physical structure of the instruments involved, the sound waves they produce, or the attunement of the audience's ears is for Wagner a matter of complete indifference. The crucial point is that any dramatic opera seeking to make optimal use of both voice and orchestra must respect the fundamental distinction of *Klangfarbe* between them.[60]

Wagner reflects that the source of this distinction lies in the chameleonic nature of the human voice. "The vocal tone of speech," he remarks, "by the very play of its initial sounds, is always coming by another, infinitely varied coloring (*unendlich mannigfaltige Färbung bekommt*)" in comparison with which "the most complex blend of *orchestral tone-colours* (*Orchestertonfarben*) conceivable must needs seem poverty-stricken."[61] The voice, perpetually in the process of transformation, assumes different shades in accordance with the consonants breaking and shaping its sonic stream. The consonant, we read, circumscribes the vowel's "infinitely fluid element, and through the lines of this delimitation it brings to the vowel's colour, in a sense, the drawing which makes of it an exactly distinguishable shape."[62] As a line defines a shape in space, so does the consonant circumscribe the vowel's extension in time, though in so doing, it also affects the vowel's "color" (*Farbe*), "changing the character of the vowel itself" (*Bestimmung des Charakters des Vokales selbst, äußert*).[63] What Wagner observes is, in other words, a certain coloring conferred by the *consonnes d'appui*.[64] To illustrate this phenomenon, he offers the example of the professional singer who, obliged to "get the full tone out of the vowel, is acutely sensitive to the difference between the effects of energetic consonants—such as K, R, P, T—, or indeed, strengthened ones—such as Schr, Sp, St, Pr-, [. . .] upon the intoned sound."[65] A "doubling or trebling of the consonant" can sometimes cast upon a vowel "a drastic coloring" (*eine so drastische Färbung*).[66] The finest orchestra, however, bereft of "the word-determining Consonant,"[67] can only ever aspire to a pale approximation of the variegated voice. Its richest sounds, combined with even the greatest artistry, will produce but a distant echo of vocal song, resounding with only the vowels of an inchoate utterance.

What makes the voice so difficult to reconcile compositionally with the timbres of a symphony orchestra is thus less an issue of vocal timbre than vocalic. There is an argument to be made, therefore, that it was Wagner, and not Helmholtz, who first used the term *Klangfarbe* to designate differences between vowel sounds. *Oper und Drama* was composed in the winter of 1850–51, fully eight years before Helmholtz would publish his 1859 study "On the Vowel Sounds (*Ueber die Klangfarbe der Vocale*)."[68] It is even possible, though not likely, that Wagner was Helmholtz's source for the term. A musician from childhood, the Prussian physicist played Wagner's compositions by night while researching the *Tonempfindungen*—in which the composer's dissonant triads put in a cameo appearance.[69]

One could also contend that Wagner anticipated Helmholtz's demonstration of the musical structure constitutive of vowel sounds, not by recording the proper tones that characterize each one but by identifying a subtle melody intrinsic to their intonation. In Wagner's account, the voice, passing through various vowels, complicates composition by presenting an internal melody all its own, distinct from the succession of pitches that it may be made to intone.[70] The elusiveness of this melody is indicated by the multiplicity of compound terms Wagner devises in what is clearly a very strenuous effort to denote it: "tone-language" or "tone-speech" (*Tonsprache*), "Word-tone-melody" (*Worttonmelodie*), "Poetic song-melody" (*dichterische Gesangsmelodie*), and most frequently, "Verse-melody" (*Versmelodie*).[71] The existence of this melody is attested, he contends, precisely by the interference it causes for the externally imposed melodies with which it is made to coincide. When the melodic line of a work written for orchestra, for example, is "translated from the instruments onto the singing voice," the logic of its progress grows obscure to Wagner's ear—just as it does, he maintains, for the public. Such a melody is "Vocal only insofar as it [is] assigned to the human voice, to deliver in its purely instrumental capacity,—a capacity in which the voice [feels] terribly hampered by the vowels and consonants of the words."[72] And it is telling, he continues on to observe, that such melodies take hold with the public only once they have been "rid of the play of vowels and consonants"[73]: "played to the public by the Orchestra, [. . .] or on some harmonic instrument," or sung as intelligent opera singers have come to sing them: "sacrificing the words entirely to the song."[74] Only then, Wagner contends, "have our most favourite operatic melodies really been understood by the public"[75] who, again tellingly, tend not to *sing* such songs but to "hum them without words."[76] Composed without regard for the quiet melody sounding through the variegated *Klangfarben* of the voice, such "absolute"[77] melodies make musical sense only when that melody has been removed: when its various vocalic overtones have been suppressed. A musical composition committed to using the singing voice and the dramatic verse it supports organically would therefore need to reverse the order of composition. It would have to begin not with successions of pitches or harmonic progressions but by attending to the nuances of vowels: discerning the melodies latent in their progression and composing on the basis of that song.

This compositional principle situates vocalic *Klangfarben* at the very point of origin of Wagner's drama of the future, or, as the critical tradition would come to call it, the *Gesamtkunstwerk*.[78] Wagner's response to the contemporary operas whose translated librettos bore little relation to the musical scores they accompanied, the *Gesamtkunstwerk* was conceived as a dramatic genre whose overwhelming affective power would derive from its reconception of all existing arts—from music to poetry, dance, architecture, and painting—as a single, organic whole. Modeled on the classical Greek drama Wagner imagined to mark the rhythms of communal, spiritual life, the *Gesamtkunstwerk* was to harness the affective capacities of all art forms into a quasi-religious experience whose instantiation would, in turn, shape political organization.[79] The starting point for this stunningly ambitious undertaking, however, was minute. It lay in the originary medium of the two arts whose union would lay the foundation for the whole: music and dramatic verse.[80] The point of departure was to be found, quite literally, in the colors of vowels.

The vowel emerges as the necessary origin for the Total Work of Art because it simultaneously addresses human feeling and understanding. Wagner describes its extraordinary affective power as he deliberates over which vowels should coincide with prominent downbeats. He envisions a syllable type that would be distinguished by both its sonic and semantic significance: a "root-syllable" (*Wurzelsilbe*) whose lexical stress signals its status as the etymological root of the word of which it forms the most prominent part.[81] Although cloaked in consonants, this syllable is essentially and fundamentally "the intoned sound" (*der tönende Laut*) that forms its "heart," and which echoes with the "emotion that an innermost Necessity bade clothe itself in this vowel and no other."[82] Beneath both consonantal cloak and vocalic clothing, this "open" or "intoned" sound is none other than emotion itself: "the embodied inner feeling"[83] emanating outward into the physical form of a vocal sound "invented or found through the Necessity of Man's earliest emotional stress."[84] One can hear a whisper here of the position Wagner famously advanced nearly two decades later in his 1870 essay on Beethoven: that every musical act is a weakening of a scream.[85]

Like that scream, Wagner's intoned sound bears a distinct affinity with music. Enunciated fully, it "becomes quite of itself a musical tone (*Dieser tönende Laut, der bei vollster Kundgebung der in ihm enthaltenen Fülle ganz von selbst zum musikalischen Tone wird*)."[86] But as the composer's transformative verb *werden* signals, the intoned sound is coterminous with that musical tone no more than with the signifying vowel that clothes it.[87] Built upon the German substantive used for speech sounds (*Laut*), the intoned sound is introduced in contradistinction to *Mitlaute* (consonants).[88] But Wagner's *tönende Laut* differs from *Mitlaute*'s more intuitive opposing term, *Selbstlaute* ("vowels," or more precisely, independently articulable speech sounds), just as it does from the imported *Vokale* ("vowels")—another term that Wagner frequently employs. The expression *der tönende Laut* emerges both to focus attention on the musicality of vocalic sound—identified with its emotional tenor—and to distinguish that sound from any abstract musical tone. It finds its echo in the orchestra but is produced by the human voice alone. For Wagner, it is the "primal tone of all human speech, which only with the advent of the consonant condensed itself into the genuine vowel (*Urtone der menschlichen Sprache, der sich erst am Konsonanten zum wirklichen Vokale verdichtete*)."[89]

Generally stifled by the signification of the vowel in which it is clothed, the tone of the intoned sound most often goes unheard. It is only the poet who, as "knower of the unconscious" (*der Wissende des Unbewußten*), intuitively finds his way to the root-syllable whose sound and sense strike simultaneously on the emotion the poet would convey. For Wagner, the path to such words may be indicated by intuition alone, though the poet may retrospectively "pry into the nature of the word" "in order to track the emotion-swaying force he knows must dwell within it," perceiving at last "the fountain of that force in the purely sensuous body of this root, whose most primal substance is the intoned sound."[90] The power of the poet, then, as Sarah Pourciau has observed, resides quite precisely in his "intimate familiarity with the *Ur*-font, conceived here as the universal alphabet of tones and feelings."[91]

In Wagner's conception, loosely inspired by the Indo-European linguistics of his era, this universal alphabet is displaced in time: it takes shape in an originary language and persists in etymological roots.[92] But it is not difficult to see its affinity with the supreme language of Stéphane Mallarmé. In Mallarmé's supreme language, also the impetus to verse, sound and sense are undivided—but they are not displaced in time.[93] The fundamental difference may be most plain in Mallarmé's playful pedagogical manual *The Words of English* (*Les Mots anglais*, 1877)—a work Paul Valéry famously called "the most revelatory document we possess on Mallarmé's private work."[94] Here, Mallarmé observes, "It happens frequently that a link between a word's form and its signification is so perfect that it creates only one impression on the mind and the ear: that of its success; this is the case above all in what is called ONOMATOPOEIA." After lamenting the marginal status of such words "for lack of immemorial, nobiliary titles," he launches into an imaginary dialogue with the rootless riff-raff:

> Your origins? we ask them; and they show nothing but their justness. They should not be humiliated, however, as they perpetuate a creative technique in our idioms that may have been the first of them all.[95]

The "justness" of the upstart words derives neither from an uncorrupted Indo-European lineage nor from a sound-sense association of English radicals reinforced by convention.[96] It derives from nothing other than speaking beings' sense that their sounds say—sometimes, indeed, *are*—precisely what they mean. This mimetic technique *may* have been how language began (*un procédé de création qui fut peut-être le premier de tous*)—but then again, maybe not. There is no way to know. The author of *Les Mots anglais* does not precisely contest the validity of Indo-European linguistics, but his limited confidence in its capacity to illuminate *le mystère dans les lettres* is clear.[97] Were the science of language to possess the vast repertory of idioms ever spoken on earth, Mallarmé concedes, perhaps it might reveal something of letters' relationship to signification.[98] But in that distant future, at least in Mallarmé's vision, "there will no longer be any Science to summarize it all, nor anyone to say it." The belief that empirical evidence will ever resolve the mystery is unequivocally cast out. "Chimera," Mallarmé concludes; "let us content ourselves, presently, with the glimmers of light cast on this subject by magnificent writers."[99]

Acknowledgments

This book began as a dissertation in the Department of Comparative Literature at Princeton University, where an exceedingly fortuitous assemblage of individuals encouraged me to set down a much steeper path than I would otherwise have dared. My thanks to David Bellos, Sandra Bermann, Ann Smock, Susan Stewart, and, especially, Daniel Heller-Roazen for getting me started and for being there every step of the way.

The MLA Convention, Nineteenth-Century French Studies Colloquia, and Annual Meetings of the Henry Sweet Society afforded me important opportunities to rehearse various portions of this text; I am grateful to all the scholars who organized those events and especially to John Joseph, Beata Stawarska, Katherine Bergeron, Seth Whidden, and Catherine Witt for their encouragement and engagement.

I am deeply grateful to the US Fulbright Scholar Program, the Fulbright Finland Foundation, the University of Helsinki, and the research collective CALLIOPE (ERC StG2017), whose support made it possible for me to take a research leave to write this book. Josephine Hoegaerts, Karen Lauwers, Monique Horstmann, and Ludovic Marionneau kept me and this project alive through the darkest days of the pandemic. Dr. Silke Grallert of the Berlin-Brandenburg Academy of Sciences and Humanities, the archivists at the Marbach Literaturarchiv, and Daniel Bowles of Boston College offered invaluable assistance with the Lepsius manuscripts; Richard Hutchins deserves special thanks for keeping my Latin in line.

This project benefited greatly from the Research Incentive Grant and Manuscript Workshop afforded to me by Boston College, whose congenial hospitality I am happy to recognize here. I extend my heartfelt thanks to Rob St. Clair, Sarah Pourciau, Kevin Ohi, Margaret Thomas, and especially Kevin Newmark for their careful reading and learned suggestions at the workshop and beyond. I would also like to thank Erin Dunbar, Hannah Vinande, Andrew Clark, Viktoryia Liashynskaya, Marie Duic, and Lucile Coneau for their translation and research assistance.

Elise Wang and Amelia Worsley deserve trophies for their formidable endurance in cheering me on all the way to the ever-receding finish line, and Philip Tidwell deserves two: one for indulging my at-times costly perfectionism and another for embracing my consistently imperfect productions.

And last but very far from least, I would like to express my gratitude to the American Comparative Literature Association for the support it has offered this book in the form of a Helen Tartar First Book Subvention; the Vice Chancellor for Research at the University of California, Berkeley, thanks to whom it has color plates; editors Haun Saussy, Lazar Fleischmann, and Tom Lay; and everyone behind the scenes at Fordham University Press.

Notes

Introduction: After "Voyelles"

1. "Voyelles," signed manuscript copy held at the Musée Rimbaud Charleville-Mézières, rpt. in the *Œuvres complètes d'Arthur Rimbaud*, ed. André Guyaux and Aurélia Cervoni (Paris: Gallimard, 2009), 167. Henceforth *ŒCAR*. The poem, probably composed between autumn 1871 and winter 1872, first appeared in print in a slightly different version as a part of Paul Verlaine's *Les poètes maudits* (*Lutèce*, September 1883). The signed manuscript copy is held to be the definitive text. Translation adapted from that of Martin Sorrell in Arthur Rimbaud, *Collected Poems* (Oxford: Oxford University Press, 2001), 135; and Oliver Bernard in Arthur Rimbaud, *Collected Poems* (London: Penguin Classics, 1997), 171–72.

2. "Une saison en enfer," in *ŒCAR*, 263. Translations are mine unless otherwise noted.

3. The prominence of Rimbaud's sonnet in *The New Princeton Encyclopedia of Poetry and Poetics*'s entry on "Synesthesia" may be taken as generally indicative; T. V. F. Brognan and Alfred Garvin Engstrom, "Synesthesia," in *The New Princeton Encyclopedia of Poetry and Poetics*, ed. Alex Preminger et al. (Princeton, NJ: Princeton University Press, 1993), 1259. For a sense of the Rimbaud reference's reach across disciplines beyond literary studies, see, for example, John E. Joseph, "Coloured Hearing," in *Saussure* (Oxford: Oxford, 2012), 394; Lawrence E. Marks, "On Colored-Hearing Synesthesia: Cross-Modal Translations of Sensory Dimensions," *Psychological Bulletin* 82, no. 3 (1975): 304; Roman Jakobson and Linda R. Waugh, "Synesthesia," in *The Sound Shape of Language* (The Hague: De Gruyter, [1979] 1987), 194.

4. William Bright and Peter T. Daniels, *The World's Writing Systems* (Oxford: Oxford University Press, 1996), 265 and 490–91.

5. "Revelation I:8," *The Holy Bible*, King James Version (KJV), www.kingjamesbible.org.

6. Here and throughout, // designates phonemes, <> graphemes, and [] linguistic sounds that may or may not precisely match the aural contours of the phonemes of a given language.

7. The reading of "I" as lips forms part of Robert Faurisson's infamous proposal that the poem offers an elaborate analogy for the female body; Robert Faurisson, "A-t-on lu Rimbaud?," *Bizarre* 21–22 (1961): 1–48; Robert Faurisson, *A - t - on lu Rimbaud? suivi de l'affaire Rimbaud* (Paris: La Vieille Taupe, 1991).

8. Early readers of the poem often asserted that Rimbaud drew his inspiration from psychological surveys on colored hearing; see, for example, Gustave Kahn's influential assertion that "Sans doute Rimbaud était au courant des phénomènes d'audition colorée," in "Arthur Rimbaud," *La revue blanche* 16 (1898): 596. The chronology known to contemporary scholars, however, reveals this assertion to be based on an erroneous dating of the poem. Although first published in *Lutèce* in October 1883, the sonnet had already been composed by the winter of 1872; Arthur Rimbaud, *Oeuvres complètes facsimiles*, ed. Steve Murphy (Paris: Champion, 2002), 543–44. Psychological surveys into colored hearing did not begin to circulate in earnest until the 1880s. As Kevin Dann has pointed out, the vectors of influence may have run in the opposite direction: an average of three papers per year were published on *audition colorée* between 1870 and 1883, a number that shot up to sixteen in the year following the publication of "Voyelles"; Kevin Dann, *Bright Colors Falsely Seen* (Cambridge, MA: MIT Press, 1998), 31. By the time Ferdinand Suárez de Mendoza published the first book-length study of the phenomenon in 1890, there were just under fifty studies to cite, and that number had risen above eighty-five within three years; Ferdinand Suárez de Mendoza, *L'audition colorée: Études sur les fausses sensations secondaires physiologiques et particulièrement sur les pseudo-sensations de couleurs associées aux perceptions objectives des sons* (Paris: Octave Doin, 1890); Théodore Flournoy, *Des phénomènes de synopsie* (Paris and Geneva: Alcan and Eggimann, 1893). The wealth of scientific material on colored hearing published after 1889 could certainly be attributed to a decision by the *Congrès International de psychologie physiologique* to establish a committee dedicated to the systematic study of colored hearing, but the sharp rise in interest leading up to that meeting bears no obvious explanation; Théodule Ribot and Léon Marillier, *Congrès International de psychologie physiologique: première session* (Paris: Bureau des revues, 1890); and Jewanski et al., "Recognizing Synesthesia on the International Stage: The First Scientific Symposium on Synesthesia at the International Conference of Physiological Psychology, Paris, 1889," *Journal of the History of the Neurosciences* 29, no. 4 (2020): 357–87. More recent readings of "Voyelles" have also sought, inconclusively, to derive its idea of colored vowels from literary and linguistic precedents. It is possible but not likely that Rimbaud spotted the vowel-color analogy in linguistics, where it is attested as early as 1840; another plausible hypothesis traces the analogy to Charles Cros; David Steel, "Autour des *Voyelles* de Rimbaud: Poésie et linguistique," *French Cultural Studies* 22, no. 1 (2011): 3–11. Stéphanie Boulard suggests another possible source in Victor Hugo, though she deems it unlikely that Rimbaud had access to Hugo's then-unpublished notebooks; Stéphanie Boulard, "Hugo/Rimbaud—Voyelles," *Parade Sauvage* 31 (2020): 189–214.

9. For the colored alphabets of children's books, see Kathy Kuiper, "Voyelles (poem by Rimbaud)," *The Encyclopaedia Britannica*, February 24, 2017, https://www.britannica.com/topic/Voyelles; for the conflict with a reader's preexisting system of vowel-color association that set the tone for a whole critical tradition, see René Ghil, *Traité du Verbe* (Paris: Giraud, 1886), 27–28. A detailed account of the poem's early reception is recounted by Jean-Jacques Lefrère in *Arthur Rimbaud* (Paris: Fayard, 2001), 889–91; René Étiemble's *Le sonnet des voyelles: de l'audition colorée à la vision érotique* (Paris:

Gallimard, 1968) offers an impressively exhaustive (if expressly dismissive) account of the critical reception through the late 1960s; and the indicative bibliography assembled in Alain Bardel's entry "Voyelles," in *Dictionnaire Rimbaud*, ed. Adrien Cavallaro, Yann Frémy, and Alain Vaillant (Paris: Classiques Garnier, 2021), 790–94, covers most major publications of the past half century, with the notable exceptions of Claude Lévi-Strauss's "Des sons et des couleurs," in *Regarder, écouter, lire* (Paris: Plon, 1993), 126–37; and Jacques Rancière's "Les voix et les corps," in *Le Millénnaire Rimbaud*, ed. Alain Badiou, Jacques Borreil, and Jacques Rancière (Paris: Belin, 1993), 11–42. The November 1991 colloquium organized by Badiou, Borreil, and Rancière for the centennial of Rimbaud's death marks the last major, multidisciplinary burst of energy around "Voyelles," whose appeal in the twenty-first century extends little beyond specialists in French (even, perhaps, Rimbaldian) poetics. To Bardel's indicative bibliography, one could nonetheless add Boulard's "Hugo/Rimbaud"; my "Correspondances: La couleur des voyelles chez Lévi-Strauss, Jakobson, Rimbaud et Banville," *Parade Sauvage* 30 (2019): 121–42; Steel's "Autour des *Voyelles*," 3–11; Yann Frémy's *Je m'évade! Je m'explique: Résistances d'Une saison en enfer* (Paris: Classiques Garnier, 2011) and his *Te voilà, c'est la force: Essai sur Une saison en enfer de Rimbaud* (Paris: Classiques Garnier, 2009), 313–15.

10. Jonathan Culler, "Apostrophe," *diacritics* 7, no. 4 (1977): 63.

11. Rimbaud's famous declaration "Le Poète se fait *voyant* par un long, immense et raisonné *dérèglement* de *tous les sens* [. . .] il devient entre tous le grand malade, le grand criminel, le grand maudit,—et le suprême Savant!" (*ŒCAR*, 344; emphasis in original) lays out the poetic project undertaken in "Voyelles" (described in *Une saison en enfer* as part of an attempt to invent "un verbe poétique accessible, un jour ou l'autre, à *tous les sens*"; *ŒCAR*, 263; emphasis mine).

12. "Au commencement était le Verbe, et le Verbe était auprès de Dieu, et le Verbe était Dieu"; *Les quatre évangiles*, trans. A. Crampon (Paris: Tolra et Haton, 1864), 401–2. Rimbaud's hubristic ambitions permeate "Voyelles" ("C'est moi l'Alpha et l'Oméga, dit Seigneur Dieu," *Apocalypse* 1, no. 8) as well as the May 15, 1871, letter to Paul Démy ("il devient [. . .] le suprême Savant!"). Vowels have been identified with the divine for about as long as they have existed as an idea; Joshua T. Katz, "Gods and Vowels," in *Poetic Language and Religion in Greece and Rome*, ed. J. Virgilio García and Angel Ruiz (Newcastle upon Tyne: Cambridge Scholars Publishing, 2013), 2–28.

13. Culler cautions against generalizing Harold Bloom's suggestion regarding Shelley that apostrophe, by means of its odd, absent objects, actually addresses an "ultimate Thou" (God). He contends that "The student of apostrophe must resist this reduction. Whatever sort of pantheism the poems embody, when they address natural objects, they formally will that these particular objects function as subjects"; Culler, "Apostrophe," 62. Culler does not appear to have considered apostrophes directed at vowels, which are neither "natural objects" nor, as apostrophe typically requires, absent.

14. Ibid.

15. W. H. Auden, "In Memory of W. B. Yeats," in *Collected Poems* (London: Faber, 1976), cit. Culler, "Apostrophe," 62.

16. Rancière, "Les voix et les corps," in *Le Millénnaire Rimbaud*, ed. Alain Badiou, Jacques Borreil, and Jacques Rancière (Paris: Belin, 1993), 19.

17. Ibid., 12.

18. Richard Cytowic, "Synesthesia: Phenomenology and Neuropsychology, A Review of Current Knowledge," *Psyche* 2, no. 10 (July 1995): 1.

19. American Psychiatric Association, *Diagnostic and Statistical Manual of Mental Disorders*, 5th ed., Text Revision (Washington, DC: American Psychiatric Association, 2022).

20. Jamie Ward and Julia Simner, "Synesthesia: The Current State of the Field," in *Multisensory Perception: From Laboratory to Clinic*, ed. K. Sathian and V. S. Ramachandran (Cambridge, MA: Academic Press, 2020), 296–97.

21. Lawrence E. Marks, "*Bright Colors Falsely Seen* by Kevin Dann (book review)," *Isis* 91, no. 2 (2000): 390.

22. Saul Kripke, *Wittgenstein on Rules and Private Language: An Elementary Exposition* (Oxford: Basil Blackwell, 1982).

23. Ludwig Wittgenstein, *Philosophical Investigations*, trans. G. E. M. Anscombe, P. M. S. Hacker, and Joachim Schulte, 4th ed. (Oxford: Blackwell, 2009), 87–88 (§202).

24. Noam Chomsky, *Syntactic Structures* (The Hague: Mouton, 1957), 15.

25. The term "synesthesia" begins appearing in its modern sense over this period, but the dominant term for the concept now associated with that word was, in the 1890s "audition colorée" (colored hearing). See Jewanski et al., "The Evolution of the Concept of Synesthesia in the Nineteenth Century as Revealed through the History of Its Name," *Journal of the History of the Neurosciences* 29, no. 3 (2020): 259–85.

26. Sachs is cited as the first case of synesthesia writ large in Jörg Jewanski, Sean A. Day, and Jamie Ward, "A Colorful Albino: The First Documented Case of Synaesthesia, by Georg Tobias Ludwig Sachs in 1812," *Journal of the History of the Neurosciences* 18, no. 3 (2009): 293–396; see also Jörg Jewanski, Julia Simner, Sean A. Day, and Jamie Ward, "The Development of a Scientific Understanding of Synesthesia from Early Case Studies (1849–1873)," *Journal of the History of the Neurosciences: Basic and Clinical Perspectives* 20, no. 4 (2011): 284–305; and Dann, *Bright Colors*, 18. In his classic article "On Colored-Hearing Synesthesia," 303–31, Marks makes the more modest claim that Sachs represents the first case of linguistic colored hearing. For a discussion of the controversial status of cases before Sachs, see Jewanski et al., "Possible Documented Cases of Synaesthesia Prior to 1812," *Journal of the History of the Neurosciences* 18, no. 3 (2009): 294–96. None of these cases appears to involve language.

27. It seems probable that Sachs's *obscura* (translated as "dark" by Jewanski et al.) is intended in the sense promulgated by Gottfried Wilhelm Leibniz the *Nouveaux Essais sur l'entendement humain* (1765). In Book 2, Chapter 29, Leibniz distinguishes between "clear," "complex," and "obscure" perceptions using color as his primary example. "Obscure perceptions" are, in Leibniz's definition, less "dark" than they are dim: lacking clear distinction, not brightness; Gottfried Wilhelm Leibniz, *Nouveaux essais sur l'entendement humain* (Paris: Flammarion, 1921), 205.

28. G. L. T. Sachs, *Historiae naturalis duorum leucaetiopum* (PhD dissertation, University of Erlangen, 1812), 81–82. Translations modified from page 297 of the partial English translation available in Jewanski et al., "Colorful Albino," 293–303.

29. The most frequent examples are Locke's blind man in the *Essay Concerning Human Understanding* (1690), who reports the sound of a trumpet as "red"; Newton's analogy of the musical and spectral chromatic scales in the *Opticks* (1704); and Father Castel's colored harpsichord (1725). Emily Dolan has traced the migration of the colored terms as applied to music from notes to instrumental timbres over the course of the eighteenth century; Emily I. Dolan, *The Orchestral Revolution: Haydn and the Technologies of Timbre* (Cambridge: Cambridge University Press, 2013), 23–52. Overviews of the history of colored hearing are offered from a scientific standpoint in

Marks, "On Colored-Hearing Synesthesia"; and Dann, *Bright Colors*, 18–26; for a more humanist perspective, see John Gage's "The Sound of Colour," in *Colour and Culture: Practice and Meaning from Antiquity to Abstraction* (London: Thames and Hudson, 1993), 227–36 and "Making Sense of Colour," in *Color and Meaning* (Berkeley and Los Angeles: University of California Press, 1999), 261–68.

30. Perroud, "De l'hyperchromatopsie," *Mémoires et compte-rendus de la société des sciences médicales de Lyon* 2 (1863): 37.

31. Gustav Theodor Fechner, *Vorschule der Aesthetik*, Vol. 2 (Leipzig: Breitkopf und Härtel, 1876), 315–19; E. Bleuler and K. Lehmann, *Zwangsmässige Lichtempfindungen durch Schall und verwandte Erscheinungen auf dem Gebiete der andern Sinnesempfindungen* (Leipzig: Fues, 1881); William O. Krohn, "Pseudo-Chromesthesia, or the Association of Colors with Words, Letters, and Sounds," *American Journal of Psychology* 5, no. 1 (1892): 20–41; Flournoy, *Phénomènes*, 47.

32. Jewanski et al. observe that their research tools privilege publication types available only from the nineteenth century onward; Jewanski, Jörg, "Synesthesia in the Nineteenth Century: Scientific Origins," in *The Oxford Handbook of Synesthesia*, ed. Julia Simner and Edward M. Hubbard, 372.

33. See particularly Jörg Jewanski, Julia Simner, Sean A. Day, Nicolas Rothen, and Jamie Ward, "From 'Obscure Feeling' to 'Synesthesia': The Development of the Term for the Condition We Today Name 'Synesthesia,'" in *Proceedings VI International Congress Synesthesia Science and Art* (Granada: Artecittà, 2018), 1–8; Jewanski et al., "Evolution of the Concept of Synesthesia," 259–85.

34. Jewanski et al., "Colorful Albino"; Jewanski et al., "Scientific Understanding of Synesthesia"; Jörg Jewanski, Julia Simner, Sean A. Day, Nicolas Rothen, and Jamie Ward, "The 'Golden Age' of Synesthesia Inquiry in the Late Nineteenth Century (1876–1895)," *Journal of the History of the Neurosciences* 29, no. 2 (2019): 175–202; Jewanski et al., "Evolution of the Concept of Synesthesia." For more on the limitations of the retrospective-diagnosis method, see "Remarks on 'Synesthesia,'" the conclusion to this book.

35. Jean-Jacques Rousseau, *Essai sur l'origine des langues* (Paris: A. Belin, [1781] 1817), 19–20.

36. "Nuance," in *Dictionnaire de l'Académie française*, 4th ed. (Paris: B. Brunet, 1762).

37. Richard Sieburth, "The Music of the Future," in *A New History of French Literature*, ed. Denis Hollier (Cambridge, MA: Harvard University Press, 1994), 791.

38. Jakobson and Waugh, *Sound Shape*, 197.

39. Ibid. The hypothesis was an old one: it appears at least as early as Bleuler and Lehmann's 1881 study, which considers the phenomenon of colored hearing to be "existent in the predisposition of everyone"; Bleuler and Lehmann, *Zwangsmässige Lichtempfindungen*, 50–51; translated Jewanski et al., "Evolution of the Concept of Synesthesia," 264.

40. Édouard Claparède, "Sur l'audition colorée," *Revue philosophique de la France et de l'Étranger* 49 (1900): 515–17.

41. Jakobson, "Linguistics and Poetics" (1958), rpt. in *Selected Writings III*, ed. Stephen Rudy (The Hague: Mouton, 1981), 44.

42. Jakobson, "Linguistics and Poetics," 44.

43. Ibid.

44. Ibid.

45. Arby Ted Siraki, "Problems of a Linguistic Problem: On Roman Jakobson's Coloured Vowels," *Neophilologus* 93 (2009): 1–9.

46. Jakobson, *Kindersprache, Aphasie und allgemeine Lautgesetze* (Uppsala: Språkvetenskapliga Sällskapets i Uppsala Förhandlingar, 1941); rpt. in Jakobson, *Selected Writings I*, 3rd ed. (Berlin: Mouton de Gruyter, 2002), 328–401; translated by Allen Keiler, *Child Language, Aphasia, and Phonological Universals* (The Hague: Mouton, 1968). Citations henceforth give the page numbers for the German in *SW I* followed by the English.

47. Jakobson, *Kindersprache*, 375/69.

48. The second step can alternatively involve "a third more central degree of opening, e.g., *papa-pipi-pepe*" ("einen dritten, mittleren Öffnungsgrad, z.B. *papa-pipi-pepe*"; ibid., 358/49.

49. Ibid.

50. Ibid., 379/74. Jakobson refers to Chapter 13 of Carl Stumpf, *Die Sprachlaute: experimentell-phonetische Untersuchungen nebst einem Anhang über Instrumentalklänge* (Berlin: Springer, 1926), 326–48.

51. Jakobson, *Kindersprache*, 386/82.

52. Ibid.

53. Ibid., 386–87/82.

1 / *Klangfarbe*: Vowels in Helmholtz's *Sensations of Tone*

1. The question may be traced at least as far back as Nicole Oresme's *Tractatus de configurationibus qualitatum et motuum* (Book 2, §18), which Marshall Clagett has dated to 1351–55; Nicole Oresme, *Tractatus de configurationibus qualitatum et motuum* (Madison: University of Wisconsin Press, 1968), 315–19.

2. Hermann von Helmholtz, *Die Lehre von den Tonempfindungen als Physiologische Grundlage für die Theorie der Musik* (Braunschweig: Vieweg and Sohn, [1863] 1913), 1. English edition translated by Alexander J. Ellis, *On the Sensations of Tone as a Physiological Basis for the Theory of Music* (New York: Dover, [1870] 1954), 1. Translations modified throughout. For more on the difficulties of translating the *Tonempfindungen* into English, see Julia Kursell, "Alexander Ellis's Translation of Helmholtz's *Sensations of Tone*," *Isis* 109, no. 2 (2018): 339–45.

3. Helmholtz, *Tonempfindungen*, 2/2. Helmholtz first presented the material published in this chapter of the *Tonempfindungen* at the Royal Bavarian Academy of Sciences in 1859 and published it as "Ueber die Klangfarbe der Vocale," *Annalen der Physik und Chemie* 108 (1859): 280–90. His critique echoes that of Denis Diderot, who wonders in his 1748 "Principes généraux d'acoustique," "How can it be [...] that the pleasure of consonance consists in the perception of relationships between sounds? [...] Does the soul possess this knowledge [of ratios] unwittingly?" (106). Unlike Helmholtz, however, Diderot locates the question in the soul rather than the ear: for him, the perception of relationships forms the basis for all aesthetic pleasure, not just for the experience of harmony, and thus lies outside the parameters of his study; Denis Diderot, "Principes généraux d'acoustique," *Œuvres complètes* (Paris: Garnier, 1875), 83–131.

4. Hence Veit Erlmann's contention in *Reason and Resonance* (New York: Zone, 2010) that it is instructive to situate Helmholtz's work within "a tradition that sought, in denial of its own claims to enlightenment and reason, to deduce the interior from

the exterior" (220). Erlmann figures among a veritable fleet of twenty-first-century scholars interested in understanding Helmholtz's scientific work as (1) reflective of his sociohistorical position, (2) decisive in the history of listening and sound technology, and (3) formative in shaping European intellectual history. An indicative though far from exhaustive list would include Kenneth L. Caneva, *Helmholtz and the Conservation of Energy: Contexts of Creation and Reception* (Cambridge, MA: MIT Press, 2021); Julia Kursell, *Epistemologie des Hörens: Helmholtz' physiologische Grundlegung der Musiktheorie* (Paderborn: Fink, 2018); David Cahan, *Helmholtz: A Life in Science* (Chicago: University of Chicago Press, 2018); M. Norton Wise, *Aesthetics, Industry, and Science: Hermann von Helmholtz and the Berlin Physical Society* (Chicago: University of Chicago Press, 2018); Benjamin Steege, *Helmholtz and the Modern Listener* (Cambridge: Cambridge University Press, 2012); Edwin Hiebert, *The Helmholtz Legacy in Physiological Acoustics* (Cham: Springer, 2015); Alexandra Hui, "Sound Materialized and Music Reconciled: Hermann Helmholtz," in *The Psychophysical Ear: Musical Experiments, Experimental Sounds, 1840–1910* (Cambridge, MA: MIT Press, 2012), 55–76; Myles Jackson, *Harmonious Triads: Physicists, Musicians, and Instrument Makers in Nineteenth-Century Germany* (Cambridge, MA: MIT Press, 2006); Jonathan Sterne, "Machines to Hear for Them," in *The Audible Past* (Durham, NC: Duke University Press, 2003), 31–85, esp. 62–67. Scholarship in French has been less singularly motivated by the will to historicize; see, for example, Michel Meulders, *Helmholtz, des lumières aux neurosciences* (Paris: Éditions Odile Jacob, 2001); Patrice Bailhache, *Une histoire de l'acoustique musicale* (Paris: CNRS, 2001); and Bailhache, *Helmholtz, du son à la musique*, co-edited with Antonia Soulez and Céline Vautrin (Paris: Vrin, 2011).

5. Helmholtz, *Tonempfindungen*, 168–93/103–19.

6. "The sensation of sound is, therefore, a species of reaction against external stimulus, peculiar to the ear, and excitable in no other organ of the body, and is completely distinct from the sensation of any other sense"; ibid., 13/7.

7. Ibid., 14/7.

8. Helmholtz thus considers "sensations of tone" in relation to tones' isolated middles, which is to say, removed from onset and decay. See Chapter 2, "The Interaction of Color."

9. Helmholtz, *Tonempfindungen*, 14/7, 8.

10. Ibid., 14/8.

11. Ibid., 37–39/23–24. Ellis's decision to use "musical tones" over "musical sounds" probably reflects a desire to distinguish *Klänge* from *Schall* and stress the nature of a *Klang* as the product of a single source rather than the combined sound of several instruments. However, the shift is not without complications.

12. This definition originates not with Helmholtz but with G. S. Ohm, the first to offer the mathematical equation of a single tone as a simple sine curve. Ohm, "Ueber die Definition des Tons, nebst daran geknüpfter Theorie der Sirene und ähnlicher tonbildener Vorrichtungen," *Poggendorffs Annalen der Physik* 59 (1843): 513–65 and "Noch ein Paar Worte über die Definition des Tons," *Poggendorffs Annalen der Physik* 62 (1844): 1–17.

13. Helmholtz, *Tonempfindungen*, 77–78/46.

14. Ibid., 77/45.

15. For the development of this calculation from antiquity through the seventeenth century, see Bailhache, *Histoire*, 63–66.

16. Joseph Sauveur, *Collected Writings on Musical Acoustics*, ed. Rudolf Rasch (Utrecht: Diapason Press, 1984), 152. An awareness that one and the same string produces tones lying at consonant intervals to the tone corresponding to its full length is attested as early as Plato. The novelty of Sauveur's observations lies in his use of the open string, as opposed to a string artificially held by a movable bridge, as in the canons and monochords of the ancients. Árpád Szabó, *Anfänge der griechischen Mathematik*, (Budapest: Akadémiai Kiadó, 1969), 128–34; see also Bailhache, *Histoire*, 13–39, 104–5, and 144–47.

17. See, for example, Oresme's discussion of "sono apparenti uno ex sonis partialibus mixto" in the *Tractatus*, 314–17.

18. Bailhache, *Histoire*, 145–47.

19. Helmholtz, *Tonempfindungen*, 77/45.

20. Ibid., 37. In introducing the overtones, Helmholtz limits his scale to the first ten overtones, though the upper extension of their production would appear to be theoretically unbounded. Ellis's decision in the English translation (22) to extend Helmholtz's scale to the first sixteen overtones, however, invites the question of whether Helmholtz's limitation to ten is entirely arbitrary. Comparison of the two scales reveals at least one reason why the eleventh overtone was to be avoided: lying at the problematic interval of the semitone, it marks the first rupture in the tonal key described by the first ten tones. As Helmholtz proceeds to identify these first ten overtones as "harmonic," later to discuss clearly dissonant "Klänge mit unharmonische Obertönen" (Helmholtz, *Tonempfindungen*, 120–27/70–74), it would seem that in his usage, "harmonisch" and "unharmonisch" do not coincide with "consonant" and "dissonant," but rather are distinguished by the appearance of the semitone.

21. The German physicist August Seebeck appears to have been the first to introduce sympathetic resonance into the physical and mathematical discussion of music; Seebeck, "Akustik," *Repertorium der Physik* 8 (1849): 60–66. Helmholtz does not cite Seebeck's work directly in his chapter on sympathetic resonance, but he does cite it elsewhere in the *Tonempfindungen* (Helmholtz, *Tonempfindungen*, 623/391), so it seems likely that Seebeck is his source for this material.

22. Helmholtz, *Tonempfindungen*, 61/36.

23. Ibid., 60/36.

24. Ibid., 82/47–48.

25. Ibid., 37/22.

26. "τόνος," d1 and d2, *An Intermediate Greek-English Lexicon* by Henry George Liddell and Robert Scott (Oxford: Clarendon Press, 1889), https://www.perseus.tufts.edu/hopper/text?doc=Perseus%3Atext%3A1999.04.0058%3Aentry%3Dto%2Fnos.

27. Szabó, *Anfänge*, 128–34.

28. Ibid., 128–34.

29. In the Pythagorean tale related by Boethius in the early sixth century, the single tone may be traced to the fourth hammer, which serves only to introduce the dissonant interval by which the diapente and diatessaron differ; Boethius, *Fundamentals of Music*, trans. Calvin M. Bower (New Haven, CT: Yale University Press, 1966), 17–19. See also Daniel Heller-Roazen, *The Fifth Hammer: Pythagoras and the Disharmony of the World* (New York: Zone, 2011), 11–17. As Szabó has shown, the history of the single "tone" may be traced not only etymologically, but also archaeologically, by means of the marked notch on the canon: the essential distinction between this instrument and the older monochord; Szabó, *Anfänge*, 128–34.

30. Neither the unit nor the harmonic system is necessary to music, of course, as Helmholtz points out: "Harmony has become essential to Western Europeans during the last three centuries, and to our taste, an indispensable means of strengthening melodic relations, but finely developed music existed for thousands of years and still exists in ultra-European nations, without any harmony at all"; Helmholtz, "Preface to the Third German Edition," *Tonempfindungen*, vii/vii. See also Helmholtz's lecture "Ueber die arabisch-persische Tonleiter," *Verhandlungen des naturhistorisch-medizinischen Vereins zu Heidelberg* 2 (1862): 216–17; and Julia Kursell, "Fine-Tuning Philology: Helmholtz's Investigation into Ancient Greek and Persian Scales," *History of Humanities* 2, no. 2 (Fall 2017): 345–59.

31. Ellis, *Sensations*, 24.

32. Helmholtz, *Tonempfindungen*, 37/22. Of course, not all musical tones are compound: tuning forks, for example, produce a tone almost entirely bereft of overtones, and those that remain can be more or less eliminated if the fork is struck at the mouth of the proper resonator.

33. Ibid., 78–79/46.

34. Ibid., 79/46.

35. Ibid., 96/55.

36. Helmholtz, "Ueber die physiologischen Ursachen der musikalischen Harmonie," in *Populäre wissenschaftliche Vorträge*, Vol. 1 (Braunschweig: Vieweg und Sohn, 1865), 83. Translated by Alexander Ellis, "On the Physiological Causes of Harmony in Music," in *Popular Lectures on Scientific Subjects*, Vol. 1 (New York: Appleton, 1885), 94.

37. Helmholtz, *Tonempfindungen*, 36/21.

38. Duration is also frequently noted but considered irrelevant to studies of harmony—harmony being the study of simultaneous sounds and melody, that of successive ones; Jean-Philippe Rameau, *Traité de l'harmonie réduite à ses principes naturels* (Paris: Ballard, 1722), 2; James Beattie, "An Essay on Poetry and Musick as They Affect the Mind" (1762), rpt. in *The Works of James Beattie* (Philadelphia: Hopkins and Earle, 1809), 321. It bears noting that duration is implied in the notion of speed, however, from which pitch is demonstrated to derive.

39. See, for example, Leonhard Euler, "Eclaircissemens plus détaillés sur la génération et la propagation du son et sur la formation de l'echo" (1764–65): "on sait que les sons, quoiqu'ils soyent également graves ou aigus et aussi également forts, admettent encore plusieurs variations er différences, comme sont celles des différentes voyelles, dont personne n'a encore entrepris d'expliquer la nature"; Euler, *Mémoires de l'académie des sciences de Berlin* 21 (1767): 547.

40. Robert Willis, "On the Vowel Sounds, and on Reed Organ-Pipes," *Transactions of the Cambridge Philosophical Society* 3 (1830): 234.

41. Helmholtz, *Tonempfindungen*, 113–14/66.

42. Ibid., 74/43.

43. Ibid., 73/43. Steege pursues an extended discussion of the subjectivity thus introduced into Helmholtz's research in *Helmholtz and the Modern Listener*, 43–79, and esp. 60–68.

44. Helmholtz, *Tonempfindungen*, 168/103.

45. Willis, "Vowel Sounds," 235.

46. Ibid., 235.

47. Samuel Reyher, *Mathesis Mosaica, sive Loca Pentateuchi Mathematica Mathematicè explicata*, (Kiel: Kilia Holsatorum, 1679).

48. Franciscus Mercurius van Helmont, *Alphabeti verè naturalis hebraici brevissima delineatio* (Sulzbach: Abraham Lichtenthaler, 1667). Helmont took the agreement between these two sets of shapes as conclusive evidence of their shared, divine design. Reyher was less than convinced; the tactful mathematician had but to allude to the glaring difficulty of Helmont's theory—namely, that the vowel notation considered therein had appeared in written Hebrew no less than a millennium after even the latest plausible dates put forth for the life of Moses; Reyher, *Mathesis Mosaica*, 432. For Ancient Hebrew, as is well known, boasts no written symbols for vowel sounds. Though the ancient tongue was the one Helmont sought to equate with divine language, he had included in his study the vowel symbols developed in the early medieval period, brushing over the temporal discrepancy with a brief explanation that "whoever devised these [vowel] figures, whoever they were and at whatever time they lived, did not stray from the nature of the vowels"; F. M. Helmont, *The Alphabet of Nature: A Short Sketch of the Truly Natural Hebrew Alphabet*, trans. Allison Coudert and Taylor Corse (Boston: Brill, 2007), 136–37.

49. Reyher, *Mathesis Mosaica*, 432.

50. Ibid., 432–33.

51. Reyher's scale, appearing as it does amid a commentary purportedly bearing on an Ancient Hebrew text, might also draw its inspiration from the diacritical dots that accompany consonants in Ancient Hebrew, indicating the presence of the vowels. These diacritical markings resemble the neumes marking melodic ascent and descent in early music and may, therefore, have suggested an association of vowels with tones through their graphic congruence.

52. The knowledge reformation that characterized Europe's early modern period disrupted this division remarkably little. See Ann Moyer, "Musical Scholarship in Italy at the end of the Renaissance, 1500–1650: From Veritas to Verisimilitude" in *History and the Disciplines: The Reclassification of Knowledge in Early Modern Europe*, ed. Donald R. Kelley (Rochester: Rochester University Press, 2000), 185–202; as well as Moyer's *Musica Scientia* (Ithaca, NY: Cornell University Press, 1992), 139–40.

53. See, for example, Kenneth Levy, "On the Origin of Neumes," *Early Music History* 7 (1987): 59–90; Leo Treitler, "The 'Unwritten' and 'Written Transmission' of Medieval Chant and the Start-Up of Musical Notation," *Journal of Musicology* 10, no. 2 (Spring 1992): 131–91; and Marie-Elisabeth Duchez, "Des neumes à la portée: Elaboration et organisation rationnelles de la discontinuité musicale et de sa représentation graphique, de la formule mélodique à l'échelle monocordale," *Canadian University Music Review* 4 (1983): 22–65.

54. Christoph Friedrich Hellwag, *Dissertatio de formatione loquelae* (Heilbronn: Gebr. Henninger, [1781] 1886), 45–53.

55. Ibid., 45–46.

56. Heinrich Gustav Flörke, "Tonleiter der Vokale," *Neue Berlinische Monatschrift* 10 (September 1803): 161–84; see also Flörke, "Nachtrag zu dem Aufsatze: Die Tonleiter der Vokale," *Neue Berlinische Monatschrift* 10 (February 1803): 343–71.

57. Flörke, "Nachtrag," 371.

58. Ibid., 349.

59. Flörke, "Tonleiter," 185.

60. Willis, "Vowel Sounds," 247. Kratzenstein's talking machine, capable of producing all the human vowels, came to light upon winning the annual prize contest held by the Imperial Academy of St. Petersburg in 1779. The challenge questions,

presumably traceable to those proposed by Leonhard Euler in his studies of sound there thirty years prior, were: "First, What is the nature and character of the sounds of the vowels A E I O U, so different from each other?" and "Secondly, Can an instrument be constructed like the *vox humane* pipes of the organ, which shall accurately express the sounds of the vowels?" C. G. Kratzenstein, *Testamen Coronatum de Voce* (St. Petersburg: Imperial Academy, 1780); see also Charles Wheatstone, "Reed Organ-Pipes, Speaking Machines, etc.," *London and Westminster Review* 27 (October 1837): 16. Wolfgang von Kempelen's lively defense of his talking machine gives reason to believe that the absence of such ingenious inventions before the late eighteenth century may have been due, at least in part, to religious scruple. The Hungarian scientist goes to great lengths to reconcile the possibility of artificial speech with John I.1–5 of the Christian Bible; Kempelen, *Mechanismus der menschlichen Sprache* (Wien: J. B. Degen, 1791), 50–56.

61. Willis, "Vowel Sounds," 240.

62. Ibid.

63. Willis notes one exception to this—namely, "When the pitch of the reed is high, some of the vowels [U] become impossible"; ibid.

64. Ibid., 247–48. This excerpt, like many from Willis's essay, suggests a certain anxiety on the part of the author in distinguishing between human and nonhuman sounds. Kempelen's anxiety over the potentially blasphemous nature of speaking machines, in other words, seems to be present in Willis's text as well, albeit more subtly. One wonders whether the essay that lay the foundation for the modern study of vowels might not have been motivated by a desire to articulate the distinction between human speech and the sounds articulable by organ pipes. The likeness between the human speech apparatus and reeds and flues of organs had been long noted, as the upper and lower "lips" of the flue, and "tongue" of the reed attest, but the implications of this correlation had come under newly intense scrutiny in the early nineteenth century. Just three years before Willis delivered his paper (in November of 1828), the French surgeon Félix Savart had advanced an elaborate comparison of the human voice, organ sounds, and birdsong that caused considerable controversy close to Willis's Cambridge circles; Savart, "Nouvelles recherches sur les vibrations de l'air," *Annales de chimie* 29 (August 1825): 404–26; "Mémoire sur la voix humaine," *Annales de chimie* 30 (September 1825): 64–87; "Mémoire sur la voix des oiseaux," *Annales de chimie* 32 (May–June 1826): 5–24.

65. Kempelen, *Mechanismus*, 196; see also Table X, figure 3 in the appendix. In Kempelen's usage, the term "vowels" (*Selbstlaute*) refers to all elements of speech whose production does not require the presence of another sound; i.e., /a/, /m/, and /l/ are all *Selbstlaute*, /b/ and /k/ are not.

66. Willis, "Vowel Sounds," 248.

67. Ibid., 244 and 247.

68. Ibid., 247.

69. Ibid., 248.

70. "[. . .] vowels, it must be considered, are not definite sounds, like the different harmonics of a note, but on the contrary glide into each other by almost imperceptible gradations, so that it becomes extremely difficult to find the exact length of pipe belonging to each, confused as we are by the difference of quality between the artificial and natural vowels"; ibid., 243. Willis also observes that "the difference between the vowels, depends entirely upon contrast, [. . .] they are therefore best distinguished by quick transitions from one to the other, and by not dwelling for any length of time

upon any one of them. A simple trial will convince any person, that even in the human voice, if any given vowel be prolonged by singing, it soon becomes impossible to distinguish what vowel it is"; ibid., 234.

71. Helmholtz, *Tonempfindungen*, 174/107. Helmholtz may well have gleaned this idea from Flörke, who observes that some vowels seem to possess two tones, corresponding to the smaller and larger cavities of the mouth; Flörke, "Tonleiter," 179.

72. The higher proper tones of Ä, E, and I, a subject of much contention, elude even Helmholtz's bottle-shaped resonators, and had escaped his—though not his critics'—notice in his 1859 paper. At the cost of "much trouble," however, Helmholtz is able to observe them in women's voices singing high notes and men's falsettos and offers the pitches thus discerned; Helmholtz, *Tonempfindungen*, 179/111.

73. Ibid., 178/110.

74. Ibid., 105, 176/61, 108.

75. The "secondary pulse" of Willis's account remains vague in his text; it would appear to correspond to the first overtone in the harmonic series, but as it moves while the reed's pitch remains constant, it cannot stand in a fixed relation to the prime tone as the overtones do; see Helmholtz, *Tonempfindungen*, 179–80/117–18.

76. Ibid., 171/104.

77. Ibid., 182–83/113.

78. Ibid., 183–84/113.

79. Ibid., 184/113.

80. Ibid., 184/113–14.

81. Ibid., 184/114.

82. Willis, "Vowel Sounds," 247.

83. Ibid., 234.

84. Noam Chomsky, "Preface to the Third Edition," in *Language and Mind* (Cambridge: Cambridge University Press, 2006), x.

85. Helmholtz, *Tonempfindungen*, 13–14/7–8.

86. Ibid., 20/10. Helmholtz specifies his meaning very clearly at the outset of the *Sensations of Tone*—a work that goes to great pains to be accessible to a broad audience—but he provides no such clarification in his 1859 essay "On the Vowel Sounds (*Ueber die Klangfarbe der Vocale*)," where he uses the term fluently. This suggests he assumed his scientific colleagues to be able to understand the term intuitively, even if none of them had used it.

87. Helmholtz, "Physiological Causes," 83/93–94. Note that although *Klangfarbe* is ostensibly an aspect of sound proper only to "musical sounds" (*Klänge*), in Helmholtz's usage here it extends well beyond the confines of music (to a dog's howl).

88. The "colors of vowels" thus partakes of a discourse nearly homonymous with yet appreciably distinct from one that may equate "the colors of voices" with the metonymic "colors" (races) of the bodies that produce them. For the second, see Nina Sun Eidsheim, *The Race of Sound: Listening, Timbre and Vocality in African American Music* (Durham, NC: Duke University Press, 2019).

89. Emily I. Dolan, *Orchestral Revolution: Haydn and the Technologies of Timbre* (Cambridge: Cambridge University Press, 2013), 23–52, esp. 47–52.

90. Ibid., 51–52.

91. The compound neologism *Klangfarbe* first appeared in print in 1834, making its way into specialized lexica of 1835 and 1838 as a possible translation of the French "timbre"; Daniel Muzzulini, "Timbre vs Klangfarbe," *Musiktheorie* 16, no. 1 (2001):

81–82. The definitions implied or offered by these texts place the term in the general semantic area of Helmholtz's definition, but they are only very approximately congruent. Emily Dolan may well be correct in observing that "While the word *Klangfarbe* only entered regular use in the middle of the nineteenth century, the concept was in place fifty years earlier," but the "concept" she identifies with *Klangfarbe* (associating colors with particular instrumental timbres) is not quite commensurate with the one advanced by Helmholtz, as evidenced by the *Klangfarbe* of vowels; Dolan, *Orchestral Revolution*, 48.

92. Dieter Ullmann, "Ohm-Seebeck-Helmholtz und das Klangfarbenproblem," *NTM-Schriftenr. Gesch. Naturwiss., Techn., Med.* 25 (1988): 65–68.

93. Willis, "Vowel Sounds," 234. Willis's explicit definition indicates the nebulousness of the existing English-language discourse on the topic, which Helmholtz's translator, Alexander Ellis, would bemoan half a century later. According to Ellis, the most evident and "time-honoured expression" in English before his 1875 translation of Helmholtz's "*Klangfarbe*" is "quality of tone," though his lively rejections of the terms "clangtint," "register," "colour," and "timbre" suggest that even by 1875 this claim was not uncontested; Ellis, *Sensations*, 24.

94. Willis, *Ueber Vocaltöne und Zungenpfeifen, Annalen der Physik und Chemie* 24, no. 3 (1832): 401.

95. F. C. Donders, "Ueber die Natur der Vocale," *Archiv für die Holländischen Beiträge für Natur- und Heilkunde* 1 (1857): 157–62. It may be that the foreign origin of *timbre* made it less palatable in Helmholtz's immediate milieu than in Donders'; in any case, Donders adopted the new term after the publication of the *Tonempfindungen* in 1863; F. C. Donders, "Zur Klangfarbe der Vocale," *Annalen der Physik und Chemie* 123 (1864): 527–28.

96. In 1802, the pioneering acoustician Ernst Theodor Chladni noted "the manifold modifications and articulations of a noise or a sound, which are called 'timbre' in French" but have no name in German; Ernst Theodor Chladni, *Die Akustik* (Leipzig: Breitkopf und Härtel, 1802); cit. Muzzulini, "Timbre vs Klangfarbe," 81. Returning to the problem again in 1827, Chladni proposed the term *Laut* as a possible translation; Ernst Theodor Chladni, *Kurze Uebersicht der Schall- une Klanglehre, nebst einem Anhange, die Entwickelung und Anordnung der Tonverhältnisse betreffend* (Mainz: Schott's Söhne, 1827); cit. Muzzulini, "Timbre vs Klangfarbe," 81.

97. First attested in French c1170 in Chrétien de Troyes' *Erec et Enide*, *timbre* derives from the Latin *tympănum* ("timbre," *Trésor de la langue française*). For the classic text on the term's many resonances, see Jacques Derrida's "tympan" in *Marges de la philosophie* (Paris: Éditions de minuit, 1972), 1–25; for its particular status in the late nineteenth century, see Katherine Bergeron, "A Bugle, a Bell, a Stroke of the Tongue: Rethinking Music in Modern French Verse," *Representations* 86 (Spring 2004): 53–72.

98. "TIMBRE. On appelle ainsi, par métaphore, cette qualité du son par laquelle il est aigre ou doux, sourd ou éclatant, sec ou moelleux. Les sons doux ont ordinairement peu d'éclat, comme ceux de la flûte et du luth; les sons éclatans sont sujets à l'aigreur comme celle de la vielle ou du hautbois: il y a même des instrumens, tels que le clavecin, qui sont à la fois sourds et aigres; et c'est le plus mauvais *timbre*: le plus beau *timbre* est celui qui réunit la douceur à l'éclat; tel est le *timbre* du violon"; Jean-Jacques Rousseau, *Dictionnaire de musique*, rpt. in *Œuvres complètes de J. J. Rousseau*, Vol. 7 (Paris: Hachette, [1767] 1906), 324.

99. Jean-Jacques Rousseau, "Son," in D. Diderot and J. d'Alembert (eds.), *Encyclopédie: ou Dictionnaire raisonné des sciences, des arts et des métiers* (Paris, 1751–72), Vol. 15, 345; translated by Dolan, *Orchestral Revolution*, 55.

100. "Timbre," *Trésor de la langue française*, accessed December 15, 2022, http://www.le-tresor-de-la-langue.fr.

101. Helmholtz, *Handbuch der physiologischen Optik* (Leipzig: Leopold Voss, 1867); English ed. James P. C. Southall, *Treatise on Physiological Optics*, 3 vols. (Wisconsin: The Optical Society of America and George Banta Publishing, 1924). The German work first appeared in three separate volumes released in 1856, 1860, and 1866.

102. Helmholtz, *Tonempfindungen*, 244/148. Other examples include but are far from limited to Helmholtz, *Tonempfindungen* 94/54, 209/128, 281–84/169–70; Helmholtz, "Physiological Causes," 65/70 and 90/104–5; and Helmholtz, *Optik*, 236/II: 76–77.

103. Helmholtz, "Thatsachen in der Wahrnehmung," *Vorträge und Reden*, Vol. 2 (Brauschweig: Vieweg und Sohn, [1878] 1884), 224. Translated by Malcolm F. Lowe, "Facts in Perception," in *Epistemological Writings*, ed. Robert S. Cohen and Yehuda Elkana (Boston: D. Reidel, 1977), 120.

104. Helmholtz, "Thatsachen," 224/120.

105. Helmholtz, *Optik*, 236/II: 76.

106. The term "tone" appears in reference to visual sensations at least as early as Pliny the Elder's *Natural History* (c. 77–79 CE). Here it specifically designates brightness: "The gradation between lustre and light on the one hand and shade on the other, is called 'tonos'; while the blending of various colors, and their passing into one another, is designated 'harmŏgĕ' (*quod inter haec et umbras esset, appellarunt tonon, commissuras vero colorem et transitus harmogen*)"; Gaius Plinius Secundus, *Natural History* [*Naturalis Historia*, 77–79 AD] 35, no. 11, trans. John Bostock and H. T. Riley (London: Taylor and Francis, 1855); available online at perseus.tufts.edu/hopper/text?doc=urn:cts:latinLit:phi0978.phi001.perseus-eng1:35.11. In German, "Ton" appears in reference to visual sensation only in the first half of the eighteenth century, at which point it begins to mimic the metaphorical extensions of the French *ton*; "Ton," *Grimms Wörterbuch: T* (Leipzig: S. Hirzel, [1913] 1935), 749.

107. Helmholtz, *Optik*, 237/v. 2, 77.

108. Ibid., 237/v. 2, 77.

109. Ibid., 270/v. 2, 118.

110. Helmholtz, "Physiological Causes," 90–91/105–6.

111. Helmholtz, "Preface to the Third German Edition," vii/vii.

112. Carl Stumpf, "Hermann von Helmholtz and the New Psychology," trans. John Grier Hibben, *Psychological Review* 2, no. 1 (1895): 10. The similar, but distinct, division of musical knowledge into "the science of sounding bodies (later known as acoustics)" and "the art of music" dates from the Renaissance; see Ann Moyer, *Musica scientia* (Ithaca, NY: Cornell University Press), 3.

113. For a stimulating study of this threshold in the early twentieth century and its stakes in the twenty-first, see Ana Hedberg Olenina, *Psychomotor Aesthetics: Movement and Affect in Modern Literature and Film* (New York: Oxford University Press, 2020), esp. 315–18.

114. Wallace Stevens, "The Idea of Order at Key West" (1934), in *Collected Poems* (New York: Knopf, 1955), 129.

2 / The Interaction of Color

1. Joseph Albers, "A color has many faces— the relativity of color," in *Interaction of Color* (New Haven, CT: Yale University Press, 2009), 11.
2. Emily I. Dolan, *The Orchestral Revolution: Haydn and the Technologies of Timbre* (Cambridge: Cambridge University Press, 2013), 53–54.
3. Julia Kursell, "Experiments on Tone Color in Music and Acoustics: Helmholtz, Schoenberg, and *Klangfarbenmelodie*," *Osiris* 28, no. 1 (January 2013): 192.
4. Robert Willis, "On the Vowel Sounds, and on Reed Organ-Pipes," *Transactions of the Cambridge Philosophical Society* 3 (1830): 234.
5. Théodore Flournoy, *Des Phénomènes de synopsie* (Paris: Alcan and Geneva: Eggiman, 1893), 2.
6. Flournoy, *Phénomènes*, 46.
7. Ibid., 9.
8. "L'audition colorée et les phénomènes similaires (Report by Professor Ed. Gruber and remarks by Mr. F. Galton," *Second Session of the International Congress of Experimental Psychology—London, 1892* (London: Williams and Norgate, 1892), 10; see also the English-language review article by F. B. D., "L'audition Colorée et les Phénomènes Similaires. Communications de Mm. Francis Galton et Edouard Grüber," *American Journal of Psychology* 6, no. 2 (January 1894): 305.
9. *Second Session*, 12. For more on Gruber, see "Colored Hearing and Similar Phenomena" in Chapter 4, "The Colors of the Universal Alphabet."
10. Francis Galton, *Inquiries into Human Faculty and Its Development* (London: J. M. Dent [1883] 1907), 110–11. For more on Galton and Key, see "Colored Hearing and Similar Phenomena" and "Distinctive Phonic Properties" in Chapter 4, "The Colors of the Universal Alphabet."
11. Galton, *Inquiries*, 110.
12. Ibid., 111.
13. Flournoy, *Phénomènes*, 95.
14. Galton, *Inquiries*, 110–11.
15. Jörg Jewanski, "Synesthesia in the Nineteenth Century: Scientific Origins," in *Oxford Handbook of Synesthesia*, ed. Julia Simner and Edward M. Hubbard (Oxford: Oxford University Press, 2013), 389–90.
16. Jamie Ward and Julia Simner, "Synesthesia: The Current State of the Field," in *Multisensory Perception*, ed. K. Sathian and V. S. Ramachandran (Cambridge, MA: Academic Press, 2020), 283–300.
17. See Jörg Jewanski, Julia Simner, Sean A. Day, Nicolas Rothen, and Jamie Ward, "The Evolution of the Concept of Synesthesia in the Nineteenth Century as Revealed Through the History of Its Name," *Journal of the History of the Neurosciences* 29, no. 3 (2020): 259–85.
18. Flournoy, *Phénomènes*, 95.
19. The role of the word-initial letter in determining synesthetic effects is identified as a general rule at least as early 1892; William O. Krohn, "Pseudo-Chromesthesia, of the Association of Color with Words, Letters, and Sounds," *American Journal of Psychology* 5, no. 1 (October 1892): 32. It remains an active area of research in something of an exception to the general absence of studies of interaction noted. See especially Julia Simner, "Beyond Perception: Synesthesia as a Psycholinguistic Phenomenon," *Trends in Cognitive Science* 11 (2007): 23–29; Julia Simner, Louise Glover, and Alice Mowat,

"Linguistic Determinants of Word Colouring in Grapheme-Colour Synaesthesia," *Cortex* 42, no. 2 (February 2006): 281–89; and Wan-Yu Hung, "Synesthesia in Non-Alphabetic Languages," in *Oxford Handbook of Synesthesia*, ed. Edward Hubbard and Julia Simner (Oxford: Oxford University Press, 2013), 212–21.

20. Flournoy, *Phénomènes*, 95.

21. The example is Théodore de Banville's, drawn from Victor Hugo; Théodore de Banville, *Petit traité de poésie française* (Paris: Éditions d'aujourd'hui, [1872] 1978), 50.

22. Banville, *Petit traité*, 44.

23. Louis Becq de Fouquières, *Traité général de versification française* (Paris: G. Charpentier, 1879), 223.

24. Letter to Coppée (December 5, 1866); Stéphane Mallarmé, *Œuvres complètes de Stéphane Mallarmé I*, ed. Bertrand Marchal (Paris: Gallimard, 1998), 709. Henceforth *ŒC I*.

25. Mallarmé also evokes the color of words in *Les Mots anglais*, where, in discussing Italian loan words that came into English by way of French, he notes that the English tend to "restore the original color to the words (*rendre aux mots leur couleur originelle*)"; Stéphane Mallarmé, *Œuvres complètes de Stéphane Mallarmé II*, ed. Bertrand Marchal (Paris: Gallimard, 2003), 1082. Henceforth *ŒC II*. The examples offered make it clear that by color, Mallarmé means vowels, as the consonantal structures of the words remain more or less consistent.

26. Mallarmé, "Crise de vers," *ŒC II*, 211.

27. Quoted from the 1923 reprinting of the 1895 text; Stéphane Mallarmé, "Préface," *Sang des crépuscules* par Charles Guérin, rpt. in *Premiers et derniers vers* (Paris: Mercure de France, 1923), 87. *ŒC II* has "son feu plus nu presque plus précieux que la rime (its barer light amost more precious than rhyme)," which seems slightly dubious; "Préface au *Sang des crépuscules* de Charles Guérin," Mallarmé, *ŒC II*, 679.

28. Banville, *Petit traité*, 42–43.

29. Banville's poetic legacy has been overwhelmingly reduced to these provocative proclamations on rhyme, as David Evans has demonstrated; David Evans, *Théodore de Banville: Constructing Poetic Value in Nineteenth-Century France* (Oxford: Legenda, 2014). Writing against the entire reception history of the *Petit traité* (which he meticulously assembles), Evans reads Banville's declarations on rhyme as comically disingenuous (see particularly his "Introduction," 1–28 and "The Music and the Mechanism: Theorizing the Unanalysable," 29–86). Evans is certainly right to bring out the contradictions between Banville's proclamations and his poetic practice. However, his unequivocal conclusion that Banville's precepts on rhyme are pure parody seems difficult to square with the fact that Banville's peers (Mallarmé amongst them) took them quite seriously. Banville's bombastic text would seem, paradoxically, to be more ambiguous than either Evans or the dismissive critical tradition would have it.

30. Flournoy, *Phénomènes*, 95.

31. Daniel Heller-Roazen, "Arismétriques: De la musique aux arts rhythmiques," in *Sens, Rhétorique et Musique: Études réunies en hommage à Jacqueline Cerquiglini-Toulet*, ed. Sophie Albert, Mireille Demaules, Estelle Doudet, Sylvie Lefèvre, Christopher Lucken, and Agathe Sultan (Paris: Champion, 2015), 275–88.

32. Milner's argument is based on the behavior of the *e muet* within the body of the line and at the end of the line; Jean-Claude Milner, "Réflexions sur le fonctionnement du vers français," in *Ordres et raisons de langue* (Paris: Seuil, 1978), 283–301.

33. Mallarmé, "Crise de vers," *ŒC II*, 213.

34. For example, Gérard Genette, "Le jour, la nuit," *Cahiers de l'Association internationale des études françaises* 20 (1968): 160; Roman Jakobson, "Linguistics and Poetics," in *Selected Writings III*, ed. Stephen Rudy (The Hague: Mouton, 1981), 44–45.

35. Susan Harrow, "Colour Concept and Practice: Mallarmé's Monochromes," in *Colourworks: Chromatic Innovation in Modern French Poetry and Art Writing* (New York: Bloomsbury, 2021), 13–66.

36. J. Duchesne-Guillemin, "Encore le divin Cygne," *Empreintes* 5 (1948): 46; Émilie Noulet, *Vingt poèmes de Stéphane Mallarmé* (Paris: Minard and Geneva: Droz, 1967), 143. Thibaudet offers the variant "harmonie en blanc majeur"; Albert Thibaudet, *La poésie de Stéphane Mallarmé* (Paris: Gallimard, [1911] 1926), 250. The three Whistler paintings were completed between 1861 and 1865.

37. Mallarmé, *ŒC II*, 36–37.

38. Translated by Peter Manson, *Stéphane Mallarmé: The Poems in Verse* (Oxford, OH: Miami University Press, 2012), 161. Translation modified.

39. For "stupefying," see Paul Bénichou, *Selon Mallarmé* (Paris: Gallimard, 1995), 246.

40. Duchesne-Guillemin, "Encore le divin Cygne," 46; Noulet, *Vingt poèmes*, 143; Guy Michaud, *Mallarmé* (Paris: Hatier, 1971), 132; Marchal, *ŒC I*, 1186.

41. Duchesne-Guillemin, "Encore le divin Cygne," 46.

42. Henri Morier, *Dictionnaire de poétique et de rhétorique* (Paris: Presses universitaires de France, 1998), 329.

43. Mallarmé, "Crise de vers," *ŒC II*, 208. See Chapter 3, "Mallarmé and the Tension of Timbre."

44. Genette, "Le jour, la nuit," 158.

45. Genette seems at pains to evoke the idea of a natural synesthetic connection without subscribing to it himself: "Cette remarque de Mallarmé se fonde sur une des données, disons les moins fréquemment contestées, de l'expressivité phonique, à savoir qu'une voyelle dite aïgue, comme le /y/ semi-consonne et le /i/ de nuit, peut évoquer, par une synesthésie naturelle, une couleur claire ou une impression lumineuse"; ibid., 158.

46. Victor Hugo, *La Légende des siècles*, ed. Jacques Truchet (Paris: Gallimard, 1950), 857; cit. Paul Valéry, *Cahiers*, Vol. 25 (Paris: Centre national de la recherche scientifique, 1957), 517. See also Suzanne Nash, "Other Voices: Intertextuality and the Art of Pure Poetry," in *Reading Paul Valéry* (Cambridge: Cambridge University Press, 1998), 187–99.

47. Valéry, *Cahiers*, 517.

48. The article preceding "voit" is difficult to decipher; I quote after the transcription provided by the BN. See also Stéphanie Boulard, "Hugo/Rimbaud: Voyelles," *Parade sauvage* 31(2020): 189–214; Stéphanie Boulard and Pierre Georgel, *Hugographies*; Jean Maurel, "L'alphabet analphabète ou Victor Hugo de A à Z (idéologie et idéographie)," *La nouvelle critique* (1971): 101–10; Meschonnic, "Ce que Hugo dit de la langue," 57–73; and Gérard Genette, "Mimophonie restreinte," *Mimologiques* (Paris: Seuil, 1976), 395–428, esp. 398–403.

49. There is little consensus on the dating. The Bibliothèque nationale de France has the fragment "daté des années 1836–1838 par Cécile Daubray," Stéphanie Boulard places it "10 ans avant Rimbaud" (so presumably 1862 or so), and Henri Meschonnic suggests 1846–47; Victor Hugo, "Note sur la couleur des voyelles," *Océan prose. Tas de pierres*,

Bibliothèque nationale de France, Manuscrit autographe NAF 13423, fol. 81; Stéphanie Boulard and Pierre Georgel, *Hugographies: Rêveries de Victor Hugo sur les lettres de l'alphabet* (Paris: Hermann, 2022), 65; Henri Meschonnic, "Ce que Hugo dit de la langue," *Romantisme* 25, no. 6 (1979): 68.

50. Tristan Corbière, "Le poète contumace," in *Les amours jaunes* (Paris: Vanier, 1891), 71.

51. Mallarmé, "Crise de vers," *ŒC II*, 206.

52. Paul Verlaine, "Un mot sur la rime" (March 1888), in *Oeuvres en prose complètes*, ed. Jacques Borel (Paris: Gallimard, 1972), 697. Richard Wagner makes precisely the same argument in *Oper und Drama* (1851), pointing out that "Where, as among the Romanic peoples, a *Rhythmik* based on prosodic longs and shorts has never been attempted in spoken verse, and the verse-line therefore has only been governed by the number of syllables, *end-rhyme* has been set fast as an indispensable condition of the verse's very existence. [. . . without a musical setting, this verse] would have been wholly unrecognizable as Verse, without its end-rhyme" (*Da, wo eine auf prosodische Längen und Kürzen zu begründende Rhythmik im Sprachverse nie versucht wurde, wie bei den romanischen Völkern, und wo die Verszeile daher nur nach der Zahl der Sylben bestimmt ward, hat sich der Endreim also unerläßliche Bedingung für den Vers überhaupt festgesetzt [. . .] Der von dieser Melodie durch den weltlichen Dichter endlich losgetrennte Wortvers wäre ohne Endreim als Vers völlig unkenntlich gewesen*)"; Richard Wagner, *Gesammelte Schriften und Dichtungen*, Vol. 4 (Leipzig: Fritzsch, 1872), 137; Richard Wagner, *Opera and Drama*, trans. William Ashton Ellis (Lincoln: University of Nebraska Press, 1995), 244–45.

53. Eric Weiskott, *Meter and Modernity in English Verse, 1350–1650* (Philadelphia: University of Pennsylvania Press, 2021), 113. Weiskott does not hazard a first meaning of "blank," but he does hypothesize that the "blank" of "blank verse" might form a pun with OED definition 2a of "blank, *n*": "The white spot in the centre of a target" (113, 242). In other words: blank verse is the verse at which critics take aim. Alternatively, 'Blank' could be associated with liberation, following the sixteenth-century British idea that "the troublesome and modern bondage of Rimeing" should be cast off, and "ancient liberty recover'd," as Milton famously put it in his note on "The Verse" of *Paradise Lost* (1667); cit. O. B. Hardison Jr., *Prosody and Purpose in the English Renaissance* (Baltimore: Johns Hopkins University Press, 1989), 267. In any case, it is clear that the expression distinguishes English unrhymed verse from the unrhymed *verso sciolto* ("open" or "untied" verse) of the Italian tradition; O. B. Hardison Jr., "Blank Verse Before Milton," *Studies in Philology* 81, no. 3 (Summer 1984): 253–74.

54. Derek Attridge, *Well-Weighted Syllables: Elizabethan verse in classical metres* (Cambridge: Cambridge University Press, 1974), 95.

3 / Mallarmé and the Tension of Timbre

1. Stéphane Mallarmé, "Crise de vers," in *Oeuvres complètes de Stéphane Mallarmé II*, ed. Bertrand Marchal (Paris: Gallimard, 2003), 211. Henceforth *ŒC II*. Translations are adapted from Barbara Johnson, *Divagations* (Cambridge, MA: Harvard University Press, 2007).

2. Mallarmé, "La musique et les lettres," in *ŒC II*, 64. An earlier version of this chapter appeared in "Mallarmé and the Tension of Timbre," *Hyperion: On the Future of Aesthetics* 9, no. 3 (2015): 111–39; a continuation of its line of inquiry has been published

in Thomas C. Connolly and Liesl Yamaguchi, "Incipit: On Poetry and Crisis," *Nineteenth-Century French Studies* 50, nos. 1–2 (Fall–Winter 2021–22): 1–49.

3. Ibid.

4. I am aware of four challenges to this definition. In his 1974 essay "Réflexions sur le fonctionnement du vers français," Jean-Claude Milner argues that "une séquence poétique n'est pas seulement un *mètre*, composé de parties distinguées, mais aussi *un vers*, c'est à dire un certain espace à l'intérieur duquel des processus spécifiques peuvent être définis et dont les bornes extérieures possèdent des propriétés caractéristiques"; Milner, *Ordres et raisons de langue* (Paris: Seuil, 1978), 285. Hence Milner's argument that the line, or rather the phonological break that the end of the line instantiates in language, be considered the defining feature of verse. For Milner, what distinguishes verse from non-verse is not meter, but the possibility of enjambment, itself defined as the possibility of noncoincidence between verse-limit and syntactic limit (Milner, "Vers français," 300–301). The second challenge, inspired by the first, is advanced by Giorgio Agamben in the titular essay of his 1985 *Idea della prosa* (Macerata: Quodlibet, 2020), translated by Michael Sullivan and Sam Whitsitt as *The Idea of Prose* (NY: SUNY Press, 1995); and his 1996 essay "La fine del poema," in *Categorie italiane: Studi di poetica e di letteratura* (Rome: Laterza, 2010), 138–44, translated by Daniel Heller-Roazen as "The End of the Poem" in *The End of the Poem: Studies in Poetics* (Stanford: Stanford University Press, 1999), 109–15. Following Milner, Agamben defines poetry by the possibility of enjambment, but Agamben's "enjambment" is glossed variously as the noncoincidence of "metrical limit" and "syntactic limit" ("Idea of Prose," 39), and even as "the opposition of [. . .] a prosodic pause to a semantic pause" ("The End of the Poem," 109). Thus for Agamben, though not for Milner, metrical breaks not coincident with the end of the line (i.e., the caesura) would seem to provide sufficient grounds for poetry. The third position, also presented somewhat dubiously as "proche de celle de Jean-Claude Milner," is that of Michel Murat, who, in *Le vers libre* (Paris: Champion, 2008), maintains that free verse (verse without meter) continues to constitute "verse." Murat defines this verse as "produit par une segmentation spécifique du discours [. . .] marquée par une convention typographique qui est le passage à la ligne" (35), stressing that this "typographic convention" is not constitutive of free verse, but a conventional marker of a preexisting segmentation ("on ne peut définir le vers par la ligne," 36). To his credit, Murat acknowledges that his definition rests on "une sorte de tautologie, que le vers libre est un vers, une unité *sui generis*" (37). A fourth position is carved out by Nigel Fabb and Morris Halle, who insist on "a well-founded distinction between texts divided into lines and texts not divided into lines" and "reserve the term 'poetry' to name the former type"; Nigel Fabb and Morris Halle, *Meter in Poetry: A New Theory* (Cambridge: Cambridge University Press, 2008), 1. This would seem to make poetry coextensive with verse, as Fabb and Halle explicitly gloss "lines" as "verses": "What distinguishes all poetry from prose is that poetry is made up of lines (verses)"; Fabb and Halle, *Meter in Poetry*, 1. In their terminology, however, these lines, or verses, are not defined exclusively by meter. The authors recognize a category of "nonmetrical poetry" created through syntactic parallelism (as in the Hebrew Bible, "where corrresponding lines must be composed of syntactic constituents of the same kind") or crafted by means of varying, original types of parallelism (as in free verse, which "does not rest on a generally agreed upon set of principles and units; rather each poem – and often also each line in the poem – is based on principles and units of its own, and the poem achieves its esthetic impact by asking the reader or listener to discover the units and

principles that give shape to the line. The one aspect that Free Verse shares with other kinds of poetry is lineation: even the most experimental kind of Free Verse is composed of lines"); Fabb and Halle, *Meter in Poetry*, 1–3.

5. Mallarmé, "Solennité," in *ŒC II*, 201.

6. Ibid.

7. "CADENCE. 1. Appui de la voix sur les syllabes accentuées, marquant la répartition rythmique des éléments d'une phrase; [. . .] 2. Succession d'accords selon certaines règles harmoniques, terminant une phrase musicale" (*Trésor de la langue française*).

8. Jean-Claude Milner, *Profils perdus de Stéphane Mallarmé: Court traité de lecture 2* (Paris: Verdier, 2019), 29–30.

9. Mallarmé, "La musique et les lettres," in *ŒC II*, 64.

10. Mallarmé, *Vers et prose* (Paris: Perrin et Cie, 1893).

11. See Bertrand Marchal's commentary in the first volume of the *Oeuvres complètes de Stéphane Mallarmé I*, ed. Bertrand Marchal (Paris: Gallimard, 1999), 1177. Henceforth *ŒC I*.

12. The text, an amalgamation of several previous essays, was published in its definitive form in *Divagations* (Paris: Charpentier, 1897).

13. "crise" (*Trésor de la langue française*); "κρίσις" (Liddell and Scott, *A Greek-English Lexicon*); "crisis" (*Oxford English Dictionary*).

14. "crise" (*Trésor de la langue française*).

15. Mallarmé, "La musique et les lettres," in *ŒC II*, 64.

16. Mallarmé, "Solennité," in *ŒC II*, 201.

17. Mallarmé, "Crise de vers," in *ŒC II*, 206.

18. The paragraph first appears in "Averses ou critique" in *La Revue blanche* (Mallarmé, *ŒC II*, 1643).

19. Mallarmé, "Crise de vers," in *ŒC II*, 208.

20. While *jour* means "day" and *nuit* "night," a slight slippage in translation is worth noting. Unlike its English counterpart, the French word *jour* may sometimes be used synonymously with *lumière* (light). In French, one can *laisser entrer le jour dans une pièce*, but in English, one cannot "let the day into a room"; one can only "let the light in." Thus, the opposition between *jour* and the "dark" timbre Mallarmé attributes to it is more symmetrical in French than in English. In his reflections on the two terms, Gérard Genette suggests that the same may be said of *nuit* in relation to *obscurité* (darkness), though only by way of metaphor; he offers the example of *la nuit du tombeau* ("the darkness of the tomb"). The expression, Genette explains, does not indicate that the tomb is devoid of light, nor that it somehow possesses "night-time"; instead, it makes use of the literary metaphor by which darkness is equated with death; hence "the death of the tomb"; Gérard Genette, "Le jour, la nuit," *Cahiers de l'Association internationale des études françaises* 20 (1968): 155. The necessity of passing by way of "darkness" here seems dubious; it would seem that the passage from *la nuit du tombeau* to *la mort du tombeau* could be made more convincingly by way of the analogy between the cycle of the day and the life of a human.

21. Mallarmé's scale of brightness appears to be universal rather than language-specific, as the scale implied here is consistent with the one implied in his English pedagogical manual *Les Thèmes anglais* (1879). Describing the vocalic shift involved in the creation of certain English plurals (*tooth/teeth, goose/geese, louse/lice, mouse/mice*), Mallarmé identifies an "éclaircissement du son" (brightening of sound) in the transformation of *tooth* to *teeth* (/u:/ —> /i:/)—which may also be glimpsed, despite

the diphthong, in the juxtaposition of *jour* and *nuit* (/u/ —> /ɥi/); Mallarmé, "Thèmes anglais," in *ŒC II*, 1154–55. The originality of the expression "éclaircissement de son" is attested by the bewilderment it provoked: commenting on this precise locution, lycée instructor Paul-Gabriel Laserstein protests, "C'est du mallarméen pur. Les enfants ne comprendront pas et les termes sont même pas d'ordre philologique"; Laserstein, "Stéphane Mallarmé: Professeur d'anglais," *Les langues modernes* 43 (1949): 35. That the /iː/ and /aɪ/ of *geese* and *mice* are deemed "brighter" than the /uː/ and /aʊ/ of *goose* and *mouse* also suggests a correlation between Mallarmé's conception of vocalic brightness and a vowel's primary place of resonance in the mouth (anterior/posterior), a correlation that his French examples confirm. The "dark" /u/ and "opaque" /ɔ̃/ are vowels that resonate predominantly in the back of the mouth; the comparatively "less dark" /ɛ/ and /e/ and the "light" /i/ resonate through cavities progressively closer to the front. Jacques Rancière is certainly right to distinguish Mallarmé's poetic project from the highly programmatic one René Ghil elaborated in his *Traité du Verbe* ("affectant des timbres et des couleurs des voyelles"), but there is an undeniable affinity between Mallarmé's notion of vowels' shading and coloring and Ghil's conviction in vowel-color correspondence; Jacques Rancière, "L'intrus. La politique de Mallarmé," in *La politique de la littérature* (Paris: Galilée, 1997), 94–95; Ghil, *Traité du Verbe* (Paris: Giraud, 1886).

22. See Milner, *Profils perdus*, 23. Milner's is a critique of the structuralist tendency to read Mallarmé's *hasard* as synonymous with a Saussurean *arbitraire du signe* (see, for example, Genette, "Le jour, la nuit," 158).

23. Mallarmé, *Les Mots anglais*, in *ŒC II*, 967.

24. Ibid., 967–68. The noncorrespondence between Mallarmé's conception of language and that advanced by the *Cours de linguistique générale* is further illustrated in the oft-cited, antepenultimate passage of "Crise de vers" ("Je dis: une fleur!"). Here, the single entity negatively designated as "something other than known calyxes (*quelque chose d'autre que les calices sus*" and "the one absent from all bouquets (*l'absente de tous bouquets*)" is "mellifluous (*suave*)" and "arises "musically (*musicalement*)" but is denoted as "the idea itself (*idée même*)." What is gestured toward here is therefore not reducible to the signifier alone (because it includes "the idea itself"), nor to the signified (because it is "mellifluous" and "musical"—terms that could not be applied to the signified content of flower/*fleur*). What Mallarmé is getting at here more closely approximates the *CLG*'s "sign" (the combination of signifier and signified).

25. Largely, though not exclusively responsible for this critical legacy is the quotation of the passage in "The Task of the Translator (*Die Aufgabe des Übersetzers*)" (1923), Walter Benjamin's foreword to his translation of Charles Baudelaire's *Tableaux Parisiens* (Frankfurt am Main: Suhrkamp, 1963), 17–18.

26. Mallarmé, "Crise de vers," 208. C.f. Mallarmé's janus-faced "Hommage" to Wagner: "Le dieu Richard Wagner irradiant un sacre / Mal tu par l'encre même en sanglots sibyllins"; Mallarmé, "Hommage," in *ŒC I*, 40. This passage from "Crise de vers" reads as a direct response to Wagner's contention in his *Lettre sur la musique*—probably Mallarmé's only personal contact with Wagner's work (*ŒC II*, 1622)—that "Si, quant à la littérature, la diversité des langues européennes fait obstacle à cette universalité, la musique est une langue également intelligible à tous les hommes, et elle devait être la puissance conciliatrice, la langue souveraine, qui, résolvant les idées en sentiments, offrait un organe universel de ce que l'intuition de l'artiste a de plus intime"; Wagner, "Lettre sur la musique" (1860), in *Quatre poèmes d'opéras, traduits en prose française, précédés d'une lettre sur la musique* (Paris: Bourdilliat, 1861), XII.

27. See "The Tone of a Breath" in Chapter 1, "*Klangfarbe*: Vowels in Helmholtz's *Sensations of Tone*."

28. Maurice Blanchot disagrees on this point. In his reading, the supreme language Mallarmé describes would be one in which language coincides with "la réalité des choses": a reality inaccessible to language because language can only ever partake of "cette réalité fictive qu'est le monde humain"; Maurice Blanchot, *L'Espace littéraire* (Paris: Gallimard, 1955), 32. The textual basis for Blanchot's separation and implied hierarchy between "the reality of things" and "this fictive reality which is the human world" is not stated, and, indeed, dubious. Mallarmé would seem to be interested in "the reality of things" only insofar as that reality *is* mediated by humans: he writes, for example, that "Parler n'a trait à la réalité des choses que commercialement: en littérature, cela se contente d'y faire une allusion ou de distraire leur qualité qu'incorporera quelque idée"; Mallarmé, "Crise de vers," in *ŒC II*, 210.

29. Mallarmé, "Crise de vers," in *ŒC II* 211.

30. Ibid., 212.

31. Mallarmé, "Ballets," in *ŒC II*, 171.

32. See Milner, *Profils perdus*, 7–8.

33. Mallarmé, "Crise de vers," in *ŒC II*, 212. Mallarmé distinguishes "Music" with a capital M from "music" the art form; "Music" is synonymous with Chimera, Idea, "poem immanent to humanity," or what we have referred to as a "sign" of humanity; for an extended discussion, see Philippe Lacoue-Labarthe, *Musica Ficta: Figures de Wagner* (Paris: Christian Bourgois, 1991), 91–160. For more on the thresholds between instrument and voice, sound and music, music and speech, see the end of Chapter 1, "*Klangfarbe*: Vowels in Helmholtz's *Sensations of Tone*," as well as "*Gesamtkunstwerk*," in the Conclusion to this book.

34. Mallarmé, "Solennité," in *ŒC II*, 200.

35. Ibid.

36. Mallarmé, "Crise de vers," in *ŒC II*, 212.

37. Translated by Rosemary Lloyd in *Mallarmé: The Poet and His Circle* (Ithaca, NY: Cornell University Press, 1999), 230.

38. Translated by Johnson, *Divagations*, 205.

39. Mallarmé's expression closely resembles that of his self-declared disciple (and theorist of *vers libre*) Robert de Souza, whose article of January 1895 (nine months before the publication of "Averses ou critique") asserts that "lorsque nous parlons, nous nous efforçons de nous faire comprendre autant par le mouvement et par le ton de la parole que par le sens approprié des mots. De ce mouvement et de ce ton combinés naissent divers rythmes dont *l'allure et la couleur* commandent à leur tour la prononciation, ainsi pressée ou large, selon le cas"; Robert de Souza, "Le rôle de l'e muet dans la poésie française," *Mercure de France* 8 no. 61 (January 1895): 19 ; emphases mine.

40. "coloris," in *Dictionnaire historique de la langue française*, ed. Alain Rey (Paris: Le Robert, 1993), 450.

41. "coloris," in *Trésor de la langue française*, ed. Paul Imbs, Vol. 2 (Paris: CNRS, 1973), 1068.

42. Hippolyte Taine, *Philosophie de l'art*, Vol. 1 (Paris: G. Baillière, 1865), 2; G. Séailles, *Eugene Carrière, essai de biographie psychologique* (Paris: Armand Colin, 1911), 56; cit. *Trésor de la langue française*, 1068.

43. Mallarmé, "Berthe Morisot," in *ŒC II*, 149.

44. Translated by Johnson, *Divagations*, 205.

45. Translated by Lloyd, *Mallarmé*, 230.

46. "touches," *Trésor de la langue française*. Mallarmé uses the term frequently to signal some aspect of language other than sense, inhering in a unit smaller than a word. The term applies to English as well; in presenting English affixes in *Les Mots anglais*, Mallarmé suggests these elements be considered "rather like light touches (*touches*) applied to the word to brighten it up here or there"; Mallarmé, *Les Mots anglais*, in *ŒC II*, 964.

47. *Trésor de la langue française*, 1068.

48. See Katherine Bergeron, "L'art de dire: or Language in Performance," in *Voice Lessons: French Mélodie in the Belle Epoque* (Oxford: Oxford University Press, 2009), 183–254, esp. 192–95.

49. "La mélodie italienne d'opéra avait dépéri par indigence de structure et de forme; mais grâce aux chanteurs les mieux doués sous le rapport du talent et de l'âme, soutenue par le plus noble organe de la musique, elle avait aquis, néanmoins, pour l'oreille une grâce de coloris, une suavité de sons inconnue jusque-là aux maîtres allemands et qui manquait à leurs mélodies instrumentales"; Wagner, "Lettre sur la musique," xxxiii.

50. "palette du chanteur, aussi riche que celle du peintre, outre ses lumières et ses ombres, ses tons rompus et ses couleurs éclatantes, possède encore les variétés de rhythme et de timbres, dont les combinaisons peuvent se multiplier à l'infini"; Jean-Baptiste Faure, *La voix et le chant* (Paris: Henri Heugel, 1886), 181–82.

51. "la diversité des timbres propres aux voyelles ouvertes ou fermées, aux nasales et aux buccales, qu'il faut chercher un des précieux éléments du coloris, sans lequel le Chant n'est qu'une suite de sons monotones," Faure, *La voix*, 88; translation from Bergeron, *Voice Lessons*, 192; slightly modified. See also Faure's observation that "Le passage sans transition d'une voyelle fermée à une voyelle ouverte" offers "de précieux effets de coloris"; Faure, *La voix*, 182.

52. "il est certaines émotions qui ne s'obtiennent, et certains sentiments qui ne s'expriment que par les effets magiques du coloris"; Faure, *La voix*, 181.

53. Charles-Augustin Sainte-Beuve, *Tableau historique et critique de la poésie française et du théâtre français au XVIe siècle* (Paris: G. Charpentier, 1843), 60; cit. Imbs, ed., "allure," in *Trésor de la langue française*, Vol. 2 (Paris: CNRS, 1973), 593–95.

54. Paul Valéry, *Regards sur le monde actuel* (Paris: Librairie Stock, Delamain et Boutelleau, 1931), 309; cit. Imbs, "allure," 593–95.

55. "allure," *Trésor de la langue française*, 593–95.

56. Émile Benveniste, "La notion de 'rythme' dans son expression linguistique," *Problèmes de linguistique générale*, Vol. 1 (Paris: Gallimard, 1966), 333.

57. Mallarmé, "Crise de vers," 208.

58. Mallarmé, "Solennité," 200.

59. Despite the prominence of the passage on *jour* and *nuit*, the inclusion of this second term within Mallarmé's conception of verse has been overwhelmingly overlooked. See, for example, Philippe Lacoue-Labarthe's argument that Mallarmé's "verse" may be reduced to "a principle of rhythm": an argument Lacoue-Labarthe is able to maintain only by excising the passage on timbre entirely; Lacoue-Labarthe, *Musica Ficta*, 91–160, esp. 155–59.

60. "quelque suprême moule n'ayant pas lieu en tant que d'aucun objet qui existe"; Mallarmé, "Solennité," in *ŒC II*, 200.

61. "Les langues imparfaites en cela que plusieurs, manque la suprême . . ."; Mallarmé, "Crise de vers," in *ŒC II*, 208.

62. It is interesting to note that from the perspective of modern linguistics, Mallarmé's formulation is asymmetrical. Timbre inheres in vowel *sounds*, rather than vowels as such; measurements of timbre consider language in acoustic, rather than linguistic terms. Timbre is therefore universal, not language-specific. Meter, on the other hand, is language-specific: organizing a language by means of phonological units, meter necessarily differs in accordance with the phonology of the language at hand; hence the syllabic-accentual meters of English, the quantitative classical meters, the syllabic meters of French, the tonal meters of Chinese, and so on. In Mallarmé's formulation, however, there is such a thing as an "absolute meter." This meter seems to refer to that by which "meter" can be said to constitute a category across languages. Yet a definition of meter that makes no reference to phonology seems difficult to formulate; one would begin, presumably, with the principle of number.

63. This orientation, manifest throughout Mallarmé's theoretical texts, is also discernible in his correspondence. In setting a title for his Taylorian Lecture of 1894, for example, Mallarmé first proposes the title "Les Lettres et la Musique." The English organizers, gently reminding him that the event will form part of a lecture series on French Literature, respond by requesting that the word "français" figure in the lecture title. Though Mallarmé's letter of response to this request is now lost, it is attested by the response of Oxford tutor Charles Bonnier, which confirms that Mallarmé's lecture has been announced, in accordance with the author's wishes, as "Les Lettres et la Musique." The absence of any national or linguistic marker in the title thus appears to have been not only considered, but indeed, insisted upon; see Henri Mondor and Lloyd James Austin, eds., *Correspondance de Stéphane Mallarmé*, Vol. 6 (Paris: Gallimard, 1981), 176; and Mallarmé, *ŒC II*, 1599.

64. Genette, "Le jour, la nuit," 160. See also Roman Jakobson, "Linguistics and Poetics," in *Selected Writings III*, ed. Stephen Rudy (The Hague: Mouton, 1981), 44–45.

65. Mallarmé, "Crise de vers," in *ŒC II*, 213.

66. "rémunère le défaut des langues"; ibid., 208.

67. "défaut," *Trésor de la langue française*.

68. "rémunérer," in *Trésor de la langue française*, ed. Paul Imbs, Vol. 14 (Paris: CNRS, 1973), 780.

69. Ibid.

70. Ibid.

71. Thus, Mallarmé might well be placed within the history of poetic atheology traced by Giorgio Agamben in the essay "Expropriated Manner" in *The End of the Poem: Studies in Poetics* (Stanford: Stanford University Press, 1999), 87–101. Another reading, not incompatible, might glimpse Mallarmé's readings of Hegel here: languages are already under the sign of negation (because they are many, they signify arbitrarily, and they exclude one another); poetry negates that negation (brings remuneration) by creating the new word. Thus: poetry sublates the condition that, previously, had defined language.

72. Mallarmé, "Observation relative au poème," in *ŒC I*, 392; Mallarmé, "Crise de vers," in *ŒC II*, 213.

4 / The Colors of the Universal Alphabet

1. Vladimir Nabokov, *Speak, Memory: An Autobiography Revisited* (New York: Knopf, 1999), 22.

2. "Proceedings at New York October 1861," *Journal of the American Oriental Society* 7 (1860–63): xlix.

3. Karl Richard Lepsius, *Das allgemeine linguistische Alphabet. Grundsätze der Übertragung fremder Schriftsysteme und bisher noch ungeschriebener Sprachen in Europäischen Buchstaben* (Berlin: Hertz, 1855); *Standard Alphabet for Reducing Unwritten Languages and Foreign Graphic Systems to a Uniform Orthography in European Letters* (London: Seeley, 1855); *Das allgemeine linguistische Alphabet. Grundsätze der Übertragung fremder Schriftsysteme und bisher noch ungeschriebener Sprachen in Europäischen Buchstaben*. 2nd Ed. (Berlin: Hertz, 1863); *Standard Alphabet for Reducing Unwritten Languages and Foreign Graphic Systems to a Uniform Orthography in European Letters*, ed. J. A. Kemp. Reprint of the 2nd (1863) Edition (Amsterdam: John Benjamins, 1981). Citations refer to the 1855 editions, with English page numbers preceding the German, unless otherwise noted.

4. Max Müller, "Proposals for a Missionary Alphabet," in Christian von Bunsen, *Outlines of the Philosophy of Universal History Applied to Language and Religion* [Christianity and Mankind, Part IV], 2 vols. (London: Longmans, 1854), II: 437–88; Alexander Ellis, *The Alphabet of Nature* (Pitman: London, 1845); Isaac Pitman, *Stenographic Sound-Hand* (London: Bagster, 1837); Alexander Melville Bell, *Visible Speech: The Science of Universal Alphabetics* (London: Simpkin, Marshall; London and New York: N. Trübner, 1867); Paul Passy, *Les Sons du français* (Paris: Firmin-Didot, 1887). A general overview of the universal alphabets of the period is available in Robert W. Albright, *The International Phonetic Alphabet: Its Backgrounds and Development* (Bloomington: Indiana University Research Center in Anthropology, Folklore, and Linguistics, 1958), 18–46; for more recent contextualization of the early IPA, see Jacques Durand and Chantal Lyche, "Retour sur *Les sons du français*: la modernité de Passy," *Journal of French Language Studies* 31 no. 3 (2021): 318–37. For contextualization of Lepsius's alphabet specifically, see Floris Solleveld, "Lepsius as a Linguist: Field Work, Philology, Phonetics, and 'the Hamitic Hypothesis,'" *Language and History* 63, no. 3 (2020): 193–213; and Alan Kemp, introduction to *Standard Alphabet* by Karl Richard Lepsius (Philadelphia: John Benjamins, 1981), 1–80.

5. Whitney, W. D., "On Lepsius's Standard Alphabet," *Journal of the American Oriental Society* 7 (1861): 302.

6. Ibid., 306.

7. Ibid., 307.

8. Ibid., 306.

9. Lepsius, *Standard Alphabet*, 25/22.

10. Ibid., 27/24.

11. Ibid., 24–5/22.

12. Ibid., 27/24.

13. Ibid., 26/24.

14. Ibid., 27/24. In many respects, this enigmatic vowel answers to the one represented by contemporary linguists with the symbol ə. On the many difficulties this vowel has posed for linguistic schematization, see Daniel Heller-Roazen, *Echolalias: On the Forgetting of Language* (New York: Zone, 2005), 27–32; for its particular cultural significance in nineteenth-century French, see Katherine Bergeron, *Voice Lessons: French Mélodie in the Belle Époque* (Oxford: Oxford University Press, 2010), 201–7 and 228–32. Echoes of Lepsius's enigmatic ę might also be heard echoing through the "Zero-Phoneme" posited by Roman Jakobson a century later; Roman Jakobson and

J. Lotz, "Notes on the French Phonemic Pattern" [1949], rpt. in Jakobson, *Selected Writings I*, 3rd ed. (Berlin and New York: Mouton de Gruyter, 2002), 426–34. For more on the phoneme's significance for post-structuralism, see Catherine Diehl, "The Empty Space in Structure: Theories of the Zero from Gauthiot to Deleuze," *diacritics* 38, no. 3 (2008): 93–99, 101–19; and Sarah M. Pourciau, "Jakobson's Zeros," in *The Writing of Spirit: Soul, System, and the Roots of Language Science* (New York: Fordham University Press, 2017), 189–242.

15. Whitney, "On Lepsius's Standard Alphabet," 307.

16. Karl Richard Lepsius with W. D. Whitney, "On Lepsius's Standard Alphabet: A Letter of Explanations from Prof. Lepsius," *Journal of the American Oriental Society* 8 ([1864] 1866): 340.

17. "If there is a physiological reason for the vowel-pyramid, why is it not given us instead of this?" Whitney asks in a frustrated footnote appended to Lepsius's response; Lepsius with Whitney, "Letter of Explanations," 340.

18. Christoph Friedrich Hellwag, *Dissertatio de formatione loquelae* (Heilbron: Gebr. Henninger, [1781] 1886), 41. Hellwag is routinely cited as the father of the vowel triangle; see, for example, Alexander Ellis, *On Early English Pronunciation*, Part IV (London: Asher, 1874), 1285–89; Wilhelm Vietör, *Elemente der Phonetik* (Leipzig: Reisland, [1884] 1894), 41–65; Carl Stumpf, *Die Sprachlaute: experimentell-phonetische Untersuchungen nebst einem Anhang über Instrumentalklänge* (Berlin: Springer, 1926), 252–57; Jakobson, *SW I*, 380. A triangular arrangement of the vowels appeared in Danish more than three decades before Hellwag's dissertation, however: in Jens Pedersen Høysgaard's *Accentuered og raisonnered Grammatica: som viser det danske Sprog I sin naturlige Skikkelse saa velsom dets Riime-Konst og Vers-Regler* (Copenhagen: Groth, 1747), 5; see Solleveld, "Lepsius as a Linguist," 195.

19. Johann Heinrich Lambert, *Beschreibung einer mit dem Calauschen Wachse ausgemalten Farbenpyramide* (Berlin: Haude und Spener, 1772), 128.

20. Tobias Mayer, "Von Meßung der Farben," in *Opera Inedita Tobiae Mayeri*, ed. G. C. Lichtenberg (Göttingen: Dieterich, 1775); translated by Adriana Fiorentini, "On the Relationships Between Colors," *Color Research and Application* 25, no. 1 (2000): 71.

21. August-Ludewig Pfannenschmid, *Versuch einer Anleitung zum Mischen aller Farben aus Blau, Gelb und Roth nach beiliegendem Triangel* (Hannover: no publisher listed, 1781), fold-out appendix. An overview of the period's color models is available in Sarah Lowengard, *The Creation of Color in Eighteenth-Century Europe* (New York: Columbia University Press, 2008), 96–152 and 441–50. It is likely these models reached Lepsius via an early nineteenth-century source such as Philipp Otto Runge's *Color Sphere (Farbenkugel)* of 1810, which also features a triangular red-yellow-blue model; Philipp Otto Runge, *Farbenkugel; oder, Construction des Verhältnisses aller Mischungen der Farben zu einander, und ihrer vollständigen Affinität, mit angehängten Versuch einer Ableitung der Harmonie un den Zusammenstellungen der Farben* (Hamburg: F. Perthes, 1810), 4–6; translated by Georg Stahl, *Color Sphere: Or, Construction of the Relations of All Color Mixtures to Each Other and Their Complete Affinity, with an Attempt to Bring the Sensuous Impressions of the Different Color Combinations with the Previously Developed Scheme*, in *"On Vision and Colors" by Arthur Schopenhauer and Color Sphere by Philipp Otto Runge* (New York: Princeton Architectural Press, 2010), 121–39, esp. 125–26.

Anglophone readers might anticipate that "Goethe's color triangle" would be known to Lepsius, but this triangle appears to originate in the English translation;

Johann Wolfgang von Goethe, *Zur Farbenlehre*, 3 vols.; translated by Charles Lock Eastlake in *Theory of Colours* (London: Murray, 1840). The oft-cited "Plate I" facing page 6 of the 1840 English edition bears no resemblance whatsoever to the first plate of the *Sechszehn Tafeln nebst der Erklärung zu Goethe's Farbenlehre* that was published as part of Goethe's three-volume, 1810 original; Johann Wolfgang von Goethe, *Sechszehn Tafeln nebst der Erklärung zu Goethe's Farbenlehre* (Tübingen: Cotta'schen, 1810). Eastlake's Plate I, figure 3, featuring two color triangles creating a star circumscribed in a color circle, corresponds to no image in the German publication; the German text in fact opposes its circular color model to triangular ones, as the dismissive discussion of Lambert's *Farbenpyramide* makes plain; Goethe, *Zur Farbenlehre*, 2:574–75.

22. Lepsius's model may also owe something to the physiologically inflected account of subtractive optical mixing advanced by Hermann von Helmholtz in 1852. In endeavoring to reconcile the primaries posited in Thomas Young's 1801 physiological theory of color vision (red, green, and violet) with those cited by Mayer, Lambert, and others, Helmholtz demonstrated that color mixing with pigments or color filters produced different color impressions than resulted from the mixing of spectral colors (isolated colored lights). In subtractive color mixing, white light striking mixtures of red, yellow, and blue yields intermediary impressions of orange, green, violet, and an overall composite black, while in additive color mixing, the partially overlapping spectral colors red, green, and violet produce impressions of red, blue, yellow, and a central white. See Hermann von Helmholtz, "Die zusammengesetzten Farben," in *Handbuch der physiologischen Optik*, Vol. 2 (Leipzig: Leopold Voss, 1867), 101–44; "The Compound Colours," in *Treatise on Physiological Optics*, ed. James P. Southall, Vol. 2 (Menasha, WI: The Optical Society of America and George Banta Publishing, 1924), 120–72. See also "The Organisation of Colour: The Primary Colours" and "Hermann von Helmholtz: New Insights into Primary Colors," in Paul D. Sherman's *Colour Vision in the Nineteenth Century: The Young-Helmholtz-Maxwell Theory* (Bristol: Adam Hilger, 1981), 60–81 and 82–92. For a broad overview of the historically unstable nature and number of "primary," "prime," "simple," and "basic" colors, see John Gage, *Colour and Culture: Practice and Meaning from Antiquity to Abstraction* (London: Thames and Hudson, 1993), 29–38.

23. Jacob Grimm, *Deutsche Grammatik*, 3rd ed., 4 vols. (Göttingen: Dieterich, 1840), 1:33. A simpler version of the analogy appears in the 1822 printing of the 1819 edition: "bei einer vergleichung der vocale und der farben fällt a mit weiß, i mit roth, u mit schwarz zusammen"; Jacob Grimm, *Deutsche Grammatik*, 2nd ed. (Göttingen: Dieterich, [1819] 1822), 1076. Grimm appears to be the first to have put the two triangles in parallel, although a vowel-color analogy does appear in list form in J. C. Markwort, *Gesang-, Ton- und Rede-Vortragslehre* (Darmstadt, Leske and Mainz: Schott, 1827), 55–56. Commentaries on Grimm's analogy are available in Alexander Ellis, *Early English Pronunciation*, 1265–69; and Karl Mortiz Rapp, "Die Vocale und die Farben," in *Versuch einer Physiologie der Sprache nebst historischer Entwicklung der abendländischen Idiome nach physiologischen Grundsätzen* (Stuttgart and Tübingen: Cotta'schen, 1841), 4:257–59.

24. Lepsius with Whitney, "Letter of Explanations," 340. Whitney's lack of familiarity with Lepsius's triangles is somewhat surprising considering the student years he spent in Berlin and Tübingen in the early 1850s; Margaret Thomas, *Fifty Key Thinkers on Language and Linguistics* (Florence: Taylor and Francis, 2011), 120.

25. Edouard Gruber, "L'audition colorée et les phénomènes similaires (Report by Professor Ed. Gruber and remarks by Mr. F. Galton)," in *Second Session of the International Congress of Experimental Psychology—London, 1892* (London: Williams and Norgate, 1892), 18. Gruber refers to the case of "Miss Stones, the head teacher in a high school for girls"; Francis Galton, *Inquiries into Human Faculty and Its Development* (London: J. M. Dent [1883] 1907), 107–8.

26. Gruber, "L'audition colorée," 20.

27. Georg Moritz Ebers, *Richard Lepsius, ein Lebensbild* (Leipzig: Engelmann, 1885), 75–76; translated by Zoe Dana Underhill as *Richard Lepsius: A Biography* (New York: WS Gottsberger, 1887), 63.

28. Richard Lepsius, *Pariser Tagebuch 1833–35*, Deutsches Literaturarchiv Handschriftenabteilung (Marbach), MS 60 564. Lepsius's account of vowel colors is, in a rare oversight, absent from the history of synesthesia meticulously amassed in recent years by Jörg Jewanski et al.; Jörg Jewanski, Julia Simner, Sean A. Day, Nicolas Rothen, and Jamie Ward, "The Evolution of the Concept of Synesthesia in the Nineteenth Century as Revealed through the History of Its Name," *Journal of the History of the Neurosciences* 29, no. 3 (2020): 263; and Jörg Jewanski, "Synesthesia in the Nineteenth Century: Scientific Origins," in *The Oxford Handbook of Synesthesia*, ed. Julia Simner and Edward Hubbard (Oxford: Oxford University Press, 2013), 373.

29. Ebers, *Lebensbild*, 76/63.

30. Hartmut Mehlitz, *Richard Lepsius: Ägypten und die Ordnung der Wissenschaft* (Berlin: Kadmos, 2011), 32 and 252; Solleveld, "Lepsius as a Linguist," 197. Although the paper is frequently cited as having earned Lepsius the Volney Prize (e.g., Ebers, *Lebensbild*, 71; and Kemp, introduction, 3), the Volney Prize was not awarded in 1834; Daunou et al., "Nouvelles littéraires: Institut royal de France, Académies, sociétés littéraires," *Journal des Savants* (June 1834): 368. Lepsius was awarded the prize in 1836 for two other essays: "Über die Anordnung und Verwandtschaft des Semitischen, Indischen, Äthiopischen, Alt-Persischen und AltÄgyptischen Alphabets" and "Über den Ursprung und die Verwandtschaft der Zahlwörter in der Indogermanischen, Semitischen und der Koptischen Sprache," which were published together in Richard Lepsius, *Zwei Sprachvergleichende Abhandlungen* (Berlin: Dümmler, 1836); Solleveld, "Lepsius as a Linguist," 197.

31. Richard Lepsius, *Paläographie als Mittel für die Sprachforschung zunächst am Sanskrit nachgewiesen* (Berlin: Königliche Akademie der Wissenschaften, 1834), 26.

32. Lepsius, *Standard Alphabet*, 26/24.

33. Ibid., 27/24.

34. Lepsius, *Paläographie*, 21–22.

35. Ibid., 24–25.

36. Ellis, *Early English Pronunciation*, 1270.

37. Ellis, *Early English Pronunciation*, 1270.

38. A telling foil to Ellis's response might be that of Hermann von Helmholtz, whose *Tonempfindungen* Ellis had translated in 1870; Hermann von Helmholtz, *Die Lehre von den Tonempfindungen als Physiologische Grundlage für die Theorie der Musik* (Braunschweig: Vieweg and Sohn, [1863] 1913); translated by Alexander J. Ellis, *On the Sensations of Tone as a Physiological Basis for the Theory of Music* (New York: Dover, [1870] 1954). Helmholtz also aligns musical pitches and colors based on wavelength in his *Handbuch der physiologischen Optik* (Vol. 2, 1867), but observes that musical intervals do not correspond in any meaningful way to the colors strongly distinguished

as different by the eye; English edition translated by James P. C. Southall, *Treatise on Physiological Optics* (Menasha, WI: The Optical Society of America and George Banta, 1924), 77. One can easily imagine Ellis coming to a similar conclusion as Helmholtz regarding frequencies and vowels—whose definition, after all, resides on a great many factors beyond F_1. See "From Tone to Color" in Chapter 1, "*Klangfarbe*: Vowels in Helmholtz's *Sensations of Tone*."

39. Ellis, *Early English Pronunciation*, 1285.
40. Albright, *International Phonetic Alphabet*, 29.
41. Whitney, "On Lepsius's Standard Alphabet," 309.
42. Albright, *International Phonetic Alphabet*, 29.
43. Whitney, "On Lepsius's Standard Alphabet," 309.
44. Lepsius, *Standard Alphabet*, 27/24.
45. Whitney, "On Lepsius's Standard Alphabet," 309.
46. N. S. Trubetzkoy, *Grundzüge zur Phonologie* (Kraus Thomson: Nendeln/Lichtenstein, [1939] 1968), 59–60; translated by Christine A. M. Baltaxe, *Principles of Phonology* (Berkeley and Los Angeles: University of California Press, 1969), 66–67.
47. Trubetzkoy, *Grundzüge*, 86/96.
48. *OED*, "saturate," d8.
49. See Chapter 2, "The Interaction of Color."
50. Galton, *Inquiries*, unpaginated appendix.
51. Ibid., 110–11.
52. Trubetzkoy, *Grundzüge*, 86–87/95–97.
53. Ibid., 89/98.
54. It was Trubetzkoy's article "On Racism" (1935) that appears to have attracted the attention of the German authorities, as well as his "Thoughts on the Indo-European Problem"; Ksenia Ermishina, *Prince N. S. Trubetzkoy: Life and Work* [Князь Н.С. Трубецкой: жизнь и труды] (Moscow: Syntaksis, 2015), 172–74 and 199–203.
55. Jakobson, *Six leçons sur le son et le sens* (Paris: Les éditions de minuit, 1976), 118.
56. Jakobson, *Kindersprache, Aphasie und allgemeine Lautgesetze* (Uppsala: Språkvetenskapliga Sällskapets i Uppsala Förhandlingar, 1941); rpt. in Jakobson, *SW I*, 328–401; translated by Allen Keiler, *Child Language, Aphasia, and Phonological Universals* (The Hague: Mouton, 1968). Citations henceforth give the page numbers for the German in *SW I* followed by the English. For more on Jakobson's model, see "Spectral Sounds" in the Introduction of this book.
57. Jakobson, "Les Lois phoniques du langage enfantin," in N. S. Trubetzkoy, *Principes de phonologie*, trans. J. Cantineau (Paris, Klincksieck, 1949), 367–79; rpt. in Roman Jakobson, *SW I*, 317–27. Translated by Rodney Sangster as "The Sound Laws of Child Language" in Roman Jakobson, *Studies of Child Language and Aphasia* (The Hague: Mouton, 1971), 7–20. Jakobson wrote the paper in the summer of 1939 with the intention of presenting it at the Fifth International Linguistics Conference scheduled to take place in Brussels that September. Although the conference did take place, the German invasion of Poland appears to have prevented Jakobson's attendance; see V Kiparsky, "Le Vième Congrès International de Linguistes," *Neuphilologische Mitteilungen* 49, no. 4 (1948): 196–99.
58. Jakobson, *Kindersprache*, 386/82.
59. Ibid., 386–87/82.
60. Ibid., 387/83.

5. L'être imaginaire: Saussure's Colored Vowels

1. Théodore Flournoy, *Des phénomènes de synopsie* (Paris: Alcan and Geneva: Eggiman, 1893), 5. An earlier version of this chapter first appeared in "Sensuous Linguistics: On Saussure's Synesthesia," *New Literary History* 51, no. 1 (Winter 2019): 23–42. Copyright © 2019 Johns Hopkins University Press.

2. Mireille Cifali, "Présentation," *Le Bloc-Notes de la psychanalyse* 3 (1983): 133–34.

3. Flournoy, *Phénomènes*, 50; Cifali, "Présentation," 135.

4. Marco Mazzeo, "Les voyelles colorées: Saussure et la synesthésie," *Cahiers Ferdinand de Saussure* 57 (2004): 135.

5. Flournoy, *Phénomènes*, 50–2.

6. Flournoy, *Phénomènes*, 164. Colleagues at the University of Geneva from 1891 onward, Saussure and Flournoy occasionally collaborated professionally, most famously on the case of Hélène Smith (Catherine Elise Müller). They were also distant cousins and came to be related by marriage when Flournoy's daughter Ariane married Saussure's son Raymond in 1919. The genealogical link between Saussure and Flournoy, and thus between Saussure and Flournoy's cousin Claparède, is relevant here because Flournoy notes that Claparède "possesses most of the indicators of colored hearing to a high degree" (Flournoy, *Phénomènes*, 2), and synesthesia appears to bear a strong genetic component. See Jamie Ward and Julia Simner, "Synesthesia: The Current State of the Field," in *Multisensory Perception: From Laboratory to Clinic*, ed. K. Sathian and V. S. Ramachandran (Cambridge, MA: Academic Press, 2020), 293. For extensive documentation of Saussure's genealogy, see John Joseph, *Saussure* (Oxford: Oxford University Press, 2012), 32–69.

7. Only in 2004 did the *Cahiers* make note of the vowel-color text, which is reproduced in full in Mazzeo, "Les voyelles colorées," 132–33.

8. The anagram notebooks came to scholarly attention primarily through Jean Starobinski's *Les mots sous les mots* (Paris: Gallimard, 1971); readings imputing mental illness to their author were commonplace in the 1970s. See Ivan Callus, "A Chronological and Annotated Bibliography of Works Referring to Ferdinand de Saussure's Anagram Notebooks," *Cahiers Ferdinand de Saussure* 55 (2002): 269–95.

9. As Jonathan Culler has demonstrated, the published *Cours* distorts Saussure's nuanced position on absolute and relative arbitrariness; see Culler, "The Sign: Saussure and Derrida on Arbitrariness," in *The Literary in Theory* (Stanford: Stanford University Press, 2007), 117–36.

10. Most prominently, Johannes Fehr, "Les couleurs des voyelles," in *Saussure: Entre linguistique et sémiologie*, trans. Pierre Caussat (Paris: Presses universitaires de France, [1997] 2000), 146–79, esp. 160–71; and Joseph, *Saussure*, 392–97. An alternate version of Joseph's text appeared under the title "He Was an Englishman," *Times Literary Supplement*, November 6, 2007, 14–15. Mazzeo's "Les voyelles colorées" adopts a different approach, attempting to situate Saussure's text within quantitative studies of vowel-color synesthesia. Other studies noting, but not extensively analyzing, the vowel-color text include Herman Parret, "Métaphysique saussurienne de la voix et de l'oreille dans les manuscrits de Genève et de Harvard," in *Ferdinand de Saussure* (Paris: L'Herne, 2003), 62–78; Marco Mazzeo, *Storia naturale sinestesia: Dalla questione Molyneux a Jakobson* (Rome: Quodlibet, 2005), 87–89; Patrice Maniglier, *La vie énigmatique des signes: Saussure et la naissance du structuralisme* (Paris: Scheer, 2006), 262–66; Joshua T. Katz, "Saussure's *anaphonie*: Sounds Asunder," in *Synaesthesia and the Ancient Senses*, ed.

Shane Butler and Alex Purves (Durham: Acumen, 2013), 167–84; and Roman Jakobson and Claude Lévi-Strauss, *Correspondance 1942-82*, ed. Emmanuelle Loyer and Patrice Maniglier (Paris: Seuil, 2018), 319.

11. Flournoy, *Phénomènes*, 256.

12. Translated by Joseph, *Saussure*, 394–95, as are all translations of the vowel-color text henceforth (occasionally modified). In introducing the text to Anglophone readers, Joseph notes that "it is easy to imagine scientific interest in the topic being inspired by [Arthur Rimbaud's] poem *Voyelles*" but asserts that "studies of synaesthesia from this period do not mention Rimbaud" (394). Scientific interest in synesthesia could be said to precede "Voyelles," but scientists did not fail to take note of the poem (Flournoy, for example, refers to "Rimbaud's well known" sonnet three times within the chapter featuring Saussure's anonymous response: Flournoy, *Phénomènes*, 74, 79, 80).

13. Flournoy, *Phénomènes*, 50. Readers of the *Cours* and of Jacques Derrida's *De la grammatologie* (Paris: Minuit, 1967) may be surprised to encounter Saussure's calm reflections on orthography; for a lucid account of this misunderstanding, see Beata Stawarska's *Saussure's Philosophy of Language as Phenomenology* (Oxford: Oxford University Press, 2015), 71–84 and 251–55.

14. Flournoy, *Phénomènes*, 50.

15. Ibid.

16. Cifali titles the text "Response to a survey on colored hearing" and Joseph's chapter title "Coloured Hearing" follows suit; Cifali, *Bloc-Notes*, 137 and Joseph, *Saussure*, 392–97. The application of the well-known expression is understandable—Flournoy himself inserted a parenthetical "colored hearing" on the inside cover page of his perplexingly titled book—but it is also misleading, as Flournoy's introductory remarks explain; Flournoy, *Phénomènes*, 5.

17. Flournoy, *Phénomènes*, 50. On the complexities of analyzing texture, consistency, and color specificity in synesthesia reporting, see Yasmina Jraissati, "Reporting Color Experience in Grapheme-Color Synesthesia: On the Relation Between Color Appearance, Categories, and Terms," in *Sensory Blending: On Synaesthesia and Related Phenomena* ed. Ophelia Deroy (Oxford: Oxford University Press, 2017), 84–104.

18. Ferdinand de Saussure, *Cours de linguistique générale*, ed. Charles Bally and Albert Séchehaye with the collaboration of Albert Riedlinger, critical edition by Tullio de Mauro (Paris: Payot, 1962), 98. Henceforth *CLG*. As this chapter requires only the most basic (and more or less uncontested) principles of synchronic linguistics, I cite the classic text, though not without noting that its extraordinarily complex publication history makes any citation a risky affair. For the most extensive English-language account of the perils involved, see Stawarska's *Phenomenology*.

19. *CLG*, 150–4.

20. Ibid., 164.

21. David Abercrombie, "What Is a 'Letter?'" *Lingua* 2 (1949): 58–59.

22. *CLG*, 53.

23. In my discussion, I use // to designate phonemes, <> graphemes, and [] linguistic sounds that may or may not precisely match the aural contours of the phonemes of a given language. Saussure's account, as it appears in Flournoy's text, uses none of these symbols; letters are italicized for emphasis, but this emphasis alternately signals their graphic and phonic status. I reproduce quotations from Saussure's account precisely as rendered by Flournoy.

24. See "Distinctive Phonic Properties" in Chapter 4 of this book.

25. As Jonathan Culler has pointed out, Saussure's distinction between diachronic and synchronic perspectives enables the division between phonetics and phonology, but Saussure does not always use these terms in the modern sense outlined here; see Culler, *Ferdinand de Saussure*, rev. ed. (Ithaca, NY: Cornell University Press, [1976] 1991), 41–42. This sense was developed and advanced principally by N. S. Trubetzkoy and Roman Jakobson in the 1920s and '30s; for the early development, see N. S. Trubetzkoy, *Grundzüge zur Phonologie* (Kraus Thomson: Nendeln/Lichtenstein, [1939] 1968)/*Principles of Phonology*, trans. Christine A. M. Baltaxe (Berkeley and Los Angeles: University of California Press, 1969); and N. S. Trubetzkoy, *Studies in General Linguistics and Language Structure*, edited and introduced by Anatoly Liberman, trans. Marvin H. Taylor and A. Liberman (Durham, NC: Duke University Press, 2001); for an overview of the development of the phonetics/phonology distinction in Jakobson's thought during the twentieth century, see Linda Waugh, "Preface to the Second Edition," in *The Sound Shape of Language*, 3rd ed. (Berlin: De Gruyter, 2002), 1–5.

26. Flournoy, *Phénomènes*, 52.

27. *CLG*, 194.

28. In his provocatively titled *Économie des changements phonétiques: Traité de phonologie diachronique* (Bern: Francke, 1955), André Martinet challenges this position, proposing a study of phonetic change from the perspective of "diachronic phonology." Martinet's diachronic phonology undertakes the systematic study of the transformation and transference of distinctive features (rather than positively defined sound properties). Sound properties form the metalanguage by which phonetics studies linguistic sound change; distinctive features, Martinet contends, may form this metalanguage for diachronic phonology (see esp. 7–8 and 30–38).

29. The *i* of *chien* results from the palatalization of the word Latin /k/ (*cānem*) into the French /ʃ/ ("chien," *Trésor de la langue française*, http://www.le-tresor-de-la-langue.fr); see also Georges Straka, "Remarques sur les voyelles nasales, leur origine et leur évolution en français," *Revue de linguistique romane* 19 (1955): 258.

30. "terrain," "plein," and "matin," *Trésor de la langue française*, http://www.le-tresor-de-la-langue.fr.

31. Flournoy, *Phénomènes*, 52.

32. *CLG*, 128.

33. Saussure, *Mémoire sur le système primitif des voyelles dans les langues indo-européennes* (Leipzig: Teubner, 1879).

34. Ibid., 20.

35. Ibid., 180; emphases mine.

36. None of Saussure's sources employ a color vocabulary systematically as Saussure does, but suggestively similar terms do turn up. Georg Curtius, Eduard Sievers, and Karl Brugman all employ the German term for timbre, *Klangfarbe* (lit. "sound-color"), describing vowels' timbres as "bright" (*hell*), "dull" (*dumpf*), and "dark" (*dunkel*) (Curtius, 14; Sievers, 34–50; Brugman, 381); Brugman also notes the "chromatic accentuation" distinguishing *a* from *ä*, and once considers the potential effect of an "a-colored sonority" on neighboring vowels (Brugman, 373, 378). Georg Curtius, *Ueber die Spaltung des A-Lautes im Griechischen und Lateinischen* (Leipzig: Hirzel, 1864); Eduard Sievers, *Grundzüge der Lautphysiologie* (Leipzig: Breitkopf and Härtel, 1876); and Karl Brugman, "Zur Geschichte der stammabstufenden Declinationen," *Studien*

zur grieschen und lateinischen Grammatik, ed. Curtius and Brugman, Vol. 9 (Leipzig: Hirzel, 1876), 361–406.

37. Saussure, "Essai pour réduire les mots du grec, du latin & de l'allemand à un petit nombre de racines" (1874), *Cahiers Ferdinand de Saussure* 32 (1978): 78. As Joseph has convincingly demonstrated, Saussure's 1903 recollection of writing this text in 1872 must have been slightly off, as the essay can only have been written in the summer of 1874; Joseph, *Saussure*, 152–58.

38. Saussure, "Essai," 77.

39. Ibid., 78.

40. The pun on the technical term (*teinte* in the visual sense of "hue" and *teinte* in the acoustic sense of "timbre") is likely anachronistic, but behind it lurks an older pun: between the verbs *tinter* ("to chime") and *teinter* ("to dye, stain, color"). The verbs do not appear to share any etymological link. "Tinter, verbe," "teinter, verbe trans.," and "teindre, verbe trans.," *Trésor de la langue française*, http://www.le-tresor-de-la-langue.fr.

41. E.g., "Sounds [. . .] distinguished by their **timbre** are called 'vowels.' **Timbre** is thus the fundamental quality of a vowel, distinguishing it from the other vowels"; Georges Le Roy, *Grammaire de la diction française* (Paris: Delaplane, 1912), 39; emphases Le Roy's).

42. John Joseph, "'La teinte de tous les ciels': divergeance et nuance dans la conception saussurienne du changement linguistique," *Cahiers Ferdinand de Saussure* 63 (2010): 148.

43. Saussure, *Mémoire*, 1.

44. Ibid., 2.

45. Ibid.

46. Jean-Claude Milner, *L'amour de la langue* (Paris: Verdier, [1978] 2009), 98–99.

47. What modern linguists call "Proto-Indo-European" appears in nineteenth-century sources under the names of "Indo-European" (*indo-européen, Indoeuropäisch*) and "Indo-German" (*Indogermanisch*), as well as the "proto-language" (*Ursprache*) and "the mother language" (*la langue mère*). Saussure uses *indo-européen* and *la langue mère*; in the interest of philological specificity, I retain his terminology.

48. Milner, *L'amour de la langue*, 98–99.

49. Ibid., 99.

50. Saussure, *Mémoire*, 105; and Saussure, "Essai d'une distinction des différents *a* indo-européens," *Mémoires de la Société de Linguistique de Paris* 3, no. 5 (1877): 362. Saussure's leap from one *a* to four *as* is mediated by a considerable amount of intervening scholarship, which conceded the existence of three distinct *as* in the European languages. The originality of Saussure's thesis lay not only in its proposal of a fourth *a* but, more audaciously, in its contention that the multiplicity of European *as* could be demonstrated to have existed in Indo-European.

51. Saussure, "Essai d'une distinction," 362.

52. Saussure, *Mémoire*, 5.

53. Ibid., 51; emphasis Saussure's.

54. Ibid.; emphases mine.

55. Except when the root contains a liquid or a nasal sonant (r, l, m, n), in which case the timbre of the vowel represents a later development caused by the quality of that liquid or nasal; Saussure, *Mémoire*, 51.

56. Ibid., emphasis Saussure's.

57. Ibid., 19.

58. The Greek characters are explicitly equated with their Roman corollaries and freely interchanged with them.

59. Saussure, "Essai d'une distinction," 361.

60. Some of the speech sounds commonly referred to as "consonants" can form the basis for a syllable in the absence of a vowel (e.g., the terminal nasal of the English "rhythm" [ɹɪðm̩]).

61. Saussure, *Mémoire*, 6–7.

62. Ibid., 134–84.

63. Ibid., 134–35.

64. Jerzy Kuryłowicz, "ǝ indoeuropéen et ḫ hittite" (1926), *Symbolae grammaticae in honorem Ioannis Rozwadowski*, ed. Witold Taszycki and Witold Jan Doroszewski, Vol. 1 (Krakow: Jagiellonian University Press, 1927), 95–104. See also Katz, "Saussure's anaphonie," 170–71.

65. Saussure's expression *coefficients sonantiques* reflects his conviction that linguistics requires an algebraic vocabulary that makes no reference to the mechanics of phonation; the *Mémoire*, accordingly, never uses the term "laryngeal." This term was introduced into the discourse as the German "Kehlkopflaut" by Danish linguist Hermann Møller, who instantly perceived Saussure's resonant coefficients to correspond to Proto-Hamito-Semitic laryngeal consonants whose existence he himself had hypothesized. Saussure's notes attest to his interest in this potential correspondence; Joseph, *Saussure*, 248–49.

66. Fredrik Otto Lindeman, *Introduction to "Laryngeal Theory,"* 2nd ed. (Innsbruck: Institut für Sprachwissenschaft der Universität Innsbruck, 1997). The actual sound qualities of all the laryngeals remain disputed, but $*h_1$ is generally hypothesized to resemble a glottal stop [ʔ] or an [h]. One might be inclined to argue, therefore, that Saussure missed this laryngeal because its sound is absent from the soundscape of his native language (it is generally accepted that modern French features neither [ʔ] nor [h], disputes concerning the *h aspiré* aside). There is little evidence to suggest Saussure was less capable of studying sounds absent from modern French, however, and a great deal of evidence to the contrary; furthermore, the conjectured pronunciations of $*h_2$ and $*h_3$ can scarcely be cited as evidence that these symbols correspond to sounds realized in modern French.

Conclusion: Remarks on "Synesthesia"

1. Hubert Damisch, "Remarks on Abstraction," trans. Rosalind Krauss, *October* 127 (Winter 2009): 133.

2. Jörg Jewanski, Sean Day, and Jamie Ward, "A Colorful Albino: The First Documented Case of Synaesthesia, by Georg Tobias Ludwig Sachs in 1812," *Journal of the History of the Neurosciences* 18, no. 3 (2009): 300. The term "synesthesia"—before acquiring its contemporary clinical sense—has a much longer history; Daniel Heller-Roazen, *The Inner Touch: Archaeology of a Sensation* (New York: Zone, 2007), 79–89.

3. G. L. T. Sachs, *Historiae naturalis duorum leucaethiopum auctoris ipsius et sororis eius* (*A Natural History of Two Albinos: The Author Himself and His Sister*) (PhD Dissertation, University of Erlangen, 1812), 80–81; translated by Jewanski et al., "A Colorful Albino," 297. A German translation of the original Latin dissertation is available in Julius Heinrich Gottlieb Schlegel, *Ein Betrag zur nähern Kentniß der Albinos* (Meiningen: Keyßnerschen Hofbuchhandlung, 1824).

4. Jewanski et al., "A Colorful Albino," 300.

5. Ibid., 293.

6. "A further generally agreed defining property is the notion of automaticity, by which it is generally meant that the concurrent is a (virtually) inevitable consequence of encountering the inducer. Synesthetes have very little control over the onset or content of their experiences"; Jamie Ward, "Synesthesia," *Annual Review of Psychology* 64 (2013): 50.

7. Sachs, *Historia naturalis*, 81; Jewanski et al., "A Colorful Albino," 297.

8. William O. Krohn, "Pseudo-Chromsethesia, or the Association of Colors with Words, Letters, and Sounds," *The American Journal of Psychology* 5, no. 1 (October 1892): 38.

9. Jewanski, "Synesthesia in the Nineteenth Century: Scientific Origins," in *Oxford Handbook of Synesthesia*, ed. Julia Simner and Edward Hubbard (Oxford: Oxford University Press, 2013), 369. Jewanski's limitation of synesthesia to humans is not evident and is a long-standing point of contention. Atavistic interpretations of synesthetic experience have famously viewed the phenomenon as "a retrogression to the very beginning of organic development" and "a descent from the height of human perfection to the low level of the mollusc"; Max Nordau, *Entartung* (Berlin: Duncker, 1892), 221; translated by George L. Mosse, *Degeneration* (Lincoln, NE: University of Nebraska Press, 1993), 142. Here, indifferentiation between the senses raises the specter of indifferentiation between species, which poses an inadmissible threat to Nordau's progressivist social project grounded in a necessary human exceptionalism. Other scholars, also suspecting synesthesia to constitute a primal genre of sensory perception shared with other life forms, have viewed this possibility in a far more positive light. Claude Lévi-Strauss, for example, writing not sixty years after Nordau, sees a promising and stimulating prospect: "Space has its own values, just as sounds and perfumes have colours, and feelings weight. The search for such correspondences is not a poetical game or a practical joke (as some critic has had the audacity to say it is, in connection with Rimbaud's '*sonnet des voyelles*' which is now a classic text for linguists who know the basis, not for the color of phonemes—which is a variable depending on the individual—but of the relationship between them, which admits of only a limited scale of possibilities); it offers absolutely unexplored territory for research where significant discoveries are still to be made. If, like the aesthete, fish divide perfumes into light and dark, and bees classify luminosity in terms of weight—darkness being heavy and brightness light—the work of the painter, the poet or the musician, like the myths and symbols of the savage, ought to be seen by us, if not as a superior form of knowledge, at least as the most fundamental and the only one really common to us all"; Claude Lévi-Strauss, *Tristes tropiques* (Paris: Plon, 1955), 137–38; translated by John and Doreen Weightman (New York: Atheneum, 1974), 123. What the Weightmans translate as "practical joke" is in French "mysticisme," which strongly suggests Nordau to be the unnamed "critic" at whom Lévi-Strauss takes aim. It is in a chapter titled "Der Mysticismus" ("Le mysticisme" in Auguste Dietrich's 1894 French translation) that Nordau denigrates Rimbaud's sonnet; Max Nordau, *Dégénérescence*, trans. Auguste Dietrich (Paris: F. Alcan, 1894), 247–48. Lévi-Strauss's understanding of synesthesia owes much to Roman Jakobson; see "Spectral Sounds" in the introduction to this book, "Distinctive Phonic Properties" in Chapter 4, and, for a detailed account of the two scholars' exchanges on colored vowels, my "Correspondances: La couleur des voyelles chez Lévi-Strauss, Jakobson, Rimbaud et Banville," *Parade Sauvage* 30 (2019): 121–42.

10. Jewanski et al., "A Colorful Albino," 294.

11. Shane Butler and Alex Purves, eds., *Synaesthesia and the Ancient Senses* (Durham: Acumen, 2013), 1.

12. Ibid, 2.

13. Ibid., 3; on Baudelaire's possible borrowing from Sappho, see Yopie Prins, *Victorian Sappho* (Princeton: Princeton University Press, 1999), 99–101.

14. Jewanski, "Synesthesia in the Nineteenth Century," 372.

15. Jewanski et al., "A Colorful Albino," 294.

16. The category would thus be a fascinating one to study through the lens of Ian Hacking's looping effect, which seeks to elucidate how the social validation of various conditions influences the constitution of individual and communitarian identity (and thus, the data set in turn constitutive of information on the condition); Hacking, "The Looping Effects of Human Kinds," in *Causal Cognition: A Multidisciplinary Debate*, ed. Dan Sperber, David Premack, and Ann James Premack (Oxford: Oxford University Press, 1995), 351–94.

17. Krohn, "Pseudo-Chromesthesia," 20–41; Ferdinand Suarez de Mendoza, *L'audition colorée: Étude sur les fausses sensations secondaires physiologiques et particulièrement sur les pseudo-sensations de couleurs associées aux perceptions objectives des sons* (Paris: Octave Doin, 1890); A. Chabalier, "De la pseudochromesthésie," *Journal de médecine de Lyon* 1, no. 2 (1864): 92–102.

18. See Margot Szarke, "Testing pathological feelings," in "Modern Sensitivity: Émile Zola's Synesthetic Cheeses," *French Studies* 74 no. 2 (2020): 217–22.

19. M. Daubresse, "L'audition colorée," *Revue philosophique* 49 (March 1900): 301.

20. Maria C. Bos, "Die echte und unechte audition colorée," *Zeitschrift f. Psychologie* III, 1929.

21. Mark Bradley provides a typical example: "As we know, synaesthesia is a complicated neurological condition in which stimulation of one sensory pathway leads to automatic, involuntary experiences in a second sensory pathway. In these terms, the ancients were not synesthetic any more than they were colour-blind. However, this does not mean that we should not think about how and why associations between the different senses were taking place in ancient thought"; Mark Bradley, "Colour as Synaesthetic Experience in Antiquity," *Synaesthesia and the Ancient Senses*, 127–28.

22. Anupama Nair and David Brang, "Inducing synesthesia in non-synesthetes: Short-term visual deprivation facilitates auditory-evoked visual precepts," *Consciousness and Cognition* 70 (April 2019): 70–79; Lawrence E. Marks, "Weak Synesthesia in Perception and Language," in *Oxford Handbook of Synesthesia*, ed. Julia Simner and Edward Hubbard (Oxford: Oxford University Press, 2013), 761–89; and Jamie Ward and Julia Simner, "Synesthesia: The Current State of the Field," in *Multisensory Perception: From Laboratory to Clinic*, ed. V. S. Ramachandran and K. Sathian (Cambridge, MA: Academic Press, 2020), 283–300.

23. Paradigmatically, Susan Bernstein, *The Other Synaesthesia* (New York: SUNY Press, 2023), 1–4. Lauren Silvers offers a variation on the theme, drawing a distinction between "synesthesia" and *cénésthésie* ("the consciousness we have of our body as it is living and acting"); Lauren Silvers, "Beyond the Senses: The Cenesthetic Poetics of French Symbolism," *Modern Philology* 112 (2014): 381–404.

24. This is why Rimbaud's "Voyelles" (1871) poses such a conundrum for modern readers: it appears to adhere to the format codified after its time of writing, inviting reading in the mode of the report it never claimed to be.

25. Sachs, *Historia naturalis*, 55.

26. The context of the passage rules out the possibility of reading *oculis* in the dative. The section quoted here is preceded by Sachs's quotation of another man whose eyes reportedly produced enough light for him to read by it: "Ioannes Tac cum diutius et continuo in tenebris cogitavisset, lumen quoddam ('flammam') ex oculis suis in chartam efferri vidit, quo tamdiu et tantopere ea illustrata est ut duas lineas, scribere potuisset. Momenti esset, si sciremus, cuius generis meditationes fuerint, sub quibus oculi tantum luminis fuderunt. Num fortasse tunc de rebus visibilibus vel ad visum pertinentibus cogitatum eoque actio vitalis in eiusdem sensus organo magnopere aucta est?"; Sachs, *Historia naturalis*, 55.

27. "spargo," *Lewis and Short Latin Dictionary Online*, https://www.perseus.tufts.edu/hopper/text?doc=Perseus%3Atext%3A1999.04.0059%3Aentry%3Dspargo1. Consulted 13 June 2023.

28. Wave theories of light gained widespead traction in Europe only in the mid-nineteenth century; see Paul D. Sherman, *Colour Vision in the Nineteenth Century* (Bristol: Adam Hilger, 1981) and Jay Buchenwald, *The Rise of the Wave Theory of Light: Optical Theory and Experiment in the Early Nineteenth Century* (Chicago: University of Chicago Press, 1989).

29. Like Rimbaud's sonnet, Sachs's text leaves room for wonder as to who sees this light: the one behind the eyes, the one who looks upon them, or both. The account Sachs offers is presented as that of his parents, but Sachs's concluding remarks ("Does not, perhaps, a certain sympathy exist between the sense of hearing and seeing? There is no doubt that the senses are interconnected in various ways") imply that it is the boy—"having wholly immersed himself in bringing out and combining the hoarse tones of a certain musical instrument"—who perceives the light in conjunction with the music (and, presumably, reports his sensations to his parents).

30. Charles Baudelaire, "Richard Wagner ou Tannhäuser à Paris," in *Œuvres complètes de Charles Baudelaire II*, ed. Claude Pichois (Paris: Gallimard, 1976), 779–815. Henceforth *ŒCB II*. The bibliography on the text is vast; see amongst others Susan Bernstein, *The Other Synesthesia*, 1, 39–60; Richard Sieburth, "The Music of the Future," in *A New History of French Literature*, ed. Denis Hollier (Cambridge, MA: Harvard University Press, 1994), 789–98; Jeremy Coleman, "Wagner Without Theatre: Aporias of Translation," in *Richard Wagner in Paris: Translation, Identity, Modernity* (Woodbridge: Boydell Press, 2019), 149–54; David Michael Hertz, *The Tuning of the Word: the Musico-Literary Poetics of the Symbolist Movement* (Carbondale: Southern Illinois University Press, 1987), esp. 24–31; Philippe Lacoue-Labarthe, "Baudelaire," *Musica Ficta: figures de Wagner* (Paris: Christian Bourgois, 1991), 28–90; Margaret Miner, *Resonant Gaps: Between Baudelaire and Wagner* (Athens: University of Georgia Press, 1995); Susan Bernstein, *Virtuosity of the Nineteenth Century: Performing Music and Language in Heine, Liszt, and Baudelaire* (Stanford: Stanford University Press, 1998), 131–174; Peter Dayan, "Baudelaire's Wagner," in *Music Writing Literature, from Sand via Debussy to Derrida* (Aldershot: Ashgate, 2006), 25–38; Joseph Acquisto, "Baudelaire in Wagner's Forests, or the Persistence of the Lyric," in *French Symbolist Poetry and the Idea of Music* (Aldershot: Ashgate, 2006), 13–45; Jocelynne Loncke, *Baudelaire et la musique* (Paris: Nizet, 1975); Michela Landi, *Baudelaire et Wagner* (Firenze: Firenze University Press, 2019).

31. Baudelaire, *ŒCB II*, 1462.

32. Baudelaire, "Richard Wagner," in *ŒCB II*, 784–85; emphasis original.

33. Translated by Jonathan Mayne, "Richard Wagner and Tannhäuser in Paris," in *The Painter of Modern Life and Other Essays* by Charles Baudelaire (London: Phaidon, 1964), 116–17. Translations modified throughout.

34. This intensifying of incandescent whiteness appears already in Baudelaire's letter to Wagner on February 17, 1860: "Il semblerait difficile, impossible même d'arriver à quelque chose de plus ardent; et cependant une dernière fusée vient tracer un sillon plus blanc sur le blanc qui lui sert de fond"; *ŒCB II*, 673.

35. Miner, *Resonant Gaps*, 51, 33.

36. Bernstein, *Virtuosity*, 168–69; see also Bernstein, *Virtuosity*, 131–51.

37. Baudelaire, "Richard Wagner," 785.

38. As Jewanski et al. point out, "Sachs's colors themselves are said to appear in 'dark space.' Some synaesthetes report experiencing their colors on an "inner screen" (or mind's eye), whereas others see them externalized [. . .] Sachs's description is, in our view, more consistent with the former"; Jewanski et al., "A Colorful Albino," 300. The synesthetic visions induced by hallucinogenics usually fall within the modern clinical sense of "synesthesia"; John E. Harrison and Simon Baron Cohen, "Synesthesia as a Consequence of Psychoactive Drug Use," in *Synesthesia: Classic and Contemporary Readings*, ed. John E. Harrison and Simon Baron Cohen (Oxford: Blackwell, 1997), 7–8.

39. Baudelaire, "Richard Wagner," in *ŒCB II*, 784/116.

40. Ibid., 785; emphasis in original. Miner (*Resonant Gaps*, 25–60) and Dayan ("Baudelaire's Wagner," 25–38) read Baudelaire's argument as a wry demonstration of precisely the opposite of what it seems to argue ("that Wagner's music expresses ideas and conveys images which are positive enough to be translated"; Dayan, "Baudelaire's Wagner," 27).

41. "Il voit se former peu à peu une apparition étrange qui prend corps et figure [. . .] en se touvant toujours rapproché de *la lumineuse apparition* [. . .] *il s'abîme dans une adoration extatique, comme si le monde entier eût soudainement disparu*"; Wagner cit. Baudelaire, "Richard Wagner," in *ŒCB II*, 782; emphasis Baudelaire's; translation by Miner, *Resonant Gaps*, 34.

42. "fait miroiter à nos yeux le temple de bois incorruptible"; Liszt cit. Baudelaire, "Richard Wagner," in *ŒCB II*, 783; emphasis Baudelaire's.

43. Baudelaire, "Richard Wagner," in *ŒCB II*, 785/117; emphasis Baudelaire's.

44. Ibid., emphasis Baudelaire's. Philippe Lacoue-Labarthe also notes that "la sensation, pour Baudelaire, se divise: elle est à la fois, étrangement, spirituelle et physique, ou matérielle." He sets aside the possibility of exploring this second (physical / material) category in any serious way, however, on the grounds that "en réalité le musique ne suggère nulle qualité sensible [. . .] Sinon très secondairement, c'est-à-dire tant qu'on en reste à l'esthétique des correspondances, qui n'est peut-être pas, sous cet angle en tout cas, l'esssentiel chez Baudelaire"; Philippe Lacoue-Labathe, *Musica Ficta: Figures de Wagner* (Paris: Christian Bourgois 1991), 76.

45. Liszt cit. Baudelaire, "Richard Wagner," in *ŒCB II*, 783; emphasis Baudelaire's.

46. Ibid., 783/115; emphasis Baudelaire's.

47. Liszt's emphasis on sensory experience here makes the alternate reading of *nos sens* as "our minds" a bit less intuitive, but both readings are possible; they are also compatible.

48. Baudelaire, "Correspondances," *Œuvres complètes de Charles Baudelaire I*, (Paris: Gallimard, 1975), 11 (Henceforth *ŒCB I*); translated by Richard Howard, *Les Fleurs du Mal* (Boston: Godine, 1982), 15.

49. Charles Baudelaire, "Nouvelles notes sur Edgar Poe," in *ŒCB II*, 334; translated by Mayne, "Further Notes on Edgar Poe," in *Painter of Modern Life*, 107; Jonathan Culler, "Intertextuality and Interpretation," in *Nineteenth-Century French Poetry*, ed. Christopher Prendergast (Cambridge: Cambridge University Press, 1990), 118.

50. Baudelaire, "Richard Wagner," 784/116.

51. Leo Bersani, *Baudelaire and Freud* (Berkeley and Los Angeles: University of California Press, 1979), 32.

52. Baudelaire, "Richard Wagner," in *ŒCB II*, 785; my emphasis.

53. Baudelaire, "Correspondances," in *ŒCB I*, 11/15; my emphases, translation modified.

54. In Bernstein's reading, Wagner aims for a unity of the arts, whereas Baudelaire's *correspondances* connect without fusing; Bernstein, *The Other Synesthesia*, 45, 73–74; see also Bernstein, *Virtuosity*, 152–74.

55. In Sieburth's reading, the "confusion" consists in conflating Wagner's vision combining "poetry and music [. . .] in order to express what neither of them could articulate in isolation" with Baudelaire's idea that "the two are substitutable for or translatable into each other"; Sieburth, "The Music of the Future," 790–91.

56. Wolfgang von Kempelen, *Mechanismus der menschlichen Sprache Nebst der Beschreibung Seiner Sprechenden Maschine* (Wien: J. B. Degen, 1791), 196.

57. Richard Wagner, "Die Oper und das Wesen der Musik," *Oper und Drama*, rpt. in *Gesammelte Schriften und Dichtungen*, Vol. 4. (Leipzig: Fritzsch, 1872), 289–394 (henceforth *GSD*). For a helpful overview of the situation to which Wagner is responding, see John Hamilton Warrack, "Opera in the mid-nineteenth century," *German Opera: From the Beginnings to Wagner* (Cambridge: Cambridge University Press, 2001), 338–80, esp. 338–44; for a revisionist look at the role of nationalism in the writing of German operatic history, see Axel Körner, "Beyond *Nationaloper*. For a critique of methodological nationalism in reading nineteenth-century Italian and German opera," *Journal of Modern Italian Studies* 25, no. 4 (2020): 402–19.

58. Richard Wagner, *Quatre poèmes d'opéras, traduits en prose française, précédés d'une lettre sur la musique* (Paris: Bourdillat, 1861), vii–viii. Henceforth *Lettre sur la musique*.

59. Richard Wagner, *Opera and Drama*, trans. William Ashton Ellis (Lincoln: University of Nebraska Press, 1995), 310 (henceforth *OD*; translations occasionally modified); *GSD IV*, 210.

60. Wagner may have reversed this position in the years between reading Schopenhauer in 1854 and publishing his Beethoven essay in 1870; Reinhart Meyer-Kalkus, "Richard Wagners Theorie der Wort-Tonsprache in 'Oper und Drama' und 'Der Ring der Nibelungen,'" *Athenäum: Jahrbuch für Romantik* 6 (1996): 188. Thomas Grey, on the other hand, convincingly argues for continuity within this reversal, suggesting that it might more accurately be characterized as a "change of focus, or accent"; Thomas Grey, *Wagner's Musical Prose* (Cambridge: Cambridge University Press, 1995), 17–18.

61. *OD*, 309; *GSD IV*, 209. Translation modified. Wagner holds that the consonants preceding vowels exercise greater influence in determining their character than the consonants that follow them; *OD* 267; *GSD IV*, 163.

62. Ibid.

63. Ibid., 271/167.

64. See Chapter 2, "The Interaction of Color"; and Chapter 5, "*L'être imaginaire*: Saussure's Colored Vowels," particularly "The Colors of Vowels" and "The Laryngeal Theory."

65. *OD*, 271; *GSD IV*, 168.

66. Ibid., 258/152.

67. Ibid., 307/207.

68. Hermann von Helmholtz, "Ueber die Klangfarbe der Vocale," *Annalen der Physik und Chemie* 108 (1859): 280–90. See Chapter 1, "*Klangfarbe*: Vowels in Helmholtz's *Sensations of Tone*."

69. Robert Michael Brain, "Bürgerliche Intelligenz: Essay Review," *Studies in History and Philosophy of Science* 26 no. 4 (1996): 629; Michel Meulders, *Helmholtz, des lumières aux neurosciences* (Paris: Éditions Odile Jacob, 2001), 229–34; Hermann von Helmholtz, *Die Lehre von den Tonempfindungen als Physiologische Grundlage für die Theorie der Musik* (Braunschweig: Vieweg and Sohn, [1863] 1913), 544 and 554. There is no evidence, however, that Helmholtz read *Opera and Drama*, and the term *Klangfarbe* was in use in musical circles, albeit not evidently in relation to vowels. It features as a possible German translation of the French "timbre" in the 1835 *Musikalisches Conversationslexicon* and 1838 *Universal-Lexikon der Tonkunst*, having first appeared in print in 1834 to designate what remains constant in the sound of a single organ pipe capable of producing multiple different pitches; *Musikalisches Conversationslexicon*, ed. A. Gathy (Leipzig, 1835), *Universal-Lexikon der Tonkunst* ed. Gustav Schilling (Stuttgart, 1838), and Johann Gottlob Töpfer, *Erster Nachtrag zur Orgelbau-Kunst* (Weimar: Hoffmann, 1834), all cit. Daniel Muzzulini, "Timbre vs Klangfarbe," *Musiktheorie* 16, no. 1 (2001): 81–82.

70. See "The Tone of a Breath" in Chapter 1, "*Klangfarbe*: Vowels in Helmholtz's *Sensations of Tone*."

71. "Tone-speech (*Tonsprache*)" (*OD*, 313; *GSD IV*, 214); "Poetic Song-melody (*dichterische Gesangsmelodie*)" (*OD* 312; *GSD IV*, 212); "Word-tone-melody (*Worttonmelodie*)" (*OD*, 315; *GSD IV*, 215); "Verse-melody (*Versmelodie*)" (*OD*, 315; *GSD IV*, 216).

72. *OD*, 311–12; *GSD IV*, 212.

73. Ibid., 311/211.

74. Ibid., 311–12/212.

75. Ibid., 311/211.

76. Ibid., 313/212.

77. For extensive contextualization and interpretation of this term, see Thomas Grey, "Wagner and the Problematics of 'Absolute Music' in the Nineteenth Century," in *Wagner's Musical Prose* (Cambridge: Cambridge University Press, 1995), 1–50.

78. This subtle distinction marks the only point at which my reading of Wagner might diverge slightly from that of Robert Michael Brain, who contends that "Wagner insisted on the poetic voice as the foundation of the total work of art, arguing that composers erred when they looked to dance to replace the primordial rhythms of the voice." By Brain's account, "[t]he primacy of the voice followed Wagner's claim that the first human expression was a succession of vowels, a melodic language of emotion," so he would appear to situate vowels as in some way anterior to voice, or perhaps even synonymous with it; Robert Michael Brain, *The Pulse of Modernism* (Seattle: University of Washington Press, 2016), 163.

79. Wagner, *Lettre sur la musique*, xxviii; and "Die Kunst und die Revolution," *GSD III*, 9–50.

80. Wagner, *OD*, 239–376; *GSD IV*, 129–284.

81. Ibid., 276/172.

82. Ibid., 273–74/170–71. See also Meyer-Kalkus, "Richard Wagners Theorie," 169.

83. *OD* 266; *GSD IV*, 162.
84. Ibid., 266/161–62.
85. Richard Wagner, *Richard Wagner's 'Beethoven' 1870: A New Translation*, trans. Roger Allen (Woodbridge: Boydell Press, 2014), 55; Daniel Albright, *Untwisting the Serpent* (Chicago: University of Chicago Press, 2000), 51–52 and 152–57.
86. *OD*, 266; *GSD IV*, 162.
87. This is a subtle but decisive point. Most readers of Wagner have taken the *tönende Laut* to be synonymous with the musical tone it becomes, and therefore evidence of Wagner's subjugation of language to music. A close reading, however, reveals that Wagner goes to extravagantly awkward lengths to insist on the intoned sound as distinct from the instrumental music in which its echo may be heard and from the signifying vowel in which it appears. Partaking of both simultaneously, the intoned sound is further distinguished from the "musical tone" in that it is the exclusive product of the human voice.
88. This is presumably why William Ashton Ellis's 1893 translation renders the expression as, alternately, "the open sound" and "the vowel"; *OD*, 266 and 273; *GSD IV*, 162 and 169.
89. *OD*, 307; *GSD IV*, 207.
90. Ibid., 266/162.
91. Sarah M. Pourciau, *The Writing of Spirit: Soul, System, and the Roots of Language Science* (New York: Fordham University Press, 2017), 152.
92. Reinhart Meyer-Kalkus indicates that Wagner probably drew his inspiration from Franz Bopp's 1833 *Comparative Grammar*; Meyer-Kalkus, "Richard Wagners Theorie," 169. One can also hear echoes of Herder's 1772 contention that "the older and more original languages are, the more feelings also intersect in the roots of the words"; Johann Gottfried von Herder, "Treatise on the Origin of Language," in *Philosophical Writings*, ed. and trans. Michael N. Forster (Cambridge: Cambridge University Press, 2002), 113. Sarah Pourciau has also pointed out that Wagner's emphasis on vowels seems to respond directly to linguists like Jacob Grimm, whose focus on consonantal writing "postpone[s] the question of specifically *vocalic* sound laws" and ends up—in Wagner's view—"dissecting the organism of language at the expense of the very phonetic essence they had hoped thereby to reveal." Where Wagner diverges significantly from the linguistic establishment, of course, is in his insistence that "the identity of initial letters *necessarily implies* an identity of etymological meaning": a position that, as Pourciau diplomatically puts it, "places him definitively outside the scholarly tradition"; Pourciau, *Writing of Spirit*, 146, 145. Otherwise put, Wagner conveniently overlooks the evidence that the initial letters of etymological roots often change or disappear.
93. See Chapter 3, "Mallarmé and the Tension of Timbre."
94. Paul Valéry, *Œuvres*, ed. Jean Hytier, Vol I. (Paris: Gallimard, 1957), 686.
95. Mallarmé, *Les Mots anglais*, in *Oeuvres complètes de Stéphane Mallarmé II*, ed. Bertrand Marchal (Paris: Gallimard, 2003), 967. Henceforth *ŒC II*.
96. Mallarmé's disdain for this second "illusion" is well-known. "The fact is," he writes of his fellow countrymen, "These recluses faithful to the sonorities of their own language, whose instinct they glorify, secretly abhor admitting any other language: in this regard they remain more patriotic than anyone. A necessary infirmity, perhaps, that reinforces in them the illusion that an object put forth under the only name they know it by springs from it, native; but—don't you think? what a strange thing"; Stéphane Mallarmé, "Tennyson vu d'ici," *ŒC II*, 139. Gérard Genette has also provided

an extended analysis of Mallarmé's Cratylism, which he finds exceptional precisely for its privileging of a foreign language (English) as the more mimetic tongue; Gérard Genette, *Mimologiques: Voyage en Cratylie* (Paris: Seuil, 1976), 257–314.

97. Although it is not clear that Mallarmé ever opened Bopp's *Comparative Grammar*, the first page would surely have dissuaded him from proceeding further if he did. In the preface to his foundational study, Bopp writes, "One point alone I shall leave untouched, the mystery of the roots, or the foundation of the nomenclature of the primary ideas"; Franz Bopp, "Vorrede," in *Vergleichende grammatik des sanskrit, zend, griechischen, lateinischen, litthauischen, gothischen und deutschen* (Berlin: F. Dümmler, 1833), iii; translated by Edward Backhouse Eastwick, *A Comparative Grammar of the Sanscrit, Zend, Greek, Latin, Lithuanian, Gothic, German, and Sclavonic Languages*, Vol. 1, 3rd ed. (London: Williams and Norgate, 1862), v; translation modified. Bopp's very first gesture is set aside Mallarmé's primary point of interest: the question of sound's originary relation to signification. While Bopp considers this question a "mystery of roots (*Geheimnis der Wurzeln*)," for Mallarmé it is a *mystère dans les lettres*: "the initial characters of the alphabet, each of which like a subtle stroke corresponds to a pose of Mystery . . ."; Mallarmé, "Étalages" (1892), in *ŒC II*, 220.

98. Mallarmé cites "relations between overall signification and the letter," specifying that "if they exist, [they] do so only by the special use, in a word, of such and such speech organs"; *Mots anglais*, in *ŒC II*, 969. Gérard Genette is right that Mallarmé's Cratylism inheres on the level of the letter rather than that of the word, but his suggestion that the poet's lack of emphasis on physical motivations distinguishes him from "the Cratylian tradition" is dubious; Gérard Genette, *Mimologiques: Voyage en Cratylie* (Paris: Seuil, 1976), 257–314, esp. 270–75. On this subject, see also my "Vers le vers véridique: poésie et vérité chez Mallarmé"; translated by Annick Ettlin as *Toucher au "vrai": l'intelligence de la poésie*, ed. Annick Ettlin and Jan Baetens. *Fabula—LhT* 24 (November 2020), https://www.fabula.org/lht/24/yamaguchi.html. Finally, it should also be noted that in the hypothetical world Mallarmé puts forth, the signification of each letter would be valid for all subjects. Thus, when R. G. Cohn explains, in his attempt to render this alphabet explicit, that the associations cited pertain to letters "as they struck Mallarmé, not anyone else," it is Cohn who reconceives of this alphabet as Mallarmé's personal one; R. G. Cohn, "Significance of Letters: Symbolism in Sound and Shape," in *Toward the Poems of Mallarmé* (Berkeley and Los Angeles: University of California Press, 1965), 265.

99. Mallarmé, *Les Mots anglais*, in *ŒC II*, 968. The move offers a microcosm of Mallarmé's intellectual trajectory; he anticipated writing a thesis in Indo-European linguistics but rapidly abandoned the project. For resonances between Mallarmé's linguistic vision and Indo-European linguistics, see Mireille Ruppli and Sylvie Thorel-Cailleteau, "La linguistique en 1870," in *Mallarmé: La Grammaire et le grimoire*, (Geneva: Droz, 2005), 51–59 ; and Jean-Claude Milner, "Le linguiste," in *Profils perdus de Stéphane Mallarmé: Court traité de lecture 2* (Paris: Verdier, 2019), 43–63.

Works Cited

Abercrombie, David. "What Is a 'Letter'?" *Lingua* 2 (1949): 54–63.
Académie française. *Dictionnaire de l'Académie française*. 4th ed. Paris: B. Brunet, 1762.
Acquisto, Joseph. *French Symbolist Poetry and the Idea of Music*. Aldershot: Ashgate, 2006.
Agamben, Giorgio. *Categorie italiane: Studi di poetica e di letteratura*. Rome: Laterza, 2010. Translated by Daniel Heller-Roazen as *The End of the Poem: Studies in Poetics*. Stanford: Stanford University Press, 1999.
———. *Idea della prosa*. Macerata: Quodlibet, 2020. Translated by Michael Sullivan and Sam Whitsitt as *The Idea of Prose*. New York: SUNY Press, 1995.
Albers, Josef. *Interaction of Color*. New Complete Edition. New Haven, CT: Yale University Press, 2009.
Albright, Daniel. *Untwisting the Serpent*. Chicago: University of Chicago Press, 2000.
Albright, Robert W. *The International Phonetic Alphabet: Its Backgrounds and Development*. Bloomington: Indiana University Research Center in Anthropology, Folklore, and Linguistics, 1958.
American Psychiatric Association. *Diagnostic and Statistical Manual of Mental Disorders*. 5th ed., Text Revision. Washington, DC: American Psychiatric Association, 2022.
Attridge, Derek. *Well-Weighted Syllables*. Cambridge: Cambridge University Press, 1974.
Auden, W. H. *Collected Poems*. London: Faber, 1976.
Bailhache, Patrice. *Une histoire de l'acoustique musicale*. Paris: CNRS, 2001.
Bailhache, Patrice, with Antonia Soulez and Céline Vautrin. *Helmholtz, du son à la musique*. Paris: Vrin, 2011.

de Banville, Théodore. *Petit traité de poésie française*. Paris: Éditions d'aujourd'hui, [1872] 1978.
Baudelaire, Charles. *Les Fleurs du Mal*. Translated by Richard Howard. Boston: Godine, 1982.
———. *Œuvres complètes de Charles Baudelaire*. Edited by Claude Pichois. 2 vols. Paris: Gallimard, 1975 and 1976.
———. *The Painter of Modern Life and Other Essays*. Translated by Jonathan Mayne. London: Phaidon, 1964.
Beattie, James. *The Works of James Beattie*. Philadelphia: Hopkins and Earle, 1809.
Becq de Fouquières, Louis. *Traité général de versification française*. Paris: G. Charpentier, 1879.
Bell, Alexander Melville. *Visible Speech: The Science of Universal Alphabetics*. London: Simpkin, Marshall; London and New York: N. Trübner, 1867.
Bénichou, Paul. *Selon Mallarmé*. Paris: Gallimard, 1995.
Benjamin, Walter. "Die Aufgabe des Übersetzers" (1923). In *Charles Baudelaire, Tableaux Parisiens*, translated by Walter Benjamin, 17–18. Frankfurt am Main: Suhrkamp, 1963.
Benveniste, Émile. *Problèmes de linguistique générale*, Vol. 1. Paris: Gallimard, 1966.
Bergeron, Katherine. "A Bugle, a Bell, a Stroke of the Tongue: Rethinking Music in Modern French Verse." *Representations* 86 (Spring 2004): 53–72.
———. *Voice Lessons: French Mélodie in the Belle Epoque*. Oxford: Oxford University Press, 2009.
Bernstein, Susan. *The Other Synesthesia*. New York: SUNY Press, 2023.
———. *Virtuosity of the Nineteenth Century: Performing Music and Language in Heine, Liszt, and Baudelaire*. Stanford: Stanford University Press, 1998.
Bersani, Leo. *Baudelaire and Freud*. Berkeley and Los Angeles: University of California Press, 1979.
Blanchot, Maurice. *L'Espace littéraire*. Paris: Gallimard, 1955. Translated by Ann Smock as *The Space of Literature*. Lincoln, Nebraska: University of Nebraska Press, 1989.
Blasi, Damián E. et al., "Sound–Meaning Association Biases Evidenced across Thousands of Languages." *Proceedings of the National Academy of Sciences of the United States of America* 113, no. 39 (2016): 10818–23.
Boethius. *Fundamentals of Music*. Translated by Calvin M. Bower. New Haven, CT: Yale University Press, 1966.
Bopp, Franz. *A Comparative Grammar of the Sanscrit, Zend, Greek, Latin, Lithuanian, Gothic, German, and Sclavonic Languages*. Translated by Edward Backhouse Eastwick. 3rd ed. London: Williams and Norgate, 1862.
———. *Vergleichende grammatik des sanskrit, zend, griechischen, lateinischen, litthauischen, gothischen und deutschen*. Berlin: F. Dümmler, 1833.
Bos, Maria C. "Die echte und unechte audition colorée." *Zeitschrift f. Psychologie* III, 1929.

Boulard, Stéphanie. "Hugo/Rimbaud — Voyelles." *Parade Sauvage* 31 (2020): 189–214.
Boulard, Stéphanie, and Pierre Georgel. *Hugographies: Rêveries de Victor Hugo sur les lettres de l'alphabet*. Paris: Hermann, 2022.
Bradley, Mark. "Colour as Synaesthetic Experience in Antiquity." In *Synaesthesia and the Ancient Senses*, edited by Shane Butler and Alex Purves, 127–40. Durham: Acumen, 2013.
Brain, Robert Michael. "Bürgerliche Intelligenz: Essay Review." *Studies in the History and Philosophy of Science* 26, no. 4 (1996): 617–35.
———. *The Pulse of Modernism*. Seattle: University of Washington Press, 2016.
Bright, William, and Peter T. Daniels. *The World's Writing Systems*. Oxford: Oxford University Press, 1996.
Brognan, T. V. F., and Alfred Garvin Engstrom. "Synesthesia." In *The New Princeton Encyclopedia of Poetry and Poetics*, edited by Alex Preminger et al. Princeton, NJ: Princeton University Press, 1993.
Brugman, Karl. "Zur Geschichte der stammabstufenden Declinationen." In *Studien zur griechen und lateinischen Grammatik*, edited by Georg Curtius and Brugman, Vol. 9, 361–406. Leipzig: Hirzel, 1876.
Buchenwald, Jay. *The Rise of the Wave Theory of Light: Optical Theory and Experiment in the Early Nineteenth Century*. Chicago: University of Chicago Press, 1989.
Butler, Shane, and Alex Purves, eds. *Synaesthesia and the Ancient Senses*. Durham: Acumen, 2013.
Cahan, David. *Helmholtz: A Life in Science*. Chicago: University of Chicago Press, 2018.
Callus, Ivan. "A Chronological and Annotated Bibliography of Works Referring to Ferdinand de Saussure's Anagram Notebooks." *Cahiers Ferdinand de Saussure* 55 (2002): 269–95.
Caneva, Kenneth L. *Helmholtz and the Conservation of Energy: Contexts of Creation and Reception*. Cambridge, MA: MIT Press, 2021.
Cavallaro, Adrien, Yann Frémy, and Alain Vaillant, eds. *Dictionnaire Rimbaud*. Paris: Classiques Garnier, 2021.
Chabalier, A. "De la pseudochromesthésie." *Journal de médecine de Lyon* 1, no. 2 (1864): 92–102.
Chladni, Ernst Theodor. *Die Akustik*. Leipzig: Breitkopf und Härtel, 1802.
———. *Kurze Uebersicht der Schall- une Klanglehre, nebst einem Anhange, die Entwickelung und Anordnung der Tonverhältnisse betreffend*. Mainz: Schott's Söhne, 1827.
Chomsky, Noam. *Language and Mind*. Cambridge: Cambridge University Press, 2006.
———. *Syntactic Structures*. The Hague: Mouton, 1957.
Cifali, Mireille. "Présentation." *Le Bloc-Notes de la psychanalyse* 3 (1983): 133–34.
Claparède, Édouard. "Sur l'audition colorée." *Revue philosophique de la France et de l'Étranger* 49 (1900): 515–17.

Cohn, R. G. *Toward the Poems of Mallarmé*. Berkeley and Los Angeles: University of California Press, 1965.
Coleman, Jeremy. *Richard Wagner in Paris: Translation, Identity, Modernity*. Boydell Press, 2019.
Corbière, Tristan. *Les amours jaunes*. Paris: Vanier, 1891.
Culler, Jonathan. "Apostrophe." *diacritics* 7, no. 4 (1977): 59–69.
———. *Ferdinand de Saussure*. Rev. ed. Ithaca, NY: Cornell University Press, [1976] 1991.
———. "Intertextuality and Interpretation." In *Nineteenth-Century French Poetry*, edited by Christopher Prendergast, 118–37. Cambridge: Cambridge University Press, 1990.
———. "The Sign: Saussure and Derrida on Arbitrariness." In *The Literary in Theory*, 117–36. Stanford: Stanford University Press, 2007.
Curtius, Georg. *Ueber die Spaltung des A-Lautes im Griechischen und Lateinischen*. Leipzig: Hirzel, 1864.
Cytowic, Richard. "Synesthesia: Phenomenology and Neuropsychology, A Review of Current Knowledge." *Psyche* 2, no. 10 (July 1995): 1–22.
Damisch, Hubert. "Remarks on Abstraction." Translated by Rosalind Krauss. *October* 127 (Winter 2009): 133–54.
Dann, Kevin. *Bright Colors Falsely Seen: Synaesthesia and the Search for Transcendental Knowledge*. Cambridge, MA: MIT Press, 1998.
Daubresse, M. "L'audition colorée." *Revue philosophique* 49 (January–June 1900): 300-305.
Daunou et al., "Nouvelles littéraires: Institut royal de France, Académies, sociétés littéraires." *Journal des Savants* (June 1834): 368–69.
Dayan, Peter. *Music Writing Literature, from Sand via Debussy to Derrida*. Aldershot: Ashgate, 2006.
Derrida, Jacques. *De la grammatologie*. Paris: Minuit, 1967.
———. *Marges de la philosophie*. Paris: Éditions de minuit, 1972.
Diderot, Denis. *Œuvres complètes*. Paris: Garnier, 1875.
Diehl, Catherine. "The Empty Space in Structure: Theories of the Zero from Gauthiot to Deleuze." *diacritics* 38, no. 3 (2008): 93–99, 101–19.
Dolan, Emily I. *The Orchestral Revolution: Haydn and the Technologies of Timbre*. Cambridge: Cambridge University Press, 2013.
Donders, F. C. "Ueber die Natur der Vocale." *Archiv für die Holländischen Beiträge für Natur- und Heilkunde* 1 (1857): 157–62.
———. "Zur Klangfarbe der Vocale," *Annalen der Physik und Chemie* 123 (1864): 527–28.
Duchez, Marie-Elisabeth. "Des neumes à la portée: Elaboration et organisation rationnelles de la discontinuité musicale et de sa représentation graphique, de la formule mélodique à l'échelle monocordale." *Canadian University Music Review* 4 (1983): 22–65.
Duchesne-Guillemin, J. "Encore le divin Cygne." *Empreintes* 5 (1948): 44–50.

Durand, Jacques, and Chantal Lyche. "Retour sur *Les sons du français*: la modernité de Passy." *Journal of French Language Studies* 31, no. 3 (2021): 318–37.
Ebers, Georg Moritz. *Richard Lepsius, ein Lebensbild*. Leipzig: Engelmann, 1885. Translated by Zoe Dana Underhill, *Richard Lepsius: A Biography*. New York: WS Gottsberger, 1887.
Ellis, Alexander. *The Alphabet of Nature*. Pitman: London, 1845.
———. *On Early English Pronunciation*, Part IV. London: Asher, 1874.
Erlmann, Veit. *Reason and Resonance*. New York: Zone, 2010.
Ermishina, Ksenia. *Prince N. S. Trubetzkoy: Life and Work* [Князь Н.С. Трубецкой: жизнь и труды]. Moscow: Syntaksis, 2015.
Étiemble, René. *Le sonnet des voyelles: de l'audition colorée à la vision érotique*. Paris: Gallimard, 1968.
Euler, Leonhard. "Eclaircissemens plus détaillés sur la génération et la propagation du son et sur la formation de l'echo" (1764–65). In *Leonhardi Euleri opera omnia*, edited by Eduard Bernoulli et al., Vol. 3, 540–67. Leipzig: Teubner, 1926.
Evans, David. *Théodore de Banville: Constructing Poetic Value in Nineteenth-Century France*. Oxford: Legenda, 2014.
Fabb, Nigel, and Morris Halle. *Meter in Poetry: A New Theory*. Cambridge: Cambridge University Press, 2008.
Faure, Jean-Baptiste. *La voix et le chant*. Paris: Henri Heugel, 1886.
Faurisson, Robert. "A-t-on lu Rimbaud?" *Bizarre* 21–22 (1961): 1–48.
Faurisson, Robert, et al. *A-t-on lu Rimbaud? suivi de l'affaire Rimbaud*. Paris: La Vieille Taupe, 1991.
Fehr, Johannes. *Saussure: Entre linguistique et sémiologie*. Translated by Pierre Caussat. Paris: Presses universitaires de France, [1997] 2000.
Flörke, Heinrich Gustav. "Nachtrag zu dem Aufsatze: Die Tonleiter der Vokale." *Neue Berlinische Monatschrift* 10 (February 1803): 343–71.
———. "Tonleiter der Vokale." *Neue Berlinische Monatschrift* 10 (September 1803): 161–84.
Flournoy, Théodore. *Des phénomènes de synopsie*. Paris: Alcan and Geneva: Eggiman, 1893.
Frémy, Yann. *Je m'évade! Je m'explique: Résistances d'Une saison en enfer*. Paris: Classiques Garnier, 2011.
———. *Te voilà, c'est la force: Essai sur Une saison en enfer de Rimbaud*. Paris: Classiques Garnier, 2009.
Gage, John. *Color and Meaning*. Berkeley and Los Angeles: University of California Press, 1999.
———. *Colour and Culture: Practice and Meaning from Antiquity to Abstraction*. London: Thames and Hudson, 1993.
Galton, Francis. *Inquiries into Human Faculty and Its Development*. London: J. M. Dent [1883] 1907.
Gathy, A., ed. *Musikalisches Conversationslexicon*. Leipzig, 1835.

Genette, Gérard. "Le jour, la nuit." *Cahiers de l'Association internationale des études francaises* 20 (1968): 149–65.

———. *Mimologiques: Voyage en Cratylie*. Paris: Seuil, 1976.

Ghil, René. *Traité du Verbe*. Paris: Giraud, 1886.

von Goethe, Johann Wolfgang. *Sechszehn Tafeln nebst der Erklärung zu Goethe's Farbenlehre*, Tübingen: Cotta'schen, 1810.

———. *Zur Farbenlehre*. 3 vols. Tübingen: Cotta'schen, 1810. Translated by Charles Lock Eastlake, *Theory of Colours*. London: Murray, 1840.

Grey, Thomas. *Wagner's Musical Prose*. Cambridge: Cambridge University Press, 1995.

Grimm, Jacob. *Deutsche Grammatik*. 2nd ed. Göttingen: Dieterich, [1819] 1822.

———. *Deutsche Grammatik*. 3rd ed. 4 vols. Göttingen: Dieterich, 1840.

Grimm, Jacob, and Wilhelm Grimm. *Deutsches Wörterbuch: K*. Leipzig: S. Hirzel, 1873.

Grimms Wörterbuch: T, Leipzig: S. Hirzel, [1913] 1935.

Gruber, Edouard. "L'audition colorée et les phénomènes similaires (Report by Professor Ed. Gruber and remarks by Mr. F. Galton)." In *Second Session of the International Congress of Experimental Psychology—London, 1892*, 10–20. London: Williams and Norgate, 1892.

Hacking, Ian. "The Looping Effects of Human Kinds." In *Causal Cognition: A Multidisciplinary Debate*, edited by Dan Sperber, David Premack, and Ann James Premack, 351–94. Oxford: Oxford University Press, 1995.

Hardison Jr., O. B. "Blank Verse Before Milton." *Studies in Philology* 81, no. 3 (Summer 1984): 253–74.

———. *Prosody and Purpose in the English Renaissance*. Baltimore: Johns Hopkins University Press, 1989.

Harrow, Susan. *Colourworks: Chromatic Innovation in Modern French Poetry and Art Writing*. New York: Bloomsbury, 2021.

Harrison, John E., and Simon Baron Cohen, eds. *Synesthesia: Classic and Contemporary Readings*. Oxford: Blackwell, 1997.

Heller-Roazen, Daniel. "Arismétriques: De la musique aux arts rhythmiques." In *Sens, Rhétorique et Musique: Études réunies en hommage à Jacqueline Cerquiglini-Toulet*, edited by Sophie Albert, Mireille Demaules, Estelle Doudet, Sylvie Lefèvre, Christopher Lucken, and Agathe Sultan, 275–88. Paris: Champion, 2015.

———. *Echolalias: On the Forgetting of Language*. New York: Zone, 2005.

———. *The Fifth Hammer: Pythagoras and the Disharmony of the World*. New York: Zone, 2011.

———. *The Inner Touch: Archaeology of a Sensation*. New York: Zone, 2007.

Hellwag, Christoph Friedrich. *Dissertatio de formatione loquelae*. Heilbronn: Gebr. Henninger, [1781] 1886.

von Helmholtz, Hermann. *Handbuch der physiologischen Optik*. Leipzig: Leopold Voss, 1867. English edition by James P. C. Southall, *Treatise on Physiologi-*

cal Optics. 3 vols. Menasha, WI: The Optical Society of America and George Banta Publishing, 1924.

———. *Die Lehre von den Tonempfindungen als Physiologische Grundlage für die Theorie der Musik*. Braunschweig: Vieweg and Sohn, [1863] 1913. Translated by Alexander J. Ellis, *On the Sensations of Tone as a Physiological Basis for the Theory of Music*. New York: Dover, [1870] 1954.

———. "Thatsachen in der Wahrnehmung." *Vorträge und Reden*, Vol. 2, 215–47. Brauschweig: Vieweg und Sohn, [1878] 1884. Translated by Malcolm F. Lowe, "Facts in Perception." In *Epistemological Writings*, edited by Robert S. Cohen and Yehuda Elkana, 115–85. Boston: D. Reidel, 1977.

———. "Ueber die arabisch-persische Tonleiter." *Verhandlungen des naturhistorisch-medizinischen Vereins zu Heidelberg* 2 (1862): 216–17.

———. "Ueber die Klangfarbe der Vocale." *Annalen der Physik und Chemie* 108 (1859): 280–90.

———. "Ueber die physiologischen Ursachen der musikalischen Harmonie." In *Populäre wissenschaftliche Vorträge*, Vol. 1, 55–91. Braunschweig: Vieweg und Sohn, 1865. Translated by Alexander Ellis, "On the Physiological Causes of Harmony in Music." In *Popular Lectures on Scientific Subjects*, Vol. 1, 61–106. New York: Appleton, 1885.

Helmont, F. M. *Alphabeti verè naturalis hebraici brevissima delineatio*. Sulzbach: Abraham Lichtenthaler, 1667. Translated by Allison Coudert and Taylor Corse. *The Alphabet of Nature: A Short Sketch of the Truly Natural Hebrew Alphabet*. Boston: Brill, 2007.

von Herder, Johann Gottfried. "Treatise on the Origin of Language." In *Philosophical Writings*, edited and translated by Michael N. Forster, 65–164. Cambridge: Cambridge University Press, 2002.

Hertz, David Michael. *The Tuning of the Word: The Musico-Literary Poetics of the Symbolist Movement*. Carbondale: Southern Illinois University Press, 1987.

Hiebert, Edwin. *The Helmholtz Legacy in Physiological Acoustics*. Cham: Springer, 2015.

Holy Bible. King James Version. http://www.kingjamesbible.org

Hugo, Victor. *La Légende des siècles*. Edited by Jacques Truchet. Paris: Gallimard, 1950.

———. "Note sur la couleur des voyelles." *Océan prose. Tas de pierres*. Bibliothèque nationale de France. Signed manuscript NAF 13423, folio 81.

Hui, Alexandra. *The Psychophysical Ear: Musical Experiments, Experimental Sounds, 1840-1910*. Cambridge, MA: MIT Press, 2012.

Hung, Wan-Yu. "Synesthesia in Non-Alphabetic Languages." In *The Oxford Handbook of Synesthesia*, edited by Edward Hubbard and Julia Simner, 212–21. Oxford: Oxford University Press, 2013.

Høysgaard, Jens Pedersen. *Accentuered og raisonnered Grammatica: som viser det danske Sprog I sin naturlige Skikkelse saa velsom dets Riime-Konst og Vers-Regler*. Copenhagen: Groth, 1747.

Ishihara, Shinobu. *Tests for Colour-Blindness*. 24-Plate edition. Tokyo and Kyoto: Kanehara Shuppan, 1971.
Imbs, Paul, ed. *Trésor de la langue française*. 16 vols. Paris: CNRS, 1973.
Jackson, Myles. *Harmonious Triads: Physicists, Musicians, and Instrument Makers in Nineteenth-Century Germany*. Cambridge, MA: MIT Press, 2006.
Jakobson, Roman. *Kindersprache, Aphasie und allgemeine Lautgesetze*. Uppsala: Språkvetenskapliga Sällskapets i Uppsala Förhandlingar, 1941; rpt. in Jakobson, *Selected Writings I*, 3rd ed., 328–401. Berlin: Mouton de Gruyter, 2002. Translated by Allen Keiler, *Child Language, Aphasia, and Phonological Universals*, The Hague: Mouton, 1968.
———. "Linguistics and Poetics." In *Selected Writings III*, edited by Stephen Rudy, 18–51. The Hague: Mouton, 1981.
———. *Six leçons sur le son et le sens*. Paris: Les éditions de minuit, 1976.
Jakobson, Roman, and Claude Lévi-Strauss. *Correspondance 1942–82*. Edited by Emmanuelle Loyer and Patrice Maniglier. Paris: Seuil, 2018.
Jakobson, Roman, and J. Lotz, "Notes on the French Phonemic Pattern" [1949], rpt. in Jakobson, *Selected Writings I*, 3rd ed., 426–34. Berlin: Mouton de Gruyter, 2002.
Jakobson, Roman, and Linda R. Waugh. *The Sound Shape of Language*. The Hague: De Gruyter, [1979] 1987.
Jewanski, Jörg. "Synesthesia in the Nineteenth Century: Scientific Origins." In *The Oxford Handbook of Synesthesia*, edited by Julia Simner and Edward M. Hubbard, 370–98. Oxford: Oxford University Press, 2013.
Jewanski, Jörg, Julia Simner, Sean A. Day, Nicolas Rothen, and Jamie Ward. "The Evolution of the Concept of Synesthesia in the Nineteenth Century as Revealed through the History of Its Name." *Journal of the History of the Neurosciences* 29, no. 3 (2020): 259–85.
———. "The 'Golden Age' of Synesthesia Inquiry in the Late Nineteenth Century (1876–1895)." *Journal of the History of the Neurosciences* 29, no. 2 (2019): 175—202.
———. "From 'Obscure Feeling' to 'Synesthesia': The Development of the Term for the Condition We Today Name 'Synesthesia.'" In *Proceedings VI International Congress Synesthesia Science and Art*, 1–8. Granada: Artecittà, 2018.
———. "Recognizing Synesthesia on the International Stage: The First Scientific Symposium on Synesthesia at the International Conference of Physiological Psychology, Paris, 1889." *Journal of the History of the Neurosciences* 29, no. 4 (2020): 357–87.
Jewanski, Jörg, Julia Simner, Sean A. Day, and Jamie Ward. "The Development of a Scientific Understanding of Synesthesia from Early Case Studies (1849–1873)." *Journal of the History of the Neurosciences* 20, no. 4 (2011): 284–305.
Jewanski, Jörg, Sean A. Day, and Jamie Ward. "A Colorful Albino: The First Documented Case of Synaesthesia, by Georg Tobias Ludwig Sachs in 1812." *Journal of the History of the Neurosciences* 18, no. 3 (2009): 293–396.

Joseph, John. "He Was an Englishman." *Times Literary Supplement*, November 6, 2007, 14–15.

———. *Saussure*. Oxford: Oxford University Press, 2012

———. "'La teinte de tous les ciels': divergeance et nuance dans la conception saussurienne du changement linguistique." *Cahiers Ferdinand de Saussure* 63 (2010): 145–58.

Jraissati, Yasmina. "Reporting Color Experience in Grapheme-Color Synesthesia: On the Relation Between Color Appearance, Categories, and Terms." In *Sensory Blending: On Synaesthesia and Related Phenomena*, edited by Ophelia Deroy, 84–104. Oxford: Oxford University Press, 2017.

Kahn, Gustave. "Arthur Rimbaud." *La revue blanche* 16 (1898): 592–601.

Katz, Joshua T. "Gods and Vowels." In *Poetic Language and Religion in Greece and Rome*, edited by J. Virgilio García and Angel Ruiz, 2–28. Newcastle upon Tyne: Cambridge Scholars Publishing, 2013.

———. "Saussure's *anaphonie*: Sounds Asunder." In *Synaesthesia and the Ancient Senses*, edited by Shane Butler and Alex Purves, 167–84. Durham: Acumen, 2013.

Kemp, Alan. Introduction to *Standard Alphabet for Reducing Unwritten Languages and Foreign Graphic Systems to a Uniform Orthography in European Letters*. Edited by J. A. Kemp. Reprint of the 2nd (1863) Edition. Amsterdam: John Benjamins, 1981. In *Standard Alphabet* by Karl Richard Lepsius, 1–80. Philadelphia: John Benjamins, 1981.

von Kempelen, Wolfgang. *Mechanismus der menschlichen Sprache*. Wien: J. B. Degen, 1791.

Kratzenstein, C. G. *Testamen Coronatum de Voce*. St. Petersburg: Imperial Academy, 1780.

Kripke, Saul. *Wittgenstein on Rules and Private Language: An Elementary Exposition*. Oxford: Basil Blackwell, 1982.

Krohn, William O. "Pseudo-Chromesthesia, or the Association of Colors with Words, Letters, and Sounds." *American Journal of Psychology* 5, no. 1 (October 1892): 20–41.

Kuiper, Kathy. "Voyelles (poem by Rimbaud)." *The Encyclopaedia Britannica*, February 24, 2017. https://www.britannica.com/topic/Voyelles.

Kursell, Julia. "Alexander Ellis's Translation of Helmholtz's *Sensations of Tone*." *Isis* 109, no. 2 (2018): 339–45.

———. *Epistemologie des Hörens: Helmholtz' physiologische Grundlegung der Musiktheorie*. Paderborn: Fink, 2018.

———. "Experiments on Tone Color in Music and Acoustics: Helmholtz, Schoenberg, and *Klangfarbenmelodie*." *Osiris* 28, no. 1 (January 2013): 191–211.

———. "Fine-Tuning Philology: Helmholtz's Investigation into Ancient Greek and Persian Scales." *History of Humanities* 2, no. 2 (Fall 2017): 345–59.

Kuryłowicz, Jerzy. "ə indoeuropéen et ḫ hittite" (1926). *Symbolae grammaticae in honorem Ioannis Rozwadowski*, edited by Witold Taszycki and Witold Jan Doroszewski, Vol. 1, 95–104. Krakow: Jagiellonian Univ. Press, 1927.

Körner, Axel. "Beyond *Nationaloper*. For a Critique of Methodological Nationalism in Reading Nineteenth-Century Italian and German Opera." *Journal of Modern Italian Studies* 25, no. 4 (2020): 402–19.

Lacoue-Labarthe, Philippe. *Musica Ficta: Figures de Wagner*. Paris: Christian Bourgois, 1991.

Lambert, Johann Heinrich. *Beschreibung einer mit dem Calauschen Wachse ausgemalten Farbenpyramide*. Berlin: Haude und Spener, 1772.

Landi, Michaela. *Baudelaire et Wagner*. Firenze: Firenze University Press, 2019.

Laserstein, Paul-Gabriel. "Stéphane Mallarmé: Professeur d'anglais." *Les langues modernes* 43 (1949): 25–46.

Lefrère, Jean-Jacques. *Arthur Rimbaud*. Paris: Fayard, 2001.

Leibniz, Gottfried Wilhelm. *Nouveaux essais sur l'entendement humain*. Paris: Flammarion, 1921.

Lepsius, Karl Richard. *Das allgemeine linguistische Alphabet. Grundsätze der Übertragung fremder Schriftsysteme und bisher noch ungeschriebener Sprachen in Europäischen Buchstaben*. Berlin: Hertz, 1855.

———. *Das allgemeine linguistische Alphabet. Grundsätze der Übertragung fremder Schriftsysteme und bisher noch ungeschriebener Sprachen in Europäischen Buchstaben*, 2nd ed. Berlin: Hertz, 1863.

———. *Paläographie als Mittel für die Sprachforschung zunächst am Sanskrit nachgewiesen*. Berlin: Königliche Akademie der Wissenschaften, 1834.

———. *Pariser Tagebuch 1833–35*. Deutsches Literaturarchiv Handschriftenabteilung (Marbach). MS 60 564.

———. *Standard Alphabet for Reducing Unwritten Languages and Foreign Graphic Systems to a Uniform Orthography in European Letters*. London: Seeley, 1855.

———. *Standard Alphabet for Reducing Unwritten Languages and Foreign Graphic Systems to a Uniform Orthography in European Letters*. Edited by J. A. Kemp. Reprint of the 2nd (1863) Edition. Amsterdam: John Benjamins, 1981.

———. *Zwei Sprachvergleichende Abhandlungen*. Berlin: Dümmler, 1836.

Lepsius, Karl Richard, with W. D. Whitney. "On Lepsius's Standard Alphabet: A Letter of Explanations from Prof. Lepsius." *Journal of the American Oriental Society* 8 ([1864] 1866): 335–73.

Le Roy, Georges. *Grammaire de la diction française*. Paris: Delaplane, 1912.

Lévi-Strauss, Claude. *Regarder, écouter, lire*. Paris: Plon, 1993.

———. *Tristes tropiques*. Paris: Plon, 1955.

———. *Tristes Tropiques*. Translated by John and Doreen Weightman. New York: Atheneum, 1974.

Levy, Kenneth. "On the Origin of Neumes." *Early Music History* 7 (1987): 59–90.

Lewis, Charlton T., and Charles Short. *A Latin Dictionary*. https://www.perseus.tufts.edu/hopper/text?doc=Perseus:text:1999.04.0059.

Liddell, Henry George, and Robert Scott. *A Greek-English Lexicon*. https://www.perseus.tufts.edu/hopper/text?doc=Perseus%3atext%3a1999.04.0057.

Lindeman, Fredrik Otto. *Introduction to "Laryngeal Theory."* 2nd ed. Innsbruck: Institut für Sprachwissenschaft der Universität Innsbruck, 1997.
Lloyd, Rosemary. *Mallarmé: The Poet and His Circle*. Ithaca, NY: Cornell University Press, 1999.
Loncke, Jocelynne. *Baudelaire et la musique*. Paris: Nizet, 1975.
Lowengard, Sarah. *The Creation of Color in Eighteenth-Century Europe*. New York: Columbia University Press, 2008.
Mallarmé, Stéphane. *Correspondance de Stéphane Mallarmé*. Edited by Henri Mondor and Lloyd James Austin. 6 vols. Paris: Gallimard, 1981.
———. *Correspondance de Stéphane Mallarmé*. Edited by Bertrand Marchal. Paris: Gallimard, 2019.
———. *Divagations*. Paris: Charpentier, 1897. Translated by Barbara Johnson as *Divagations*. Cambridge, MA: Harvard University Press, 2007.
———. *Oeuvres complètes de Stéphane Mallarmé*. Edited by Bertrand Marchal. 2 vols. Paris: Gallimard, 1998 and 2003.
———. "Préface." In *Premiers et derniers vers* by Charles Guérin. Paris: Mercure de France, 1923.
———. *Stéphane Mallarmé: The Poems in Verse*. Translated by Peter Manson. Oxford, OH: Miami University Press, 2012.
———. *Vers et prose*. Paris: Perrin et Cie, 1893.
Maniglier, Patrice. *La vie énigmatique des signes: Saussure et la naissance du structuralisme*. Paris: Scheer, 2006.
Marks, Lawrence E. "*Bright Colors Falsely Seen* by Kevin Dann (book review)." *Isis* 91, no. 2 (2000): 389–90.
———. "On Colored-Hearing Synesthesia: Cross-Modal Translations of Sensory Dimensions." *Psychological Bulletin* 82, no. 3 (1975): 303–31.
———. "Weak Synesthesia in Perception and Language" (2013). In *The Oxford Handbook to Synesthesia*, 761–89. Oxford: Oxford University Press, 2018.
Markwort, J. C. *Gesang-, Ton- und Rede-Vortragslehre*. Darmstadt: Leske and Mainz: Schott, 1827.
Martinet, André. *Économie des changements phonétiques: Traité de phonologie diachronique*. Bern: Francke, 1955.
Maurel, Jean. "L'alphabet analphabète ou Victor Hugo de A à Z (idéologie et idéographie)." *La nouvelle critique* (1971): 101–10.
Mayer, Tobias. "Von Meßung der Farben." In *Opera Inedita Tobiae Mayeri*, edited by G. C. Lichtenberg. Göttingen: Dieterich, 1775. Translated by Adriana Fiorentini. "On the Relationships Between Colors." *Color Research and Application* 25, no. 1 (2000): 66–74.
Mazzeo, Marco. "Les voyelles colorées: Saussure et la synesthésie." *Cahiers Ferdinand de Saussure* 57 (2004): 129–43.
———. *Storia naturale sinestesia: Dalla questione Molyneux a Jakobson*. Rome: Quodlibet, 2005.
Mehlitz, Hartmut. *Richard Lepsius: Ägypten und die Ordnung der Wissenschaft*. Berlin: Kadmos, 2011.

de Mendoza, Ferdinand Suárez. *L'audition colorée: Études sur les fausses sensations secondaires physiologiques et particulièrement sur les pseudo-sensations de couleurs associées aux perceptions objectives des sons*. Paris: Octave Doin, 1890.

Meschonnic, Henri. "Ce que Hugo dit de la langue." *Romantisme* 25, no. 6 (1979): 57–73.

Meulders, Michel. *Helmholtz, des lumières aux neurosciences*. Paris: Éditions Odile Jacob, 2001.

Meyer-Kalkus, Reinhart. "Richard Wagners Theorie der Wort-Tonsprache in 'Oper und Drama' und 'Der Ring der Nibelungen.'" *Athenäum: Jahrbuch für Romantik* 6 (1996): 153-95.

Michaud, Guy. *Mallarmé*. Paris: Hatier, 1971.

Milner, Jean-Claude. *L'amour de la langue*. Paris: Verdier, [1978] 2009.

———. *Ordres et raisons de langue*. Paris: Seuil, 1978.

———. *Profils perdus de Stéphane Mallarmé : Court traité de lecture 2*. Paris: Verdier, 2019.

Miner, Margaret. *Resonant Gaps: Between Baudelaire and Wagner*. Athens: University of Georgia Press, 1995.

Morier, Henri. *Dictionnaire de poétique et de rhétorique*. Paris: Presses universitaires de France, 1998.

Moyer, Ann. *Musica Scientia*. Ithaca, NY: Cornell University Press, 1992.

———. "Musical Scholarship in Italy at the end of the Renaissance, 1500–1650: From Veritas to Verisimilitude." In *History and the Disciplines: The Reclassification of Knowledge in Early Modern Europe*, edited by Donald R. Kelley, 185–202. Rochester: Rochester University Press, 2000.

Müller, Friedrich Max. "Proposals for a Missionary Alphabet." In Christian von Bunsen, *Outlines of the Philosophy of Universal History Applied to Language and Religion* [Christianity and Mankind, Part IV]. 2 vols. London: Longmans, 1854, II: 437–88.

Murat, Michel. *Le vers libre*. Paris: Champion, 2008.

Muzzulini, Daniel. "Timbre vs Klangfarbe: Zu Rudolf Bockholdts Herder-Kommentar." *Musiktheorie* 16, no. 1 (2001): 81–84.

Nair, Anupama, and David Brang. "Inducing Synesthesia in Non-Synesthetes: Short-Term Visual Deprivation Facilitates Auditory-Evoked Visual Precepts." *Consciousness and Cognition* 70 (April 2019): 70–79.

Nash, Suzanne. *Reading Paul Valéry*. Cambridge: Cambridge University Press, 1998.

Nordau, Max. *Entartung*. Berlin: Duncker, 1892. Translated by George L. Mosse as *Degeneration*. Lincoln, Nebraska: University of Nebraska Press, 1993. Translated by Auguste Dietrich as *Dégénérescence*. Paris: F. Alcan, 1894.

Noulet, Émilie. *Vingt poèmes de Stéphane Mallarmé*. Paris: Minard and Geneva: Droz, 1967.

Ohm, G. S. "Noch ein Paar Worte über die Definition des Tons." *Poggendorffs Annalen der Physik* 62 (1844): 1–17.

———. "Ueber die Definition des Tons, nebst daran geknüpfter Theorie der Sirene und ähnlicher tonbildener Vorrichtungen." *Poggendorffs Annalen der Physik* 59 (1843): 513–65.

Olenina, Ana Hedberg. *Psychomotor Aesthetics: Movement and Affect in Modern Literature and Film.* New York: Oxford University Press, 2020.

Oresme, Nicole. *Tractatus de configurationibus qualitatum et motuum.* Madison: University of Wisconsin Press, 1968.

Oxford English Dictionary. www.oedonline.com.

Parret, Herman. "Métaphysique saussurienne de la voix et de l'oreille dans les manuscrits de Genève et de Harvard." In *Ferdinand de Saussure*, 62–78. Paris: L'Herne, 2003.

Passy, Paul. *Les Sons du français.* Paris: Firmin-Didot, 1887.

Perroud, "De l'hyperchromatopsie." *Mémoires et compte-rendus de la société des sciences médicales de Lyon* 2 (1863): 37–41.

Pitman, Isaac. *Stenographic Sound-Hand.* London: Bagster, 1837.

Pliny the Elder. *Natural History.* Translated by John Bostock and H. T. Riley. London: Taylor and Francis, 1855.

Pfannenschmid, August-Ludewig. *Versuch einer Anleitung zum Mischen aller Farben aus Blau, Gelb und Roth nach beiliegendem Triangel.* Hannover: no publisher listed, 1781.

Pourciau, Sarah M. *The Writing of Spirit: Soul, System, and the Roots of Language Science.* New York: Fordham University Press, 2017.

Prins, Yopie. *Victorian Sappho.* Princeton, NJ: Princeton University Press, 1999.

Proceedings at New York October 1861. *Journal of the American Oriental Society* 7 (1860–63): xliii–xlix.

Les quatre évangiles. Translated by A. Crampon. Paris: Tolra et Haton, 1864.

Ramachandran, V. S. and E. M. Hubbard, "Synaesthesia: A Window into Perception, Thought and Language." *Journal of Consciousness Studies* 8, no. 12 (2001): 3–34.

Rameau, Jean-Philippe. *Traité de l'harmonie réduite à ses principes naturels.* Paris: Ballard, 1722.

Rancière, Jacques. *La politique de la littérature.* Paris: Galilée, 1997.

———. "Les voix et les corps." In *Le Millénnaire Rimbaud*, ed. Alain Badiou, Jacques Borreil, and Jacques Rancière, 11–42. Paris: Belin, 1993.

Rapp, Karl Mortiz. "Die Vocale und die Farben." In *Versuch einer Physiologie der Sprache nebst historischer Entwicklung der abendländischen Idiome nach physiologischen Grundsätzen.* Stuttgart and Tübingen: Cotta'schen, 1841.

Rey, Alain, ed. *Dictionnaire historique de la langue française.* Paris: Le Robert, 1993.

Reyher, Samuel. *Mathesis Mosaica, sive Loca Pentateuchi Mathematica Mathematicè explicata.* Kiel: Kilia Holsatorum, 1679.

Ribot, Théodule and Léon Marillier. *Congrès International de psychologie physiologique: première session.* Paris: Bureau des revues, 1890.

Rimbaud, Arthur. *Collected Poems*. Translated by Oliver Bernard. London: Penguin Classics, 1997.

———. *Collected Poems*. Translated by Martin Sorrell. Oxford: Oxford University Press, 2001.

———. *Œuvres complètes d'Arthur Rimbaud*. Edited by André Guyaux and Aurélia Cervoni. Paris: Gallimard, 2009.

———. *Oeuvres complètes facsimiles*. Edited by Steve Murphy. Paris: Champion, 2002.

Roch, Eckhard. *Chroma – Color – Farbe: Ursprung und Funktion der Farbmetapher in der antiken Musiktheorie*. Mainz: Schott, 2001.

Rousseau, Jean-Jacques. *Dictionnaire de musique* in *Œuvres complètes de J. J. Rousseau*, Vol. 7. Paris: Hachette, (1767) 1906.

———. *Essai sur l'origine des langues*. Paris: A. Belin, [1781] 1817.

Ruppli, Mireille, and Sylvie Thorel-Cailleteau. *Mallarmé: La Grammaire et le grimoire*. Geneva: Droz, 2005.

Sachs, G. L. T. *Historiae naturalis duorum leucaetiopum (A Natural History of Two Albinos: The Author Himself and His Sister)*. PhD dissertation, University of Erlangen, 1812.

Sainte-Beuve, Charles-Augustin. *Tableau historique et critique de la poésie française et du théâtre français au XVIe siècle*. Paris: G. Charpentier, 1843.

de Saussure, Ferdinand. *Cours de linguistique générale*. Edited by Charles Bally and Albert Séchehaye with the collaboration of Albert Riedlinger, critical edition by Tullio de Mauro. Paris: Payot, 1962.

———. "Essai d'une distinction des différents *a* indo-européens." *Mémoires de la Société de Linguistique de Paris* 3, no. 5 (1877): 379–90.

———. "Essai pour réduire les mots du grec, du latin & de l'allemand à un petit nombre de racines" (1874). *Cahiers Ferdinand de Saussure* 32 (1978): 73–101.

———. *Mémoire sur le système primitif des voyelles dans les langues indo-européennes*. Leipzig: Teubner, 1879.

Sauveur, Joseph. *Collected Writings on Musical Acoustics*. Edited by Rudolf Rasch. Utrecht: Diapason Press, 1984.

Savart, Félix. "Nouvelles recherches sur les vibrations de l'air." *Annales de chimie* 29 (August 1825): 404–26; "Mémoire sur la voix humaine." *Annales de chimie* 30 (September 1825): 64–87; "Mémoire sur la voix des oiseaux," *Annales de chimie* 32 (May-June 1826): 5–24.

Séailles, G. *Eugene Carrière, essai de biographie psychologique*. Paris: Armand Colin, 1911.

Seebeck, August. "Akustik." *Repertorium der Physik* 8 (1849): 60–66.

Schilling, Gustav, ed. *Universal-Lexikon der Tonkunst*. Stuttgart, 1838.

Schlegel, Julius Heinrich Gottlieb. *Ein Betrag zur nähern Kentniß der Albinos*. Meiningen: Keyßnerschen Hofbuchhandlung, 1824.

Sherman, Paul D. *Colour Vision in the Nineteenth Century: The Young-Helmholtz-Maxwell Theory*. Bristol: Adam Hilger, 1981.

Sieburth, Richard. "The Music of the Future." In *A New History of French Literature*, edited by Denis Hollier, 789–98. Cambridge, MA: Harvard University Press, 1994.
Sievers, Eduard. *Grundzüge der Lautphysiologie*. Leipzig: Breitkopf and Härtel, 1876.
Silvers, Lauren. "Beyond the Senses: The Cenesthetic Poetics of French Symbolism." *Modern Philology* 112 (2014): 381–404.
Simner, Julia. "Beyond Perception: Synesthesia as a Psycholinguistic Phenomenon." *Trends in Cognitive Science* 11 (2007): 23–29.
Simner, Julia, Louise Glover, and Alice Mowat. "Linguistic Determinants of Word Colouring in Grapheme-Colour Synaesthesia." *Cortex* 42, no. 2 (February 2006): 281–89.
Siraki, Arby Ted. "Problems of a Linguistic Problem: On Roman Jakobson's Coloured Vowels." *Neophilologus* 93 (2009): 1–9.
Solleveld, Floris. "Lepsius as a Linguist: Field Work, Philology, Phonetics, and 'the Hamitic Hypothesis.'" *Language and History* 63, no. 3 (2020): 193–213.
de Souza, Robert. "Le rôle de l'e muet dans la poésie française." *Mercure de France* 8, no. 61 (January 1895): 3–23.
Starobinski, Jean. *Les mots sous les mots*. Paris: Gallimard, 1971.
Stawarska, Beata. *Saussure's Philosophy of Language as Phenomenology*. Oxford: Oxford University Press, 2015.
Steege, Benjamin. *Helmholtz and the Modern Listener*. Cambridge: Cambridge University Press, 2012.
Steel, David. "Autour des *Voyelles* de Rimbaud: Poésie et linguistique." *French Cultural Studies* 22, no. 1 (2011): 3–11.
Sterne, Jonathan. *The Audible Past*. Durham, NC: Duke University Press, 2003.
Stevens, Wallace. *Collected Poems*. New York: Knopf, 1955.
Straka, Georges. "Remarques sur les voyelles nasales, leur origine et leur évolution en français." *Revue de linguistique romane* 19 no. 75–76 (1955): 245–74.
Stumpf, Carl. "Hermann von Helmholtz and the New Psychology." Translated by John Grier Hibben. *The Psychological Review* 2, no. 1 (1895): 1–12.
———. *Die Sprachlaute: experimentell-phonetische Untersuchungen nebst einem Anhang über Instrumentalklänge*. Berlin: Springer, 1926.
Szabó, Árpád. *Anfänge der griechischen Mathematik*. Budapest: Akadémiai Kiadó, 1969.
Szarke, Margot. "Modern Sensitivity: Zola's Synaesthetic Cheeses." *French Studies* 74, no. 2 (2020): 203–22.
Taine, Hippolyte. *Philosophie de l'art*, Vol. 1. Paris: G. Baillière, 1865.
Thibaudet, Albert. *La poésie de Stéphane Mallarmé*. Paris: Gallimard, [1911] 1926.
Thomas, Margaret. *Fifty Key Thinkers on Language and Linguistics*. Florence: Taylor and Francis, 2011.
Treitler, Leo. "The 'Unwritten' and 'Written Transmission' of Medieval Chant and the Start-Up of Musical Notation." *Journal of Musicology* 10, no. 2 (Spring 1992): 131–91.

Trésor de la langue française. http://www.le-tresor-de-la-langue.fr.

Trubetzkoy, N. S. *Grundzüge zur Phonologie.* Kraus Thomson: Nendeln/Lichtenstein, [1939] 1968.

———. *Principles of Phonology.* Translated by Christine A. M. Baltaxe. Berkeley and Los Angeles: University of California Press, 1969.

———. *Studies in General Linguistics and Language Structure.* Edited and introduced by Anatoly Liberman. Translated by Marvin H. Taylor and A. Liberman. Durham, NC: Duke University Press, 2001.

Töpfer, Johann Gottlob. *Erster Nachtrag zur Orgelbau-Kunst.* Weimar: Hoffmann, 1834.

Ullmann, Dieter. "Ohm-Seebeck-Helmholtz und das Klangfarbenproblem." *NTM- Schriftenr. Gesch. Naturwiss., Techn., Med.* 25 (1988): 65–68.

Valéry, Paul. *Cahiers,* Vol. 25. Paris: Centre national de la recherche scientifique, 1957.

———. *Œuvres,* Vol. 1. Edited by Jean Hytier. Paris: Gallimard, 1957.

———. *Regards sur le monde actuel.* Paris: Librairie Stock, Delamain et Boutelleau, 1931.

Verlaine, Paul. *Oeuvres en prose complètes.* Edited by Jacques Borel. Paris: Gallimard, 1972.

Vietör, Wilhelm. *Elemente der Phonetik.* Leipzig: Reisland, [1884] 1894.

Wagner, Richard. *Gesammelte Schriften und Dichtungen,* Vol. 4, Leipzig: Fritzsch, 1872.

———. *Opera and Drama.* Translated by William Ashton Ellis. Lincoln: University of Nebraska Press, 1995.

———. *Quatre poèmes d'opéras, traduits en prose française, précédés d'une lettre sur la musique.* Paris: Bourdillat, 1861.

———. *Richard Wagner's "Beethoven" 1870: A New Translation.* Translated by Roger Allen. Woodbridge: The Boydell Press, 2014.

Ward, Jamie. "Synesthesia." *Annual Review of Psychology* 64 (2013): 49–75.

Ward, Jamie, and Julia Simner. "Synesthesia: The Current State of the Field." In *Multisensory Perception: From Laboratory to Clinic,* edited by K. Sathian and V. S. Ramachandran, 283–300. Cambridge, MA: Academic Press, 2020.

Warrack, John Hamilton. *German Opera: From the Beginnings to Wagner.* Cambridge: Cambridge University Press, 2001.

Waugh, Linda. "Preface to the Second Edition." In *The Sound Shape of Language,* 3rd ed., 1–5. Berlin: De Gruyter, 2002.

Weiskott, Eric. *Meter and Modernity in English Verse, 1350–1650.* Philadelphia: University of Pennsylvania Press, 2021.

Wheatstone, Charles. "Reed Organ-Pipes, Speaking Machines, etc." *London and Westminster Review* 27 (October 1837): 14–22.

Whitney, W. D. "On Lepsius's Standard Alphabet." *Journal of the American Oriental Society* 7 (1861): 299–332.

Willis, Robert. "On the Vowel Sounds, and on Reed Organ-Pipes." *Transactions of the Cambridge Philosophical Society* 3 (1830): 231–68.

———. *Ueber Vocaltöne und Zungenpfeifen, Annalen der Physik und Chemie* 24, no. 3 (1832): 397–437.

Wise, M. Norton. *Aesthetics, Industry, and Science: Hermann von Helmholtz and the Berlin Physical Society*. Chicago: University of Chicago Press, 2018.

Wittgenstein, Ludwig. *Bemerkungen über die Farben / Remarks on Colour*. Edited by G. E. M. Anscombe. Translated by Linda L. McAlister and Margarete Schättle. Oxford: Blackwell, [1977] 2007.

———. *Philosophical Investigations*. Translated by G. E. M. Anscombe, P. M. S. Hacker, and Joachim Schulte. 4th ed. Oxford: Blackwell, 2009.

Yamaguchi, Liesl. "Correspondances: La couleur des voyelles chez Lévi-Strauss, Jakobson, Rimbaud et Banville." *Parade Sauvage* 30 (2019): 121–42.

———. "Vers le vers véridique : poésie et vérité chez Mallarmé." Translated by Annick Ettlin. *Toucher au "vrai": l'intelligence de la poésie*. Edited by Annick Ettlin and Jan Baetens. *Fabula—LhT* 24 (November 2020). https://www.fabula.org/lht/24/yamaguchi.html.

Yamaguchi, Liesl, and Thomas C. Connolly. "Incipit : On Poetry and Crisis." *Nineteenth-Century French Studies* 50, nos. 1–2 (Fall–Winter 2021–2022): 1–49.

Index

Albers, Josef, 49, 157n1
alliteration, 53, 64
allure [pace/rhythm], 71, 75–78, 164n39; cadence, 67–69, 77, 162n7
alphabet, 10, 33, 51, 117–18, 121, 126; phonetic, 84, 116; standard alphabet, 84–85; universal alphabet, 14, 87, 138, 157nn *passim*, 167n4, 184n98
aperture [*Öffnungsgrad*], 16, 18, 98–100, 102
Aristotle, 123
assonance, 7, 53–55, 63–64
Attridge, Derek, 64
Auden, W. H., 6

Banville, Théodore de, 11, 13, 54, 56–57, 63, 145n9, 158n21, 158n29, 177n9
Baudelaire, Charles, 2, 54, 123, 163n25, 178n13, 180n48, 181n51; on Wagner, 12, 128–34, 179n30, 180n34, 180n40, 180n41, 180n42, 180n44, 181n54, 181n55
Becq de Fouquières, Louis, 13, 54–55, 57
Bell, Alexander Melville, 84, 167n4
Bellay, Joachim du, 77
Bernstein, Susan, 130, 133, 178n23, 179n30, 181n54
Bersani, Leo, 133
Boethius, Anicius Manlius Severinus, 10, 150n29
Bopp, Franz, 113–14, 183n92, 184n97
brightness (*Helligkeit; brillance, clarté*), 3, 6–7, 11, 13, 19, 54, 58–60, 62, 66, 71, 75, 78–80, 94, 96, 100–2, 129, 146n27, 156n106, 162n21nn *passim*, 174n36, 177n9
Butler, Shane, 123–25

caesura, 54, 67, 161n4
Castel, Louis Bertrand, 43, 146n29
Chomsky, Noam, 10, 40–41
chromatism (*Farbigkeit*), 7, 10, 19, 102
Cifali, Mireille, 14–15, 103–4, 173n16
Claparède, Édouard, 15, 50, 103, 105, 172n6
color [*couleur, Farbe*], 7, 10–11, 13, 54–55, 57, 62–63, 111, 133, 164n39; additive vs. subtractive, 169n22; color spectrum, 7, 47; color triangle/pyramid, 11, 14, 86–89, 91, 94–97, 102, 168n21nn *passim*; *coloration*, 7, 10, 11, 13, 54–55, 57, 62–63, 111; pigments [*les couleurs*], 7, 55, 60, 88, 169n22; primary colors, 85, 88, 169n22. *See also* coloring [*coloris*]
colored hearing [*audition colorée*], 13, 15, 19, 50–51, 62, 91, 102, 106, 125, 143n3, 144n8, 146n25, 146n26nn *passim*, 147n39, 172n6, 173n16; with labels *fausse, pseudo, quasi*, 125
coloring [*coloris*], 54, 62, 75–78; in music, 76–77, 132, 165n51, 165n52; in painting, 75–76; relationship to rhythm, 71, 75–78; as Wagner's translation of *Klangfarbe*, 76
consonance, 28–29, 63–64, 148n3, 150n16

consonants, 2, 18, 35, 50–54 *passim*, 70, 92, 96, 152n51, 158n25, 176n60, 176n65, 183n92; coloring of [*coloris*], 7, 12, 53; *consonne d'appui*, 53–54, 135; in Helmholtz, 22, 150n20; in music, 50, 136; in Saussure, 109, 112–13, 116–18; in Wagner, 135–38, 181n61
Coppée, François, 55
Cours de linguistique générale [*Course in General Linguistics*], 104, 108, 163n24, 173n18
Cratylism, 184n96, 184n98
Culler, Johnathan, 5–6, 145n13, 172n9, 174n25
Curtius, Georg, 114, 174n36
Cytowic, Richard E., 7–8

Damisch, Hubert, 121
Day, Sean, 10, 146n26, 147n33, 147n34, 157n17, 170n28, 176n2
Diderot, Denis, 44, 148n3
diphthong, 59, 70, 88, 163n21
distinctive features, 16–10, 97–102, 174n28
Dolan, Emily I., 43, 146n29, 155n81–82
Donders, Franciscus Cornelius, 38, 44, 155n95
Duchesne-Guillemin, Jacques, 59

Eber, Georg Moritz, 92
Ellis, Alexander, 84, 149n11; critique of Grimm's vowel-color analogy, 94–95, 169n23; as translator of Helmholtz, 23, 28, 148n2, 150n20, 155n93, 170n38
Ellis, William Ashton, 160n52, 181n59, 183n88
Euler, Leonhard, 36, 151n39, 153n60

Faure, Jean-Baptiste, 76, 165n50, 165n51
Flörke, Heinrich Gustav, 35, 38, 154n71
Flournoy, Théodore, 14–15, 50–54, 56, 103–4, 144n8, 172n6, 173n12, 173n16, 173n23
Fourier, Joseph, 25–26
Freud, Sigmund, 103–4

Galton, Francis, 14, 51–52, 54, 91–92, 99, 157n10, 170n25
Gautier, Théophile, 57
Genette, Gérard, 59–60, 62, 82, 159n34, 159n45, 159n48, 162n20, 183n96, 184n98
Gesamtkunstwerk [Total Work of Art], 9, 12, 134–38
Greene, Robert, 64
Grimm, Jacob, 88, 91, 94–95, 169n23, 183n92
Grimm, Wilhelm, 92
Gruber, Edouard, 50, 52–54, 91–92, 157n8, 157n9, 170n25

harmony, 148n3; color, 47, 76; musical, 22, 27, 29, 34–35, 47–48, 67, 136–37, 150n20, 151n30, 151n38, 153n70, 154n75, 162n7; poetic, 54, 56, 159n36; vowel, 34–35, 54, 63
Hellwag, Christoph Friedrich, 14, 34, 88, 168n18
Helmholtz, Hermann von: on color mixing, 169n22; on musical sound [*musikalische Klänge*] vs. noise [*Geräusch*], 22–23, 40–41, 154n87; account of overtones [*Obertöne*], 11, 13, 25, 27–30, 32, 38–39, 42, 44, 49, 150n20, 151n32, 154n75; proper tone [*Eigenton*], 21, 26–27, 31–32, 37–39, 154n72; resonator, 31–32, 37–39, 49, 151n32; simple tones [*einfache Töne*], 27–28, 37; sound-color [*Klangfarbe*], 11–13, 22–23, 30, 39–40, 42–44, 136, 148n3, 154n86nn *passim*; sympathetic resonance [*Phänomen des Mittönens*], 26–27, 150n21
Helmont, Franciscus Mercurius van, 33–34, 152n48
Hittite, 119, 176n64
Hrozný, Bedřich, 119
Hugo, Victor, 11, 13, 60–62, 144n8, 158n21, 159n48, 159n49; on vowel color and brightness, 60–62
Huysman, Joris-Karl, 2, 134

Jakobson, Roman, 12, 14–19, 101–2, 143n3, 145n9, 148n45, 148n50, 159n34, 166n64, 168n18, 172n10nn *passim*, 174n25, 177n9; child language / aphasia, 17–18, 101, 171n56, 171n57; chromatism [*Farbigkeit*], 19, 102; distinctive features, 101–2, 174n28; sound symbolism, 15–17; zero phoneme, 167n14
Jewanski, Jörg, 10–11, 121–24, 126, 144n8, 146n25, 146n26, 146n27, 147n32, 147n33, 147n34, 157n17, 170n28, 176n2, 177n9, 180n38

Kempelen, Wolfgang von, 36, 134, 153n60, 153n64, 153n65
Key, James, 51, 53, 99, 157n10
Klangfarbe, 6–7, 10, 100, 154n91; in Helmholtz, 11–13, 22–23, 30, 39–40, 42–44, 136, 148n3, 154n86nn *passim*; as a translation of *timbre*, 6, 13, 100, 154n91, 155n96, 174n36, 182n69; in Wagner, 76, 135–37
Kratzenstein, Christian, 36, 152n60
Krohn, William O., 122, 147n31, 157n19
Kursell, Julia, 49
Kuryłowicz, Jerzy, 119

Lambert, Johann Heinrich, 14, 88–89, 169n21nn *passim*
laryngeal theory, 9, 119–20, 176n65, 176n66
Lepsius, Karl Richard, 14, 92–96, 99, 170n30; *Standard Alphabet*, 84–85, 167n4; vowel-color pyramid, 14, 84–88, 96, 168n21, 170n28
letters: of the alphabet, 10, 33, 51, 97, 121, 126; and colors/light, 11, 50–52, 60–61, 106–8; with constitutive properties, 97–98; as graphemes, 3, 8, 10, 143n6, 173n23; historical determinacy of, 108–10, 118; immateriality of, 105–7; as a minimal unit, 97–102 *passim* (*see also* consonants; vowels); relationship to signification, 139, 184n98; and vocalism, 59, 93–94, 111, 183n92; word-initial, 157n19, 183n92 (*see also* alliteration)
linguistics, 9, 14–15, 17, 34, 40–42, 91, 96, 104–5, 107, 112, 144n8, 166n62, 183n92; Indo-European, 11, 15, 88, 105, 110–11, 113–20, 138–39, 171n54, 175n47, 175n50, 184n99; Jakobsonian, 15, 17, 19, 101, 168n14; Saussurian, 14–15, 103, 105, 109–19, 163n22, 172n10, 173n18, 175n47, 175n50, 176n65; structural, 14–15, 17, 101, 103, 172n10
Liszt, Franz, 131–32, 180n42, 180n47
Locke, John, 10, 146n29

Mallarmé, Stéphane, 9, 13–14, 17, 138, 158n27, 158n29, 159n36, 163n26, 163n39, 164n33, 165n46, 166n63, 166n71, 183n96, 184n97, 184n98, 184n99; on meter, 63, 65–67, 70, 83, 165n59, 166n62; poetry vs. verse, 65–69; on supreme language, 73–74, 80–83, 138–39, 164n28; on timbre, 13, 57, 59, 69–71, 75, 77–82, 166n62; on vowel color, 11, 13, 55–57, 59–62, 78, 158n25, 159n45, 162n21, 164n39
Marchal, Bertrand, 59, 162n11
Marks, Lawrence E., 8–9, 143n3, 146n26, 147n29, 178n22
Mayer, Tobias, 88, 90, 169n22
Mazzeo, Marco, 104, 172n7, 172n10
Mémoire sur le système primitive des voyelles dans les langues indo-européennes [*Memoir on the Original System of Vowels in the Indo-European Languages*], 15, 105, 111
meter, 13–14, 63, 65–68, 70, 74–75, 78–83, 160n53, 161n4, 166n62; absolute, 74–75, 80, 166n62; alexandrine [*alexandrin*], 59, 63, 67, 70, 81; hexameter [*hexamètre*], 63, 70; quantitative, 64, 66, 166n62; stress-timed, 66, 166n62; syllabic, 66, 160n53, 166n62; tonal, 66, 166n62
Milner, Jean-Claude, 57, 114, 158n32, 161n4, 163n22, 184n99
Miner, Margaret, 130, 179n30
Morier, Henri, 59
"La musique et les lettres" ["Music and Letters"], 65–69
Müller, Johannes, 45
Müller, Max, 84, 167n4

Nabokov, Vladimir, 84
neumes, 34, 152n51, 152n53
Newton, Issac, 10, 43, 46, 128, 146n29
Noulet, Émilie, 59, 159n36
nuance: visual, 12, 55; vocalic, 12–13, 51–56, 59–60, 62–63, 85–86, 93, 96, 137, 147n36

Ohm, Georg Simon, 25, 27–28, 43, 149n12
On the Sensations of Tone [*Die Lehre von den Tonempfindungen als Physiologische Grundlage für die Theorie der Musik*], 11–13, 22–23, 41–42, 44–46, 48–49, 148n2, 154n86
opera, 39, 76, 131, 134–37, 165n49, 181n57
overtones [*Obertöne*], 137; in Helmholtz, 11, 13, 25, 27–30, 32, 38–39, 42, 44, 49, 150n20, 151n32, 154n75; in Willis, 154n75

Passy, Paul, 84, 167n4
Pfannenschmid, August-Ludewig, 88, 90, 168n21
phonetics, 34–35, 77, 84–97, 109–10, 116, 174n25, 174n28g
phonology, 4, 10, 14, 81, 97–98, 100–1, 108–9, 116–19, 166n62, 174n25; distinctive features, 16–10, 97–102, 174n28; phoneme, 3, 15, 61, 98, 100, 107–10, 116–19, 168n14, 173n23, 177n9; vs. phonetics, 97, 109–10, 116, 174n25, 174n28; phonological structures, 16, 19, 41, 57, 67, 108, 117–18, 161n4
pigments [*couleurs*], 7, 55, 60, 88, 169n22
Pitman, Issac, 84, 167n4
poetry, 1–6, 10, 13–14, 15–20, 48, 50–64, 65–68, 77, 137, 161n4, 166n71, 181n55; free verse [*vers libre*], 14, 83, 161n4, 164n39; as opposed to verse, 65–66; sound symbolism, 7–8, 15–17
Pourciau, Sarah, 138, 168n14
private language, vii, 9–10
prose poem [*le poème en prose*], 65–68
Purves, Alex, 123–25

Rancière, Jacques, 6, 145n9, 163n21
resonant coefficients [*coefficients sonantiques*], 118–19, 176n65
Reyher, Samuel, 33–35, 38, 152n48
rhyme, 7, 54–57, 59, 62–64, 67–70, 77, 83, 109, 158n27, 158n29, 160n52, 160n53; rhythm, 47, 64, 67, 76–80, 165n50, 165n59, 176n60
rhythm, 2, 47, 64, 67, 76–80, 160n52, 165n50, 165n59; as a translation of *allure*, 77–78
Rimbaud, Arthur, 2–6, 10–11, 128, 134, 143n3, 144n7, 144n8, 144n9nn *passim*, 145n11, 145n12, 159n48, 159n49, 173n12, 177n9, 178n24, 179n29
Rousseau, Jean-Jacques, 11–12, 44, 155n98

Sachs, Georg Ludwig Tobias, 10, 12, 121–22, 124, 126–28, 130, 133, 146n26, 146n27, 176n2nn *passim*, 179n26, 179n29, 180n38
Sainte-Beuve, Charles Augustin, 77
saturation [*Sättigung*], 98–102
Saussure, Ferdinand de, 14–15, 72, 103–20, 172n6, 173n12, 174n25, 176n65; Indo-European linguistics, 15, 105, 110–20, 175n47, 175n50; linguistic arbitrariness, 14, 105, 172n9; sign, 72, 106–7, 163n24; structural linguistics, 14–15, 103, 163n24; synesthesia, 172n1, 172n6, 172n10; vowel color, 14, 172n10, 176n36
Sauveur, Joseph, 24, 150n16
Seebeck, Thomas Johann, 43, 150n21; difference of (musical) sounds [*Verschiedenheit der Klänge, Klangverschiedenheit*], 43
Sieburth, Richard, 133–34, 179n30, 181n55
signifier and signified [*signifié et significant*]: in the *Course in General Linguistics*, 72, 106–7, 163n24; in Jakobson, 17; in Mallarmé, 72, 163n24, 166n71
Simner, Julia, 8, 10, 52, 146n20, 146n26, 147n32, 147n33, 147n34, 157n16, 157n17, 157n19nn *passim*, 170n28, 172n6, 177n9, 178n22
sound symbolism, 7–8, 15–17
Standard Alphabet, 14, 84–86, 92–94, 97, 167n4
Stevens, Wallace, 48
stress, 52; lexical, 64, 86, 137; metrical, 54, 56, 64, 67; musical, 67, 137
Stumpf, Carl, 18, 48, 102, 156n112, 168n18
supreme language in Mallarmé, 73–74, 80–83, 138, 164n28
symbolists/symbolism, 12, 63, 128, 134, 179n30

synesthesia, 94; clinical definition of, 8–9, 11, 52, 123, 143n3, 177n6, 178n22, 180n38; history of the term, 7–11, 52, 97, 104, 121–26, 144n8, 146n25, 146n26, 147n32, 147n33, 147n34, 147n39, 157n19, 170n28, 172n6, 172n10, 173n12, 173n17, 176n2, 177n9; in Jakobson, 19, 101–2, 143n3, 157n19; in literature, 2–3, 8, 12, 59, 130, 133–34, 143n3, 173n12, 178n23

Thibaudet, Albert, 59, 159n36
timbre, 44, 154n91, 155n95, 155n96, 155n97; in linguistics, 85, 111, 166n62; in Mallarmé, 13–14, 59, 63, 66, 68–71, 75–83, 162n20, 163n21, 165n59, 166n62; as *teintes*, for Saussure, 106, 111–13, 175n40; vocal, 10–11, 43–44, 49, 76, 121, 136, 146n29, 155n81, 155n98, 165n50, 182n69; of vowels, 4, 6–7, 54–57, 62–64, 66, 76, 85, 100, 108–15, 120, 136, 155n93, 165n51, 166n62, 174n36, 175n41, 175n55
tone, 10–11, 13, 21–50 *passim*, 76, 100, 127, 149n12, 150n29, 156n106, 164n39; musical, 24, 27–28, 30, 44, 49, 127, 134–38, 149n8, 150n16, 150n20, 151n32, 154n71, 179n29, 183n87; vs. pitch 21, 24, 27; "prime tone" [*Grundton*], 26–27, 29–30, 32, 39, 154n75; "proper tone" [*Eigenton*], 21, 26–27, 36–39, 100, 136, 154n72; visual, 10–11, 45–47, 156n106; vocalic, 31–41, 92, 100, 104, 135–38 (*see also* overtones [*Obertöne*])
tone-color, 43. See also *Klangfarbe*
Trubetzkoy, Nikolai Sergeyevich, 14, 97–98, 100–2, 171n54, 174n25

Valéry, Paul, 60–62, 77, 139
Verlaine, Paul, 11, 13, 63–64, 143n1, 160n52
verse/versification [*le vers*], 5, 11–14, 53–57, 60, 62–64, 65–83 *passim*, 123, 133, 136–38, 158n32, 160n52, 160n53, 161n4nn *passim*, 165n59
vowel-color: coloration in poetry, 54, 62, 64, 144n8; in Jakobson, 102; in Lepsius, 14, 86–88, 91, 94, 96–97, 102, 170n28; and nuance, 11–13, 51–54, 56, 59–60, 62–63, 86, 93, 96, 129, 137; in Rimbaud, 1–6, 144n8; in Saussure, 14, 104–5, 109–13, 116–17, 172n7, 172n10, 173n12
vowels: in Ancient Greek, 3, 93, 111–13, 115–18, 176n58; as graphemes, 8, 10, 143n6, 173n23; immateriality of 106–8, 110–11; as letters, 3, 6–7, 10, 18; as minimal linguis-

tic unit, 16–17, 107, 109; musical structure of, 4, 10–11, 13, 22–23, 34–36, 39–41, 136, 138; opposable, 14, 93, 96, 107, 109–10; vs. *Selbstlaute*, 138, 153n65; and timbre, 4, 6–7, 10–11, 13–14, 54–57, 59, 62–64, 66, 70, 76, 100, 108–15, 120, 136, 155n81–82, 163n21, 165n51, 166n62, 174n36, 175n41, 175n55; undifferentiated, 41, 94, 96, 113
"Voyelles" [Rimbaud's sonnet, "Vowels"], 1–6, 128, 143n, 144n8, 144n9, 145n11, 145n12, 173n12, 177n9, 178n24

Wagner, Richard, 134–38, 160n52, 163n26, 165n49, 181n57, 181n60, 181n61, 182n78, 183n92; and Baudelaire, 12, 128–34, 179n30, 180n34, 180n40, 180n41, 181n54, 181n55; on *coloris* as a translation of *Klangfarbe*, 76; intoned sound [*der tönende Laut*], 137–38, 183n87; root syllable [*Wurzelsilbe*], 137; Total Work of Art [*Gesamtkunstwerk*], 9, 12, 134, 137

waves, 3, 48; light, 95, 128, 132, 170n30, 179n28; sound, 22, 24, 27–29, 36–37, 42–43, 45, 48–49, 95, 135, 170n30; strings, 24–27, 29; wavelength, 26–27, 31, 36–37, 46, 95, 170n30

Whistler, James, 57, 159n36

Whitney, William Dwight, 84–87, 91, 94–96, 168n17, 169n24

Willis, Robert, 32–33, 35–40, 43, 50, 152n60, 153n63nn *passim*, 153n70, 154n75, 155n93

Wittgenstein, Ludwig, vii, 9

Liesl Yamaguchi is Assistant Professor of French at the University of California, Berkeley.

VERBAL ARTS :: STUDIES IN POETICS

Lazar Fleishman and Haun Saussy, series editors

Kiene Brillenburg Wurth, *Between Page and Screen: Remaking Literature Through Cinema and Cyberspace*
Jacob Edmond, *A Common Strangeness: Contemporary Poetry, Cross-Cultural Encounter, Comparative Literature*
Christophe Wall-Romana, *Cinepoetry: Imaginary Cinemas in French Poetry*
Marc Shell, *Talking the Walk and Walking the Talk: A Rhetoric of Rhythm*
Ryan Netzley, *Lyric Apocalypse: Milton, Marvell, and the Nature of Events*
Ilya Kliger and Boris Maslov (eds.), *Persistent Forms: Explorations in Historical Poetics*. Foreword by Eric Hayot
Ross Chambers, *An Atmospherics of the City: Baudelaire and the Poetics of Noise*
Haun Saussy, *The Ethnography of Rhythm: Orality and Its Technologies*
Andrew Hui, *The Poetics of Ruins in Renaissance Literature*
Peter Szendy, *Of Stigmatology: Punctuation as Experience*. Translated by Jan Plug
Ben Glaser and Jonathan Culler (eds.), *Critical Rhythm: The Poetics of a Literary Life Form*
Craig Dworkin, *Dictionary Poetics: Toward a Radical Lexicography*
Harald Weinrich, *Tempus: The World of Discussion and the World of Narration*. Translated by Jane K. Brown and Marshall Brown
Liesl Yamaguchi, *On the Colors of Vowels: Thinking through Synesthesia*

www.ingramcontent.com/pod-product-compliance
Lightning Source LLC
Chambersburg PA
CBHW071158070526
44584CB00019B/2840